Library of
Davidson College

THE VICTORIAN MUSE

Selected Criticism and Parody of the Period

A thirty-nine-volume facsimile set essential to the study of one of the most prolific periods in English literature

Edited by
William E. Fredeman, Ira Bruce Nadel, John F. Stasny

A Garland Series

Victorian Prefaces and Introductions
A Facsimile Collection

Edited by
William E. Fredeman

Garland Publishing, Inc.
New York & London
1986

For a complete list of the titles in this series
see the final pages of this volume.

The facsimiles of the prefaces to *Philip Van Artevelde, Festus*, and the Shelley collections and the excerpt from *Literary Anecdotes* are from a private collection. The facsimiles of the Prefatory Notice to *Poems of Walt Whitman* is from a copy in the New York Public Library; that of the Preface to *The Book of Ballads* is from a copy in the British Library. The remaining facsimiles are from copies in the libraries of Yale University.

Introduction © 1986 by William E. Fredeman

Library of Congress Cataloging-in-Publication Data

Victorian prefaces and introductions.

(The Victorian muse)
Reprint of works originally published 1834–1903.
1. English prose literature—19th century.
2. Prefaces.   3. English poetry—19th century—
History and criticism.   4. American poetry—19th
century—History and criticism.   5. Poets, English—
19th century—Biography.   6. Poetry.   I. Fredeman,
William E. (William Evan), 1928–   .   II. Series.
PR1304.V54   1986   821'.7'09   86-12025
ISBN 0-8240-8627-9 (alk. paper)

Design by Bonnie Goldsmith

The volumes in this series are printed on
acid-free, 250-year-life paper.

Printed in the United States of America

Contents

Prefaces to Original Editions and Collections

"Preface," *Philip Van Artevelde*, 1834
Henry Taylor

"Preface," *Poems*, 1854
Matthew Arnold

"Preface," *The Golden Treasury*, 1861
Francis Turner Palgrave

"Introduction to Part II," *The Early Italian Poets*, 1861
D. G. Rossetti

Retrospective Prefaces

"Brief Commentary," *Orion*, 1872
R. H. Horne

"Preface," *Festus*, Fiftieth-Anniversary Edition, 1889
Philip James Bailey

"The Author of 'Festus' and the Spasmodic School," *Literary Anecdotes of the Nineteenth Century*, 1896
W. Robertson Nicoll and Thomas J. Wise, eds.

"Preface," *The Book of Ballads*, 1903
Theodore Martin

Prefaces to Major Victorian Editions of Romantic and American Poets

"Memoir of John Keats," *The Poetical Works of John Keats*, 1854
Richard Monckton Milnes

"Prefatory Memoir," *The Poetical Works of William Blake*, 1875
W. M. Rossetti

"Preface to the Revised Edition," *The Poetical Works of Percy Bysshe Shelley*, 1870
W. M. Rossetti

"Editor's Preface," *The Poetical Works of Percy Bysshe Shelley*, 1886
H. Buxton Forman

"The Life and Genius of Edgar Allan Poe," *The Poetical Works of Edgar Allan Poe*, 1853
James Hannay

"Prefatory Notice," *Poems by Walt Whitman*, 1868
W. M. Rossetti

Memoirs to the Poems of Arthur Hugh Clough

"Memoir," *Poems of Arthur Hugh Clough*, 1862
F. T. Palgrave

"Arthur Hugh Clough," *The Atlantic Monthly*, 1862
[Charles Eliot Norton]

"Memoir of Arthur Hugh Clough," *Poems by Arthur Hugh Clough*, 1871
[Mrs. A. H. Clough]

Introduction

The Victorians are noted, among other things (and in no particular order), for the remarkable range of their interests; for their aesthetic innovativeness in creating new and exciting genres in both the fine and useful arts, while at the same time building on both classical and modern models; for their gradual liberalism, witnessed by increasing social reforms throughout the century; for their indefatigability, as evidenced by such prodigious and seemingly impossible publishing schemes as the multi-volumed *Dictionary of National Biography* and the *Oxford English Dictionary*, and their verbal prodigality (mirroring perhaps their biological fecundity) to which the collected writings of Carlyle, Macaulay, Ruskin, Dickens, Mill, Arnold, Thackeray, and Morris provide ample testimony; for their "high seriousness," which found its ironic counterpart in parody, caricature, and comic spoof characterized by such works as *Punch*, the *Bon Gaultier Ballads*, the *Nonsense* verses of Edward Lear, and the comic operas of Gilbert and Sullivan; for their blending of antiquarianism with the hard pragmatism and practical concerns of the market place, a blending that found at least one outlet in an architectural revolution capable of adapting classical forms to functional buildings like train stations, libraries, theaters, and other public edifices; for their pride in the literary and cultural past of England, which manifested itself in a series of revivals, among them the medieval, which later translated into the arts and crafts movement and many areas of social reform, and a number of societies devoted to resuscitating the masterworks of earlier centuries, of which the Early English Text Society was perhaps the most prominent, and even of the immediate past, such as the Browning and Shelley Societies; and, finally, for their scholarship, which laid the groundwork for the sophisticated methods of modern textual editing.

The sixteen prefaces and introductions reprinted in this edition, which are at least suggestive of the range of Victorian interests, have been chosen from a variety of sources and an almost infinite number of possibilities and are grouped under four distinct headings. The first, prefaces to original editions and collections, reprints four essays that introduced an experimental dramatic romance, a volume of poems by one of the three major poets of the period, an anthology destined to become the supreme example of the genre, and a collection of translations of Italian poets contemporary with Dante made by the Pre-Raphaelite poet and painter Dante Gabriel Rossetti. The earliest, Henry Taylor's *Philip Van Artevelde*, appeared three years before Victoria's accession, but its popularity was sufficient to take it through no less than six editions by 1872; Taylor's discussion of the "present state of poetical literature" throws valuable light on his own and later Victorian poetic practices. Arnold's preface to *Poems* (1854) amounts to a literary manifesto from the third member of the triumvirate of major Victorian poets. It also anticipates the dilemma that would ultimately lead Arnold, applying standards similar to those he later used to dismiss Keats, to abandon the writing of poetry for criticism and cultural commentary. Palgrave's preface to *The Golden Treasury* is curiously short given the reputation that the *Treasury* eventually attained as the most popular anthology ever compiled, but its brevity may reflect Palgrave's own reservations about the book at the time of its publication. Differing in kind is Dante Gabriel Rossetti's Introduction to the second part of his *Early Italian Poets*, containing translations of Dante's *Vita Nuova* and of the Italian lyrical poets contemporary with Dante that for the first time made this corpus of poetry available to the English reading public. The volume is doubly important, however, since it serves as an iconographic source book for Rossetti's own pictures and poems, whose themes and imagery are so heavily indebted to this body of literature.

The three commentaries in the second group—by Richard Hengist Horne on his "Farthing Epic" *Orion*, by Theodore Martin on his *Bon-Gaultier Ballads*, and by Philip James Bailey on his *Festus*, the original editions of which were published in 1843, 1845, and 1839 respectively, all of which were enormously popular in their day—provide different, and distanced, perspectives on the works in question, which, having already stood the test of time, contrast dramatically with the essays appended to volumes that appeared on the occasion of their original publication.

Perhaps the most important selection of essays are those in the third group containing introductory notices to four important Victorian editions of the works of the major Romantic poets, Keats, Blake, and Shelley, and to two editions of leading American poets, Poe and Whitman. It is as difficult from the perspective of the 1980's to imagine that the works of poets so recent as the Romantics were at mid-century so little known and their texts so tentatively established as it is to comprehend how daring in its day was the printing of Whitman's work, even in an expurgated edition, for an English audience.

Keats's reputation suffered during his lifetime from the attacks of the reviewers, and following his death in 1821 until the fourth decade of the century—his collected poems were reprinted in 1840—his poetry was generally neglected and largely unknown. Shelley's "Adonais," with its pale portrait of the poet, and Byron's depiction of him as having been "killed off by one critique" in *Don Juan* (Canto XI) led critics, like Carlyle, who dismissed him as a "miserable creature" with a "weak-eyed maudlin sensibility," to underestimate his poetic powers. But Keats's name and fame were not wholly "writ in water"; his seminal influence on Tennyson and the group of Cambridge Apostles, which included Richard Monckton Milnes, later Lord Houghton, kept his reputation alive. By 1850, as George Ford in his invaluable *Keats and the Victorians* (1944) has shown, Keats's reputation had undergone a remarkable rise. The first full-scale biographical account of Keats was Lord Houghton's (Richard Monckton Milnes) *Life, Letters and Literary Remains*, published in two volumes in 1848, followed in 1854 by his edition of the poems, with a memoir, here reprinted, condensing the material in his *Life*. These two works—Milnes reissued the poetry in 1876—in combination with the rising popularity of Tennyson's poetry, so heavily indebted to Keats, led Swinburne in an *Athenaeum* notice of 1877 to acclaim "Lord Houghton as the one man who had done for Keats and for us all the one service most truly and most thoroughly worth doing and worth thanks" (James Pope-Hennessy, *Monckton Milnes: The Flight of Youth 1851–1885* [1955], 135).

William Michael Rossetti's Aldine Edition of William Blake, published in 1875, was attended by controversy with both the editor and publisher of a rival edition issued in the same year, Richard Herne Shepherd's combined edition, for Basil Montague Pickering, of his two previous editions of 1866 and 1868 of *The Songs of Innocence and Experience* and *Poetical Sketches*, which was itself based on the edition of the *Songs* by Dr. Garth Wilkinson in 1839, published by William Pickering. At the core of the controversy were questions of copyright involving manuscripts owned by Basil Pickering. But even more contentious were the textual liberties taken by Dante Gabriel Rossetti in his edition of selections from Blake's poetry made in the second volume of Gilchrist's *Life of Blake* (1863) and followed in large extent by William Michael, to which Swinburne had at least given his tacit assent in following Dante Gabriel's text in the passages quoted in his *Critical Essay on Blake* (1868), dedicated to William Michael. The nature of the corruptions introduced into Blake's poems by both Rossettis and the adverse effects their editing had on the evolution of Blake's texts is too complicated to rehearse here, but it should be noted that such practices were not uncommon among Victorian editors. When it was published, William Michael's edition was the most complete selection of Blake's poetry available, and together with his prefatory memoir, which was both biographical and critical, it provided Victorian readers with a convenient and inexpensive introduction to Blake's poetry and art.

Less controversial but equally vexing textually was the

Shelley canon, which was first addressed seriously by the poet's widow, Mary Wollstonecraft Shelley, in her four-volume edition of 1839. Preceded by her own suppressed edition of the *Posthumous Poems* in 1824, two unauthorized editions (by Benbow and Ascham, 1826 and 1834), and the Galignani edition of 1829, this edition, which became for later editors what might be called a "scapegoat" text, went through a number of revisions and reprintings in both England and America, to which were added in 1854 Shelley's essays and letters. William Michael Rossetti's two-volume "revised" edition of 1870 (expanded to three volumes in 1878) was intended to rectify the textual inaccuracies in previous editions, which he attributes in his preface to three specific sources: "Shelley himself, Casualty, and Mrs. Shelley." Rossetti's edition was followed two years later by Herne Shepherd's edition (1872–75), with a memoir by Leigh Hunt, and in 1876–77 by the four-volume annotated library edition of H. Buxton Forman, the text of which purported to have been collated against "many manuscripts and all authorized editions." Forman's "Editor's Preface" is reprinted from the second edition of 1886; in it he summarizes the problems posed by Shelley's poetry and traces briefly its textual history. Rossetti's and Forman's prefaces are interesting complementary documents by two of the leading Victorian editors of Shelley, whose later revised editions remained in print well into the twentieth century.

Hannay's *Poe* (1853) and William Michael Rossetti's *Whitman* (1868) have in common that they both first made generally accessible to the English reader the works of America's two most original and able nineteenth-century poets. Both books have interesting publication histories, centering on their respective dedications. Hannay's interest in Poe came through Rossetti and the PRB, who were themselves probably introduced to Poe by the minor American poet Thomas Buchanan Read. Rossetti and Holman Hunt projected with Hannay as early as 1850 an illustrated edition of Poe, from which they later defected. Hannay's edition is the first book dedicated to Dante Gabriel. The PRB connection doubtless explains the somewhat cryptic reference in the concluding paragraph in Hannay's remarks to a "select band"—"three-times-three"—"of admirers." Introduced by a preface whose title, "The Life and Genius of Edgar Allan Poe," conveys the bias of the essay, Hannay's selection consists of forty-three poems, illustrated by twenty engravings cut by the Brothers Dalziel. That Hannay was successful in his purpose of widening Poe's readership in England is indicated by the fact that the book went through three further editions (at least two of them reset and issued by different publishers) in the succeeding decade.

William Rossetti's *Whitman* is dedicated to William Bell Scott, from whom William received a copy of *Leaves of Grass* as early as 1856, the year following its publication in America, where it went ignored, even unmarketed. The circumstances of Scott's acquisition are described in his *Autobiographical Notes* (1892), in which he states that he had the book from his eccentric friend Thomas Dixon, the cork-cutter poet from Sunderland, to whom Ruskin addressed his famous letters in *Time and Tide* (1867) and who later corresponded with Dante Gabriel, introducing him to the poetry of the coal-miner poet Joseph Skipsey. Scott's response to Whitman's work—"Instantly, I perceived the advent of a new poet, a new Americanism, and a new teacher"—was echoed by William Michael in acknowledging the news of Scott's gift, which came through Woolner, who with others denounced the book in the "savagest of terms": "I suspect," William wrote, "I shall find a great deal to like, a great deal to be surprised and amused at, and not a little to approve,—all mingled of course with a lot of worse than worthless eccentricity" (2:32). William's expectations were more than fulfilled, and he wrote Scott that even Dante Gabriel, "who has had nothing but abuse for it hitherto, tends even towards enthusiasm. You could not," he concludes a later letter, "have given me anything I should better like to receive" (2:33). William's letter to Scott anticipates, though somewhat less hyperbolically, his treatment of Whitman's poetry in his prefatory notice to the edition, though much of that notice is devoted to explaining the omissions, which amount to something like half the canon then available, including "Song of Myself." An unwilling bowdlerizer, who refused to excise lines from individual poems, William nevertheless felt constrained to bow to middle-class British tastes, and one of the delights of his preface is his attack on "mealy-mouthed British nineteenth century" morality. William Michael Rossetti must be credited with winning Whitman his first poetic recognition, long before he was accepted in America, and with generating a group of British enthusiasts for his poetry. Together with Anne Gilchrist, the widow of Blake's editor, William Michael became a lifelong champion of Whitman, with whom he regularly corresponded. Following Whitman's paralysis and during the long years of his convalescent retirement in Camden, New Jersey, William Michael led two subscriptions (in 1876 and 1885) to assist the ailing poet. On 13 June 1885 he took the unprecedented step of writing directly to President Cleveland entreating him to intercede on Whitman's behalf—a poet, William advised the president, whom many Europeans would "decisively pronounce . . . to be the poet of largest scope, strongest initiative, and widest future, alive in the world" (C. Gohdes & P. F. Baum, *Letters of William Michael Rossetti* [1934], 181). That some Americans were displeased that subscriptions for the "Great Gray Poet" came from abroad is placed in ironic perspective by a letter William Michael wrote on 3 April 1885 to the American writer Charles Aldrich:

> To show you the inveterate animus which Americans exhibit against their patriotic poet Whitman, I will mention the following fact. In the English editions my book concludes with a sentence saying that not Longfellow but Whitman is properly the national poet of America (perhaps you don't agree with the opinion). When the publishers in 1878 treated with American houses to circulate an American edition of my book, they found that no American would do so as long as that sentence stood in print. My publishers consulted me: and I told them that, so far as I am concerned with the book, the sentence must remain as it stands: but that, if their own trade-interests in

America required an alteration, they could act as they chose . . .: and I believe that all copies sold in America omit that final sentence, while all copies sold in England retain it. (187)

The final group of critical essays consists of three prefaces to the posthumous collections of the poetry of Arthur Hugh Clough. While the essays are cast as memoirs and each was prepared by persons close to the poet—his Balliol college friend Francis Turner Palgrave, his American editor and friend, Charles Eliot Norton, and his wife—they represent three distinctive critical points of view with which to evaluate Victorian contemporary reaction to Clough, perhaps the most eccentric Victorian poet, leaving aside Gerard Manley Hopkins, who, though chronologically a Victorian, is more often associated with the poets of the twentieth than of the nineteenth century.

While each of the essays in this selection stands alone, it is interesting to note the interrelationships that many of the poets and editors had both with each other and with the subjects of the several editions. Buxton Forman, for example, brought out multiple editions of Keats's poetry and letters between 1883 and 1906, including the first edition of the poet's letters to Fanny Brawne (1878), and Francis Turner Palgrave edited Keats for the Golden Treasury Series in 1884. Most surprising, however, (and quite unsuspected) is the direct and peripheral association of the Rossetti brothers with so many of the authors and works included. Besides their specific contributions already discussed, the Rossettis have some connection with no fewer than ten of the selections or poets. On the most superficial level, William Michael reviewed Clough's *Bothie* and Arnold's *Strayed Reveller* in the first and second numbers of *The Germ* (January and February 1850) and was thus instrumental in bringing their early works to the attention of the reading public. And Dante Gabriel, who read Henry Taylor's *Philip Van Artevelde* in the early 50's, quoted four lines from the poem to describe his friendship with William Holman Hunt in presenting a daguerreotype of his first exhibited oil, *The Girlhood of Mary Virgin*, to his Pre-Raphaelite brother on his departure for the Holy Land in 1854 (reproduced in *Pre-Raphaelitism and the Pre-Raphaelite Brotherhood* 1:268–69). Rossetti and the Pre-Raphaelites were also fascinated with *Festus*, which is regarded by most critics as one of the key works of the Spasmodic School of Poetry.

The involvement of the Rossettis with Keats and Shelley is much more critical. William Michael was not only an early devotee of the poet, he was, with Forman, one of the two major nineteenth-century authorities on Shelley. His two-volume edition appeared six years before Forman's, and the two joined forces in correspondence over the preparation of their respective later editions, sharing information and details on Shelley's life and poetry; and both were charter members of the Shelley Society, founded by Frederick Furnivall in 1886. The Rossetti brothers read Keats as early as 1845, three years before the formation of the PRB. Dante Gabriel, who regarded himself as one of the first to rediscover the poet, was enthusiastic in praising and recommending him to his colleagues, and Keats's works inspired a number of Pre-Raphaelite paintings. Indeed, Keats may even have been instrumental in naming the Brotherhood. George Ford has traced in meticulous detail Rossetti's role as a proselytizer of Keats, and it was his influence that converted William Michael, who both edited Keats for the Moxon Popular Poets series and wrote a rather perfunctory biography of the poet in the "Great Writers" series in 1887.

Finally, it must be said that no examination of the revival of Blake in the nineteenth-century can ignore the crucial role of the Rossettis. Dante Gabriel's acquisition of the famed Blake notebook (known as the Rossetti Manuscript) from a minion of the British Museum in 1848 placed him in a fortuitous position to provide vital material for Alexander Gilchrist's monumental *Life of William Blake* in 1863. On Gilchrist's untimely death, the task of composing the "Supplementary" chapter to volume one fell to him, and he was singly responsible for the "Selections" from the poetry, which occupy nearly two hundred pages of volume two. The remainder of that volume is taken up mainly with William's "Descriptive Catalogue" of Blake's visual art, the first checklist of the artist's pictures, drawings, and engravings.

Both brothers worked closely with Anne Gilchrist, the writer's widow, on the second edition of the *Life* (1880), and while they are given no title-page credit for their contributions to this pioneer work in Blake scholarship, they must be regarded in every sense as collaborators, though as mentioned above, their gratuitous tampering with the texts of Blake's poems seriously, and adversely, affected future scholarship.

This stricture notwithstanding, the prominence of Dante Gabriel and William Michael Rossetti in Victorian art and literature has never been in serious doubt. The evidence of their liaison with so many of the poetic and scholarly projects of the century—over and above their involvement in the Pre-Raphaelite Movement—perhaps places them, more centrally than has heretofore been recognized, in the vanguard of many of those formative activities that shaped to so great an extent Victorian and modern literary taste.

PREFACE.

As this work, consisting of two Plays and an Interlude, is equal in length to about six such plays as are adapted to representation, it is almost unnecessary to say that it was not intended for the stage. It is properly an Historical Romance, cast in a dramatic and rythmical form. Historic truth is preserved in it, as far as the material events are concerned—of course with the usual exception of such occasional dilatations and compressions of time as are required in dramatic composition.

This is, perhaps, all the explanation which is absolutely required in this place; but, as there may be readers who feel an inclination to learn something of an author's tastes in poetry before they proceed to the perusal of what he has written, I will take the opportunity which a preface affords me of expressing my opinions upon two or three of the most prominent features in the present state of poetical literature; and I shall do so the more gladly, because I am apprehensive, that without some previous intimations of the kind, my work might occasion disappointment to the admirers of that highly coloured poetry which has been popular in these latter years. If in the strictures, which, with this object, I may be led to make upon authors of great reputation, I should appear to be wanting in the respect due to prevalent opinions,—opinions which, from the very circumstance of their prevalence, must be assumed to be partaken by many to whom deference is owing,—I trust that it will be attributed, not to any spirit of dogmatism, far less to a love of disparagement; but simply to the desire of exercising, with a discreet freedom, that humble independence of judgment in matters of taste, which it is for the advantage of literature that every man of letters should maintain.

My views have not, in truth, been founded upon any predisposition to depreciate the popular poetry of the times. It will always produce a powerful impression upon very young readers, and I scarcely think that it can have been more admired by any than by myself, when I was included in that category. I have not ceased to admire this poetry in its degree; and the interlude which I have inserted between these plays will show, that, to a limited extent, I have been desirous even to cultivate and employ it: but I am unable to concur in opinion with those who would place it in the foremost ranks of the art: nor does it seem to have been capable of sustaining itself quite firmly in the very high degree of public estimation in which it was held at its first appearance, and for some years afterwards. The poetical taste to which some of the popular poets of this century gave birth, appears at present to maintain a more unshaken dominion over the writers of poetry, than over its readers.

These poets were characterised by great sensibility and fervour, by a profusion of imagery, by force and beauty of language, and by a versification peculiarly easy and adroit, and abounding in that sort of melody, which, by its very obvious cadences, makes itself most pleasing to an unpractised ear. They exhibited, therefore, many of the most attractive graces and charms of poetry—its vital warmth not less than its external embellishments; and had not the admiration which they excited, tended to produce an indifference to higher, graver, and more various endowments, no one would have said that it was, in any evil sense, excessive. But from this unbounded indulgence in the mere luxuries of poetry, has there not ensued a want of adequate appreciation for its intellectual and immortal part? I confess, that such seems to me to have been both the actual and the natural result; and I can hardly believe the public taste to have been in a healthy state, whilst the most approved poetry of past times was almost unread. We may now, perhaps, be turning back to it; but it was not, as far as I can judge, till more than a quarter of a century had expired, that any signs of re-action could be discerned. Till then, the elder luminaries of our poetical literature were obscured, or little regarded; and we sate with dazzled eyes at a high festival of poetry, where, as at the funeral of Arvalan, the torch-light put out the star-light.

So keen was the sense of what the new poets possessed, that it never seemed to be felt that any thing was deficient in them. Yet their deficiences were not unimportant. They wanted, in the first place, subject matter. A feeling came more easily to them than a reflection, and an image was always at hand when a thought was not forthcoming. Either they did not look upon mankind with observant eyes, or they did not feel it to be any part of their vocation to turn what they saw to account. It did not belong to poetry, in their apprehension, to thread the mazes of life in all its classes and under all its circumstances, common as well as romantic, and, seeing all things, to infer and to instruct: on the contrary, it was to stand aloof from every thing that is plain and true; to have little concern with what is rational or wise; it was to be, like music, a moving and enchanting art, acting upon the fancy, the affections, the passions, but scarcely connected with the exercise of the intellectual faculties. These writers had, indeed, adopted a tone of language which is hardly consistent with the state of mind in which a man makes use of his understanding. The realities of nature, and the truths which they suggest, would have seemed cold and incongruous, if suffered to mix with the strains of impassioned sentiment and glowing imagery in which they poured themselves forth. Spirit was not to be debased by any union with matter, in their effusions; dwelling, as they did, in a region of poetical sentiment which did not permit them to walk upon the common earth, or to breathe the common air.

Writers, however, whose appeal is made so exclusively to the excitabilities of mankind, will not find it possible to work upon them continuously without a diminishing effect. Poetry of which sense is not the basis, though it may be excellent of its kind, will not long be reputed to be poetry of the highest order. It may move the feelings and charm the fancy; but failing to satisfy the understanding, it will not take permanent possession of the strong-holds of fame. Lord Byron, in giving the most admirable example of this species of poetry, undoubtedly gave the strongest impulse to the appetite for it. Yet this impulse is losing its force, and even Lord Byron himself repudiated, in the latter years of his life, the poetical taste which he had espoused and propagated. The constitution of this writer's mind is not difficult to understand, and sufficiently explains the growth of his taste.

Had he united a philosophical intellect to his peculiarly poetical temperament, he would probably have been the greatest poet of his age. But no man can be a very great poet who is not also a great philosopher. Whatever Lord Byron's natural powers may have been, idleness and light reading, an early acquisition of popularity by the exercise of a single talent, and an absorbing and contracting self-love, confined the field of his operations within narrow limits. He was in knowledge merely a man of Belles-lettres; nor does he appear at any time to have betaken himself to such studies as would have tended to the cultivation and discipline of his reasoning powers, or the enlargement of his mind. He had, however, not only an ardent and brilliant imagination, but a clear understanding; and the signs both of what he had and of what he wanted, are apparent in his poetry. There is apparent in it a working and moulding spirit, with a want of material to work up, — a great command of language, with a want of any views or reflections which, if unembellished by imagery, or unassociated with passionate feelings, it would be very much worth while to express. Page after page throughout his earlier poems, there is the same uninformed energy at work upon the same old feelings; and when at last he became conscious that a theme was wanting, it was at a period of life when no man will consent to put himself to school; he could change his style and manner, but he could not change his moral and intellectual being, nor extend the sphere of his contemplations to subjects which were alien in *spirit* from those with which he had been hitherto, whether in life or in literature, exclusively conversant: in short, his mind was past the period of growth; there was (to use a phrase of Ben Jonson's) an *ingeni-stitium,* or wit-stand: he felt, apparently, that the food on which he had fed his mind had not been invigorating; but it could no longer bear a stronger diet, and he turned his genius loose to rove over the surface of society, content with such light observations upon life and manners as any acute man of the world might collect upon his travels, and conscious that he could recommend them to attention by such wit, brilliancy, dexterity of phrase, and versatility of fancy, as no one but himself could command.

His misanthropy was probably, like his tenderness, not practical, but merely matter of imagination, assumed for purposes of effect. But whilst his ignorance of the better elements of human nature may be believed to have been in a great measure affected, it is not to be supposed that he knew of them with a large and appreciating knowledge. Yet that knowledge of human nature which is exclusive of what is good in it, is, to say the least, as shallow and imperfect as that which is exclusive of what is evil. There is no such thing as philosophical misanthropy; and if a misanthropical spirit, be it genuine or affected, be found to pervade a man's writings, that spirit may be poetical as far as it goes, but being at fault in its philosophy, it will never, in the long run of time, approve itself equal to the institution of a poetical fame of the highest and most durable order.

These imperfections are especially observable in the portraitures of human character (if such it can be called) which are most prominent in Lord Byron's works. There is nothing in them of the mixture and modification,—nothing of the composite fabric which Nature has assigned to Man.

They exhibit rather passions personified, than persons impassioned. But there is a yet worse defect in them. Lord Byron's conception of a hero is an evidence, not only of scanty materials of knowledge from which to construct the ideal of a human being, but also of a want of perception of what is great or noble in our nature. His heroes are creatures abandoned to their passions, and essentially, therefore, weak of mind. Strip them of the veil of mystery and the trappings of poetry, resolve them into their plain realities, and they are such beings as, in the eyes of a man of masculine judgment, would certainly excite no sentiment of admiration, even if they did not provoke contempt. When the conduct and feelings attributed to them are reduced into prose, and brought to the test of a rational consideration, they must be perceived to be beings in whom there is no strength, except that of their intensely selfish passions,—in whom all is vanity; their exertions being for vanity under the name of love, or revenge, and their sufferings for vanity under the name of pride. If such beings as these are to be regarded as heroical, where in human nature are we to look for what is low in sentiment, or infirm in character?

How nobly opposite to Lord Byron's, was Shakspeare's conception of a hero:—

" Give me that man
That is not passion's slave, and I will wear him
In my heart's core; aye, in my heart of heart."

Lord Byron's genius, however, was powerful enough to cast a highly romantic colouring over these puerile creations, and to impart the charms of forcible expression, fervid feeling, and beautiful imagery, to thoughts in themselves not more remarkable for novelty than for soundness. The public required nothing more; and if he himself was brought latterly to a sense of his deficiencies of knowledge and general intellectual cultivation, it must have been more by the effect of time in so far maturing his very vigorous understanding, than by any correction from without. No writer of his age has had less of the benefits of adverse criticism. His own judgment, and that of his readers, have been left equally without check or guidance; and the decline in popular estimation which he has suffered for these last few years, may be rather attributed to a satiated appetite on the part of the public, than to a rectified taste: for those who have ceased to admire his poetry so ardently as they did, do not appear in general to have transferred their admiration to any worthier object.

Nor can it be said that anything better, or indeed anything half so good, has been subsequently produced. The poetry of the day, whilst it is greatly inferior in quality, continues to be like his in kind. It consists of little more than a poetical diction, an arrangement of words implying a sensitive state of mind, and therefore more or less calculated to excite corresponding associations, though, for the most part, not pertinently to any matter in hand; a diction which addresses itself to the sentient, not the percipient, properties of the mind, and displays merely symbols or types of feelings, which might exist with equal force in a being the most barren of understanding.

It may be proper, however, to take a distinction between the ordinary Byronian poetry, and that which may be considered as the offspring, either in the first or second generation, of the genius of Mr. Shelley. Mr. Shelley was a person of a more powerful and expansive imagination than Lord Byron, but he was inferior to him in those practical abilities, which (unacceptable as such an opinion may be to those who believe themselves to be writing under the guidance of inspiration) are essential to the production of consummate poetry. The editor of Mr. Shelley's posthumous poems apologises for the publication of some fragments in a very incomplete state, by remarking how much " more than every other poet of the present day, every line and word he wrote is instinct with peculiar beauty." Let no man sit down to write with the purpose of making every line and word beautiful and peculiar. The only effect of such an endeavour will be to corrupt his judgment and confound his understanding. In Mr. Shelley's case, besides an endeavour of this kind, there seems to have been an attempt to unrealise every object in nature, presenting them under forms and combinations in which they are never to be seen through the mere medium of our eye-sight. Mr. Shelley seems to have written under the notion that no phenomena can be perfectly poetical, until they shall have been so decomposed from their natural order and coherency, as to be brought before the reader in the likeness of a phantasma or a vision. A poet is, in his estimation, (if I may venture to infer his principles from his practice,) purely and pre-eminently a visionary. Much beauty, exceeding splendour of diction and imagery, cannot but be perceived in his poetry, as well as exquisite charms of versification; and a reader of an apprehensive fancy will doubtless be entranced whilst he reads: but when he shall have closed the volume, and considered within himself what it has added to his stock of permanent impressions, of recurring thoughts, of pregnant recollections, he will probably find his stores in this kind no more enriched by having read Mr. Shelley's poems, than by having gazed on so many gorgeously coloured clouds in an evening sky. Surpassingly beautiful they were whilst before his eyes; but forasmuch as they had no relevancy to his life, past or future, the impression upon the memory barely survived that upon the senses.

I would by no means wish to be understood as saying that a poet can be too imaginative, provided that his other faculties be exercised in due proportion to his imagination. I would have no man depress his imagination, but I would have him raise his reason to be its equipoise. What I would be understood to oppugn, is the strange opinion which seems to prevail amongst certain of our writers and readers of poetry, that good sense stands in a species of antagonism to poetical genius, instead of being one of its most essential constituents. The maxim that a poet should be " of imagination all compact," is not, I think, to be adopted thus literally. That predominance of the imaginative faculty, or of impassioned temperament, which is incompatible with the attributes of a sound understanding and a just judgment, may make a rhapsodist, a melodist, or a visionary, each of whom may produce what may be admired for the particular talent and beauty belonging to it: but imagination and passion, thus unsupported, will never make a poet, in the largest and highest sense of the appellation:—

" For Poetry is Reason's self sublimed;
'Tis Reason's sovereignty, whereunto
All properties of sense, all dues of wit,
All fancies, images, perceptions, passions,
All intellectual ordinance grown up
From accident, necessity, or custom,
Seen to be good, and after made authentic;
All ordinance aforethought, that from science
Doth prescience take, and from experience law;
All lights and institutes of digested knowledge,
Gifts and endowments of intelligence
From sources living, from the dead bequests,—
Subserve and minister*."

Mr. Shelley and his disciples, however,—the followers (if I may so call them) of the PHANTASTIC SCHOOL, labour to effect a revolution in this order of things. They would transfer the domicile of poetry to regions where reason, far from having any supremacy or rule, is all but

* MS.

unknown, an alien and an outcast; to seats of anarchy and abstraction, where imagination exercises the shadow of an authority, over a people of phantoms, in a land of dreams.

In bringing these very cursory criticisms to a close, I must beg leave to warn the reader against any expectation that he will find my work free either from the faults which I attribute to others, or from faults which may be worse, and more peculiarly my own. The actual works of men will not bear to be measured by their ideal standerds in any case; and I may observe, in reference to my own, that my critical views have rather resulted from composition than directed it. If, however, I have been unable to avoid the errors which I condemn, or errors not less censurable, I trust that, on the other hand, I shall not be found to have deprived myself, by any narrowness or perversity of judgment, of the advantage which the study of these writers, exceptionable though they be, may undoubtedly afford to one who, whilst duly taking note of their general defects, shall not have closed his mind to a perception of their particular excellences. I feel, and have already expressed, a most genuine, and I hope not an inadequate, admiration for the powers which they respectively possess; and wherever it might occur to me that the exercise of those powers would be appropriate and consistent, I should not fail to benefit by their example to the extent of my capabilities. To say, indeed, that I admire them, is to admit that I owe them much; for admiration is never thrown away upon the mind of him who feels it, except when it is misdirected or blindly indulged. There is perhaps nothing which more enlarges or enriches the mind, than the disposition to lay it genially open to impressions of pleasure from the exercise of every species of talent; nothing by which it is more impoverished than the habit of undue depreciation. What is puerile, pusillanimous, or wicked, it can do us no good to admire; but let us admire all that can be admired without debasing the dispositions or stultifying the understanding.

PREFACE.

I HAVE allowed the Preface to the former edition of these Poems to stand almost without change, because I still believe it to be, in the main, true. I must not, however, be supposed insensible to the force of much that has been alleged against portions of it, or unaware that it contains many things incompletely stated, many things which need limitation. It leaves, too, untouched the question, how far and in what manner the opinions there expressed respecting the choice of subjects apply to lyric poetry; that region of the poetical field which is chiefly cultivated at present. But neither have I time now to supply these deficiencies, nor is this the proper place for attempting it: on one or two points alone I wish to offer, in the briefest possible way, some explanation.

An objection has been ably urged to the classing together, as subjects equally belonging to a past time,

Œdipus and Macbeth. And it is no doubt true that to Shakspeare, standing on the verge of the middle ages, the epoch of Macbeth was more familiar than that of Œdipus. But I was speaking of actions as they presented themselves to us moderns: and it will hardly be said that the European mind, since Voltaire, has much more affinity with the times of Macbeth than with those of Œdipus. As moderns, it seems to me, we have no longer any direct affinity with the circumstances and feelings of either; as individuals, we are attracted towards this or that personage, we have a capacity for imagining him, irrespective of his times, solely according to a law of personal sympathy; and those subjects for which we feel this personal attraction most strongly, we may hope to treat successfully. Prometheus or Joan of Arc, Charlemagne or Agamemnon — one of these is not really nearer to us now than another; each can be made present only by an act of poetic imagination: but this man's imagination has an affinity for one of them, and that man's for another.

It has been said that I wish to limit the Poet in his choice of subjects to the period of Greek and Roman antiquity: but it is not so: I only counsel him to choose for his subjects great actions, without regarding to what time they belong. Nor do I deny that the poetic faculty can and does manifest itself in treating the most trifling action, the most hopeless subject. But it is a pity that power should be wasted; and that the Poet should be compelled to impart interest and force to his subject, instead of receiving them from it, and thereby doubling his impressiveness. There is, it has been excellently said, an immortal strength in the stories of great actions: the most gifted poet, then, may well be glad to supplement with it that mortal weakness, which, in presence of the vast spectacle of life and the world, he must for ever feel to be his individual portion.

Again, with respect to the study of the classical writers of antiquity; it has been said that we should emulate rather than imitate them. I make no objection: all I say is, let us study them. They can help to cure us of what is, it seems to me, the great vice of our intellect, manifesting itself in our incredible vagaries in literature, in art, in religion, in morals; namely, that it is *fantastic*, and wants *sanity*. Sanity — that is the great virtue of the ancient literature: the want of that is the great defect of the modern, in spite of all its variety and power. It is impossible to read carefully the great ancients, without losing something of our caprice and eccentricity; and to emulate them we must at least read them.

London, June 1, 1854.

PREFACE

TO

THE FIRST EDITION.

In two small volumes of Poems, published anonymously, one in 1849, the other in 1852, many of the Poems which compose the present volume have already appeared. The rest are now published for the first time.

I have, in the present collection, omitted the Poem from which the volume published in 1852 took its title. I have done so, not because the subject of it was a Sicilian Greek born between two and three thousand years ago, although many persons would think this a sufficient reason. Neither have I done so because I had, in my own opinion, failed in the delineation which I intended to effect. I intended to delineate the feelings of one of the last of the Greek religious philosophers, one of the family of Orpheus and Musæus, having survived his fellows, living on into a time when the habits of Greek thought and feeling had begun fast to change, character to dwindle, the influence of the Sophists to prevail. Into the feelings of a man so situated there entered much that we are accustomed to consider as exclusively modern; how much, the fragments of Empedocles himself which remain to us are sufficient at least to indicate. What those who are familiar only with the great monuments of early Greek genius suppose to be its exclusive characteristics, have disappeared; the calm, the cheerfulness, the disinterested objectivity have disappeared: the dialogue of the mind with itself has commenced; modern problems have presented themselves; we hear already the doubts, we witness the discouragement, of Hamlet and of Faust.

The representation of such a man's feelings must be interesting, if consistently drawn. We all naturally take pleasure, says Aristotle, in any imitation or representation whatever: this is the basis of our love of Poetry: and we take pleasure in them, he adds, because all knowledge is naturally agreeable to us; not to the philosopher only, but to mankind at large.

Every representation therefore which is consistently drawn may be supposed to be interesting, inasmuch as it gratifies this natural interest in knowledge of all kinds. What is *not* interesting, is that which does not add to our knowledge of any kind; that which is vaguely conceived and loosely drawn; a representation which is general, indeterminate, and faint, instead of being particular, precise, and firm.

Any accurate representation may therefore be expected to be interesting; but, if the representation be a poetical one, more than this is demanded. It is demanded, not only that it shall interest, but also that it shall inspirit and rejoice the reader: that it shall convey a charm, and infuse delight. For the Muses, as Hesiod says, were born that they might be " a forgetfulness of evils, and a truce from cares:" and it is not enough that the Poet should add to the knowledge of men, it is required of him also that he should add to their happiness. "All Art," says Schiller, "is dedicated to Joy, and there is no higher and no more serious problem, than how to make men happy. The right Art is that alone, which creates the highest enjoyment."

A poetical work, therefore, is not yet justified when

it has been shown to be an accurate, and therefore interesting representation; it has to be shown also that it is a representation from which men can derive enjoyment. In presence of the most tragic circumstances, represented in a work of Art, the feeling of enjoyment, as is well known, may still subsist: the representation of the most utter calamity, of the liveliest anguish, is not sufficient to destroy it: the more tragic the situation, the deeper becomes the enjoyment; and the situation is more tragic in proportion as it becomes more terrible.

What then are the situations, from the representation of which, though accurate, no poetical enjoyment can be derived? They are those in which the suffering finds no vent in action; in which a continuous state of mental distress is prolonged, unrelieved by incident, hope, or resistance; in which there is everything to be endured, nothing to be done. In such situations there is inevitably something morbid, in the description of them something monotonous. When they occur in actual life, they are painful, not tragic; the representation of them in poetry is painful also.

To this class of situations, poetically faulty as it

appears to me, that of Empedocles, as I have endeavoured to represent him, belongs; and I have therefore excluded the Poem from the present collection.

And why, it may be asked, have I entered into this explanation respecting a matter so unimportant as the admission or exclusion of the Poem in question? I have done so, because I was anxious to avow that the sole reason for its exclusion was that which has been stated above; and that it has not been excluded in deference to the opinion which many critics of the present day appear to entertain against subjects chosen from distant times and countries: against the choice, in short, of any subjects but modern ones.

"The Poet," it is said*, and by an intelligent critic, "the Poet who would really fix the public attention must leave the exhausted past, and draw his subjects from matters of present import, and *therefore* both of interest and novelty."

Now this view I believe to be completely false. It is worth examining, inasmuch as it is a fair sample of a class of critical dicta everywhere current at the

---

* In *The Spectator* of April 2d, 1853. The words quoted were not used with reference to poems of mine.

present day, having a philosophical form and air, but no real basis in fact; and which are calculated to vitiate the judgment of readers of poetry, while they exert, so far as they are adopted, a misleading influence on the practice of those who write it.

What are the eternal objects of Poetry, among all nations, and at all times? They are actions; human actions; possessing an inherent interest in themselves, and which are to be communicated in an interesting manner by the art of the Poet. Vainly will the latter imagine that he has everything in his own power; that he can make an intrinsically inferior action equally delightful with a more excellent one by his treatment of it: he may indeed compel us to admire his skill, but his work will possess, within itself, an incurable defect.

The Poet, then, has in the first place to select an excellent action; and what actions are the most excellent? Those, certainly, which most powerfully appeal to the great primary human affections: to those elementary feelings which subsist permanently in the race, and which are independent of time. These feelings are permanent and the same; that which interests them is permanent and the same also. The modernness or antiquity of an action, therefore, has nothing to do with its fitness for poetical representation; this depends upon its inherent qualities. To the elementary part of our nature, to our passions, that which is great and passionate is eternally interesting; and interesting solely in proportion to its greatness and to its passion. A great human action of a thousand years ago is more interesting to it than a smaller human action of to-day, even though upon the representation of this last the most consummate skill may have been expended, and though it has the advantage of appealing by its modern language, familiar manners, and contemporary allusions, to all our transient feelings and interests. These, however, have no right to demand of a poetical work that it shall satisfy them; their claims are to be directed elsewhere. Poetical works belong to the domain of our permanent passions: let them interest these, and the voice of all subordinate claims upon them is at once silenced.

Achilles, Prometheus, Clytemnestra, Dido — what modern poem presents personages as interesting, even to us moderns, as these personages of an "exhausted past?" We have the domestic epic dealing with the details of modern life which pass daily under our eyes; we have poems representing modern personages in contact with the problems of modern life, moral, intellectual, and social; these works have been produced by poets the most distinguished of their nation and time; yet I fearlessly assert that Hermann and Dorothea, Childe Harold, Jocelyn, The Excursion, leave the reader cold in comparison with the effect produced upon him by the latter books of the Iliad, by the Orestea, or by the episode of Dido. And why is this? Simply because in the three latter cases the action is greater, the personages nobler, the situations more intense: and this is the true basis of the interest in a poetical work, and this alone.

It may be urged, however, that past actions may be interesting in themselves, but that they are not to be adopted by the modern Poet, because it is impossible for him to have them clearly present to his own mind, and he cannot therefore feel them deeply, nor represent them forcibly. But this is not necessarily the case. The externals of a past action, indeed, he cannot know with the precision of a contemporary; but his business is with its essentials. The outward man of Œdipus or of Macbeth, the houses in which they lived, the ceremonies of their courts, he cannot accurately figure to himself; but neither do they essentially concern him. His business is with their inward man; with their feelings and behaviour in certain tragic situations, which engage their passions as men; these have in them nothing local and casual; they are as accessible to the modern Poet as to a contemporary.

The date of an action, then, signifies nothing: the action itself, its selection and construction, this is what is all-important. This the Greeks understood far more clearly than we do. The radical difference between their poetical theory and ours consists, as it appears to me, in this: that, with them, the poetical character of the action in itself, and the conduct of it, was the first consideration; with us, attention is fixed mainly on the value of the separate thoughts and images which occur in the treatment of an action. They regarded the whole; we regard the parts. With them, the action predominated over the expression of it; with us, the expression predominates over the action. Not that they failed in expression, or were inattentive to it; on the contrary, they are the highest models of expression, the unapproached masters of the *grand style:* but their expression is so excellent because it is so admirably kept in its right degree of prominence; because it is so simple and so well subordinated; because it draws its force directly from the pregnancy of the matter which it conveys. For what reason was the Greek tragic poet confined to so limited a range of subjects? Because there are so few actions which unite in themselves, in the highest degree, the conditions of excellence: and it was not thought that on any but an excellent subject could an excellent Poem be constructed. A few actions, therefore, eminently adapted for tragedy, maintained almost exclusive possession of the Greek tragic stage; their significance appeared inexhaustible; they were as permanent problems, perpetually offered to the genius of every fresh poet. This too is the reason of what appears to us moderns a certain baldness of expression in Greek tragedy; of the triviality with which we often reproach the remarks of the chorus, where it takes part in the dialogue: that the action itself, the situation of Orestes, or Merope, or Alcmæon, was to stand the central point of interest, unforgotten, absorbing, principal;

that no accessories were for a moment to distract the spectator's attention from this; that the tone of the parts was to be perpetually kept down, in order not to impair the grandiose effect of the whole. The terrible old mythic story on which the drama was founded stood, before he entered the theatre, traced in its bare outlines upon the spectator's mind; it stood in his memory, as a group of statuary, faintly seen, at the end of a long and dark vista: then came the Poet, embodying outlines, developing situations, not a word wasted, not a sentiment capriciously thrown in: stroke upon stroke, the drama proceeded: the light deepened upon the group; more and more it revealed itself to the rivetted gaze of the spectator: until at last, when the final words were spoken, it stood before him in broad sunlight, a model of immortal beauty.

This was what a Greek critic demanded; this was what a Greek poet endeavoured to effect. It signified nothing to what time an action belonged; we do not find that the Persæ occupied a particularly high rank among the dramas of Æschylus, because it represented a matter of contemporary interest: this was not what a cultivated Athenian required; he required that the permanent elements of his nature should be moved; and dramas of which the action, though taken from a long-distant mythic time, yet was calculated to accomplish this in a higher degree than that of the Persæ, stood higher in his estimation accordingly. The Greeks felt, no doubt, with their exquisite sagacity of taste, that an action of present times was too near them, too much mixed up with what was accidental and passing, to form a sufficiently grand, detached, and self-subsistent object for a tragic poem: such objects belonged to the domain of the comic poet, and of the lighter kinds of poetry. For the more serious kinds, for *pragmatic* poetry, to use an excellent expression of Polybius, they were more difficult and severe in the range of subjects which they permitted. Their theory and practice alike, the admirable treatise of Aristotle, and the unrivalled works of their poets, exclaim with a thousand tongues — " All depends upon the subject; choose a fitting action, penetrate yourself with the feeling of its situations; this done, everything else will follow."

But for all kinds of poetry alike there was one point on which they were rigidly exacting; the adaptability of the subject to the kind of poetry selected, and the careful construction of the poem.

How different a way of thinking from this is ours! We can hardly at the present day understand what Menander meant, when he told a man who enquired as to the progress of his comedy that he had finished it, not having yet written a single line, because he had constructed the action of it in his mind. A modern critic would have assured him that the merit of his piece depended on the brilliant things which arose under his pen as he went along. We have poems which seem to exist merely for the sake of single lines and passages; not for the sake of producing any total-impression. We have critics who seem to direct their attention merely to detached expressions, to the language about the action, not to the action itself. I verily think that the majority of them do not in their hearts believe that there is such a thing as a total-impression to be derived from a poem at all, or to be demanded from a poet; they think the term a commonplace of metaphysical criticism. They will permit the Poet to select any action he pleases, and to suffer that action to go as it will, provided he gratifies them with occasional bursts of fine writing, and with a shower of isolated thoughts and images. That is, they permit him to leave their poetical sense ungratified, provided that he gratifies their rhetorical sense and their curiosity. Of his neglecting to gratify these, there is little danger; he needs rather to be warned against the danger of attempting to gratify these alone; he needs rather to be perpetually reminded to prefer his action to everything else; so to treat this, as to permit its inherent excellences to develope themselves, without interruption from the intrusion of his personal peculiarities: most fortunate, when he most entirely succeeds in effacing himself, and in enabling a noble action to subsist as it did in nature.

But the modern critic not only permits a false practice; he absolutely prescribes false aims.—" A true allegory of the state of one's own mind in a representative history," the Poet is told, "is perhaps the highest thing that one can attempt in the way of poetry."—And accordingly he attempts it. An allegory of the state of one's own mind, the highest problem of an art which imitates actions! No assuredly, it is not, it never can be so: no great poetical work has ever been produced with such an aim. Faust itself, in which something of the kind is attempted, wonderful passages as it contains, and in spite of the unsurpassed beauty of the scenes which relate to Margaret, Faust itself, judged as a whole, and judged strictly as a poetical work, is defective: its illustrious author, the greatest poet of modern times, the greatest critic of all times, would have been the first to acknowledge it; he only defended his work, indeed, by asserting it to be "something incommensurable."

The confusion of the present times is great, the multitude of voices counselling different things bewildering, the number of existing works capable of attracting a young writer's attention and of becoming his models, immense: what he wants is a hand to guide him through the confusion, a voice to prescribe to him the aim which he should keep in view, and to explain to him that the value of the literary works which offer themselves to his attention is relative to their power of helping him forward on his road towards this aim. Such a guide the English writer at the present day will nowhere find. Failing this, all that can be looked for, all indeed that can be desired, is, that his attention should be fixed on excellent models; that he may reproduce, at any rate, something of their excellence, by penetrating himself with their works and by catching their spirit, if he cannot be taught to produce what is excellent independently.

Foremost among these models for the English writer stands Shakspeare: a name the greatest perhaps of all poetical names; a name never to be mentioned without reverence. I will venture, however, to express a doubt, whether the influence of his works, excellent and fruitful for the readers of poetry, for the great majority, has been of unmixed advantage to the writers of it. Shakspeare indeed chose excellent subjects; the world could afford no better than Macbeth, or Romeo and Juliet, or Othello: he had no theory respecting the necessity of choosing subjects of present import, or the paramount interest attaching to allegories of the state of one's own mind; like all great poets, he knew well what constituted a poetical action; like them, wherever he found such an action, he took it; like them, too, he found his best in past times. But to these general characteristics of all great poets he added a special one of his own; a gift, namely, of happy, abundant, and ingenious expression, eminent and unrivalled: so eminent as irresistibly to strike the attention first in him, and even to throw into comparative shade his other excellences as a poet. Here has been the mischief. These other excellences were his fundamental excellences *as a poet;* what distinguishes the artist from the mere amateur, says Goethe, is *Architectonicè* in the highest sense ; that power of execution, which creates, forms, and constitutes: not the profoundness of single thoughts, not the richness of imagery, not the abundance of illustration. But these attractive accessories of a poetical work being more easily seized than the spirit of the whole, and these accessories being possessed by Shakspeare in an unequalled degree, a young writer having recourse to Shakspeare as his model runs great risk of being vanquished and absorbed by them, and, in consequence, of reproducing, according to the measure of his power, these, and these alone. Of this preponderating quality of Shakspeare's genius, accordingly, almost the whole of modern English poetry has, it appears to me, felt the influence. To the exclusive attention on the part of his imitators to this it is in a great degree owing, that of the majority of modern poetical works the details alone are valuable, the composition worthless. In reading them one is perpetually reminded of that terrible sentence on a modern French poet — *il dit tout ce qu'il veut, mais malheureusement il n'a rien à dire.*

Let me give an instance of what I mean. I will take it from the works of the very chief among those who seem to have been formed in the school of Shakspeare: of one whose exquisite genius and pathetic death render him for ever interesting. I will take the poem of Isabella, or the Pot of Basil, by Keats. I choose this rather than the Endymion, because the latter work, (which a modern critic has classed with the Fairy Queen!) although undoubtedly there blows through it the breath of genius, is yet as a whole so utterly incoherent, as not strictly to merit the name of a poem at all. The poem of Isabella, then, is a perfect treasure-house of graceful and felicitous words and images: almost in every stanza there occurs one of those vivid and picturesque turns of expression, by which the object is made to flash upon the eye of the mind, and which thrill the reader with a sudden delight. This one short poem contains, perhaps, a greater number of happy single expressions which one could quote than all the extant tragedies of Sophocles. But the action, the story? The action in itself is an excellent one; but so feebly is it conceived by the Poet, so loosely constructed, that the effect produced by it, in and for itself, is absolutely null. Let the reader, after he has finished the poem of Keats, turn to the same story in the Decameron: he will then feel how pregnant and interesting the same action has become in the hands of a great artist, who above all things delineates his object; who subordinates expression to that which it is designed to express.

I have said that the imitators of Shakspeare, fixing their attention on his wonderful gift of expression, have directed their imitation to this, neglecting his other excellences. These excellences, the fundamental excellences of poetical art, Shakspeare no doubt possessed them—possessed many of them in a splendid degree; but it may perhaps be doubted whether even he himself did not sometimes give scope to his faculty of expression to the prejudice of a higher poetical duty. For we must never forget that Shakspeare is the great poet he is from his skill in discerning and firmly conceiving an excellent action, from his power of intensely feeling a situation, of intimately associating himself with a character; not from his gift of expression, which rather even leads him astray, degenerating sometimes into a fondness for curiosity of expression, into an irritability of fancy, which seems to make it impossible for him to say a thing plainly, even when the press of the action demands the very directest language, or its level character the very simplest. Mr. Hallam, than whom it is impossible to find a saner and more judicious critic, has had the courage (for at the present day it needs courage) to remark, how extremely and faultily difficult Shakspeare's language often is. It is so: you may find main scenes in some of his greatest tragedies, King Lear for instance, where the language is so artificial, so curiously tortured, and so difficult, that every speech has to be read two or three times before its meaning can be comprehended. This over-curiousness of expression is indeed but the excessive employment of a wonderful gift — of the power of saying a thing in a happier way than any other man; nevertheless, it is carried so far that one understands what M. Guizot meant, when he said that Shakspeare appears in his language to have tried all styles except that of simplicity. He has not the severe and scrupulous self-restraint of the ancients, partly no doubt, because he had a far less cultivated and exacting audience: he has indeed a far wider range than they

had, a far richer fertility of thought; in this respect
he rises above them: in his strong conception of his
subject, in the genuine way in which he is penetrated
with it, he resembles them, and is unlike the moderns:
but in the accurate limitation of it, the conscientious
rejection of superfluities, the simple and rigorous development of it from the first line of his work to the
last, he falls below them, and comes nearer to the
moderns. In his chief works, besides what he has of his
own, he has the elementary soundness of the ancients;
he has their important action and their large and broad
manner: but he has not their purity of method. He
is therefore a less safe model; for what he has of his
own is personal, and inseparable from his own rich
nature; it may be imitated and exaggerated, it cannot
be learned or applied as an art; he is above all suggestive; more valuable, therefore, to young writers as
men than as artists. But clearness of arrangement,
rigour of development, simplicity of style — these may
to a certain extent be learned: and these may, I am
convinced, be learned best from the ancients, who although infinitely less suggestive than Shakspeare, are
thus, to the artist, more instructive.

What then, it will be asked, are the ancients to be

our sole models? the ancients with their comparatively narrow range of experience, and their widely different circumstances? Not, certainly, that which is narrow in the ancients, nor that in which we can no longer sympathise. An action like the action of the Antigone of Sophocles, which turns upon the conflict between the heroine's duty to her brother's corpse and that to the laws of her country, is no longer one in which it is possible that we should feel a deep interest. I am speaking too, it will be remembered, not of the best sources of intellectual stimulus for the general reader, but of the best models of instruction for the individual writer. This last may certainly learn of the ancients, better than anywhere else, three things which it is vitally important for him to know: — the all-importance of the choice of a subject; the necessity of accurate construction; and the subordinate character of expression. He will learn from them how unspeakably superior is the effect of the one moral impression left by a great action treated as a whole, to the effect produced by the most striking single thought or by the happiest image. As he penetrates into the spirit of the great classical works, as he becomes gradually aware of their intense significance, their noble simplicity, and their calm pathos, he will be convinced that it is this effect, unity and profoundness of moral impression, at which the ancient Poets aimed; that it is this which constitutes the grandeur of their works, and which makes them immortal. He will desire to direct his own efforts towards producing the same effect. Above all, he will deliver himself from the jargon of modern criticism, and escape the danger of producing poetical works conceived in the spirit of the passing time, and which partake of its transitoriness.

The present age makes great claims upon us: we owe it service, it will not be satisfied without our admiration. I know not how it is, but their commerce with the ancients appears to me to produce, in those who constantly practise it, a steadying and composing effect upon their judgment, not of literary works only, but of men and events in general. They are like persons who have had a very weighty and impressive experience: they are more truly than others under the empire of facts, and more independent of the language current among those with whom they live. They wish neither to applaud nor to revile their age: they wish to know what it is, what it can give them, and whether this is what they want. What they want, they know very well; they want to educe and cultivate what is best and noblest in themselves: they know, too, that this is no easy task — χαλεπὸν, as Pittacus said. χαλεπὸν ἐσθλὸν ἔμμεναι — and they ask themselves sincerely whether their age and its literature can assist them in the attempt. If they are endeavouring to practise any art, they remember the plain and simple proceedings of the old artists, who attained their grand results by penetrating themselves with some noble and significant action, not by inflating themselves with a belief in the preeminent importance and greatness of their own times. They do not talk of their mission, nor of interpreting their age, nor of the coming Poet; all this, they know, is the mere delirium of vanity; their business is not to praise their age, but to afford to the men who live in it the highest pleasure which they are capable of feeling. If asked to afford this by means of subjects drawn from the age itself, they ask what special fitness the present age has for supplying them: they are told that it is an era of progress, an age commissioned to carry out the great ideas of industrial development and social amelioration. They reply that with all this they can do nothing; that the elements they need for the exercise of their art are great actions, calculated powerfully and delightfully to affect what is permanent in the human soul; that so far as the present age can supply such actions, they will gladly make use of them; but that an age wanting in moral grandeur can with difficulty supply such, and an age of spiritual discomfort with difficulty be powerfully and delightfully affected by them.

A host of voices will indignantly rejoin that the present age is inferior to the past neither in moral grandeur nor in spiritual health. He who possesses the discipline I speak of will content himself with remembering the judgments passed upon the present age, in this respect, by the men of strongest head and widest culture whom it has produced; by Goethe and by Niebuhr. It will be sufficient for him that he knows the opinions held by these two great men respecting the present age and its literature; and that he feels assured in his own mind that their aims and demands upon life were such as he would wish at any rate, his own to be; and their judgment as to what is impeding and disabling such as he may safely follow. He will not, however, maintain a hostile attitude towards the false pretensions of his age; he will content himself with not being overwhelmed by them. He will esteem himself fortunate if he can succeed in banishing from his mind all feelings of contradiction, and irritation, and impatience; in order to delight himself with the contemplation of some noble action of a heroic time, and to enable others, through his represention of it, to delight in it also.

I am far indeed from making any claim, for myself, that I possess this discipline; or for the following Poems, that they breathe its spirit. But I say, that in the sincere endeavour to learn and practise, amid the bewildering confusion of our times, what is sound and true in poetical art, I seemed to myself to find the only sure guidance, the only solid footing, among the ancients. They, at any rate, knew what they wanted in Art, and we do not. It is this uncertainty which is disheartening, and not hostile criticism. How often have I felt this when reading words of disparagement or of cavil: that it is the uncertainty as to what is really to be aimed at which makes our difficulty, not the dissatisfaction of the critic, who himself suffers from the same uncertainty. *Non me tua fervida terrent Dicta; Dii me terrent, et Jupiter hostis.*

Two kinds of *dilettanti,* says Goethe, there are in poetry : he who neglects the indispensable mechanical part, and thinks he has done enough if he shows spirituality and feeling ; and he who seeks to arrive at poetry merely by mechanism, in which he can acquire an artisan's readiness, and is without soul and matter. And he adds, that the first does most harm to Art, and the last to himself. If we must be *dilettanti :* if it is impossible for us, under the circumstances amidst which we live, to think clearly, to feel nobly, and to delineate firmly : if we cannot attain to the mastery of the great artists — let us, at least, have so much respect for our Art as to prefer it to ourselves : let us not bewilder our successors : let us transmit to them the practice of Poetry, with its boundaries and wholesome regulative laws, under which excellent works may again, perhaps, at some future time, be produced, not yet fallen into oblivion through our neglect, not yet condemned and cancelled by the influence of their eternal enemy, Caprice.

Fox How, Ambleside,
  October 1. 1853.

PREFACE

THIS little Collection differs, it is believed, from others in the attempt made to include in it all the best original Lyrical pieces and Songs in our language, by writers not living,—and none beside the best. Many familiar verses will hence be met with ; many also which should be familiar :—the Editor will regard as his fittest readers those who love Poetry so well, that he can offer them nothing not already known and valued.

The Editor is acquainted with no strict and exhaustive definition of Lyrical Poetry ; but he has found the task of practical decision increase in clearness and in facility as he advanced with the work, whilst keeping in view a few simple principles. Lyrical has been here held essentially to imply that each Poem shall turn on some single thought, feeling, or situation. In accordance with this, narrative, descriptive, and didactic poems,—unless accompanied by rapidity of movement, brevity, and the colouring of human passion,—have been excluded. Humourous poetry, except in the very unfrequent instances where a truly poetical tone pervades the whole, with what is strictly personal, occasional, and religious, has been considered foreign to the idea of the book. Blank verse and the ten-syllable couplet, with all pieces markedly dramatic, have been rejected as alien from what is commonly understood by Song, and rarely conforming to Lyrical conditions in treatment. But it is not anticipated, nor is it possible, that all readers shall think the line accurately drawn. Some poems, as Gray's Elegy, the Allegro and Penseroso, Wordsworth's Ruth or Campbell's Lord Ullin, might be claimed with perhaps equal justice for a narrative or descriptive selection: whilst with reference especially to Ballads and Sonnets, the Editor can only state that he has taken his utmost pains to decide without caprice or partiality.

This also is all he can plead in regard to a point even more liable to question ;—what degree of merit should give rank among the Best. That a Poem shall be worthy of the writer's genius,—that it shall reach a perfection commensurate with its aim,—that we should require finish in proportion to brevity,—that passion, colour, and originality cannot atone for serious imperfections in clearness, unity, or truth,—that a few good lines do not make a good poem,—that popular estimate is serviceable as a guidepost more than as a compass,—above all, that Excellence should be looked for rather in the Whole than in the Parts,—such and other such canons have been always steadily regarded. He may however add that the pieces chosen, and a far larger number rejected, have been carefully and repeatedly considered; and that he has been aided throughout by two friends of independent and exercised judgment, besides the distinguished person addressed in the Dedication. It is hoped that by this procedure the volume has been freed from that one-sidedness which must beset individual decisions :—but for the final choice the Editor is alone responsible.

It would obviously have been invidious to apply the standard aimed at in this Collection to the Living. Nor, even in the cases where this might be done without offence, does it appear wise to attempt to anticipate the verdict of the Future on our contemporaries. Should the book last, poems by Tennyson, Bryant, Clare, Lowell, and others, will no doubt claim and obtain their place among the best. But the Editor trusts that this will be effected by other hands, and in days far distant.

Chalmers' vast collection, with the whole works of all accessible poets not contained in it, and the best Anthologies of different periods, have been twice systematically read through : and it is hence improbable that any omissions which may be regretted are due to oversight. The poems are printed entire, except in a very few instances (specified in the notes) where a stanza has been omitted. The omissions have been risked only when the piece could be thus brought to a closer lyrical unity: and, as essentially opposed to this unity, extracts, obviously such, are excluded. In regard to the text, the purpose of the book has appeared to justify the choice of the most poetical version, wherever more than one exists: and much labour has been given to present each poem, in disposition, spelling, and punctuation, to the greatest advantage.

For the permission under which the copyright pieces are inserted, thanks are due to the respective Proprietors, without whose liberal concurrence the scheme of the collection would have been defeated.

In the arrangement, the most poetically-effective order has been attempted. The English mind has passed through phases of thought and cultivation so various and so opposed during these three centuries of Poetry, that a rapid passage between Old and New, like rapid alteration of the eye's focus in looking at the landscape, will always be wearisome and hurtful to the sense of Beauty. The poems have been therefore distributed into Books corresponding, I to the ninety years closing about 1616, II thence to 1700, III to 1800, IV to the half century just ended. Or, looking at the Poets who more or less give each portion its distinctive character, they might be called the Books of Shakespeare, Milton, Gray, and Wordsworth. The volume, in this respect, so far as the limitations of its range allow, accurately reflects the natural growth and evolution of our Poetry. A rigidly chronological sequence, however, rather fits a collection aiming at instruction than at pleasure, and the Wisdom which comes through Pleasure:—within each book the pieces have therefore been arranged in gradations of feeling or subject. The development of the symphonies of Mozart and Beethoven has been here thought of as a model, and nothing placed without careful consideration. And it is hoped that the contents of this Anthology will thus be found to present a certain unity, 'as episodes,' in the noble language of Shelley, 'to that great Poem which all poets, like the cooperating thoughts of one great mind, have built up since the beginning of the world.'

As he closes his long survey, the Editor trusts he may add without egotism, that he has found the vague general verdict of popular Fame more just than those have thought, who, with too severe a criticism, would confine judgments on Poetry to 'the selected few of many generations.' Not many appear to have gained reputation without some gift or performance that, in due degree, deserved it: and if no verses by certain writers who show less strength than sweetness, or more thought than mastery in expression, are printed in this volume, it should not be imagined that they have been excluded without much hesitation and regret,—far less that they have been slighted. Throughout this vast and pathetic array of Singers now silent, few have been honoured with the name Poet, and have not possessed a skill in words, a sympathy with beauty, a tenderness of feeling, or seriousness in reflection, which render their works, although never perhaps attaining that loftier and finer excellence here required, —better worth reading than much of what fills the scanty hours that most men spare for self-improvement, or for pleasure in any of its more elevated and permanent forms.—And if this be true of even mediocre poetry, for how much more are we indebted to the best! Like the fabled fountain of the Azores, but with a more various power, the magic of this Art can confer on each period of life its appropriate blessing: on early years Experience, on maturity Calm, on age, Youthfulness. Poetry gives treasures 'more golden than gold,' leading us in higher and healthier ways than those of the world, and interpreting to us the lessons of Nature. But she speaks best for herself. Her true accents, if the plan has been executed with success, may be heard throughout the following pages:—wherever the Poets of England are honoured, wherever the dominant language of the world is spoken, it is hoped that they will find fit audience.

INTRODUCTION TO PART II.

IN the second division of this volume are included all the poems I could find which seemed to have value as being personal to the circle of Dante's friends, and as illustrating their intercourse with each other. Those who know the Italian collections from which I have drawn these pieces (many of them most obscure) will perceive how much which is in fact elucidation is here attempted to be embodied in themselves, as to their rendering, arrangement, and heading: since the Italian editors have never yet paid any of them, except of course those by Dante, any such attention; but have printed and reprinted them in a jumbled and disheartening form, by which they can serve little purpose except as *testi di lingua*—dead stock by whose help the makers of dictionaries may smother the language with decayed words. Appealing now I believe for the first time, though in a new idiom, from their once living writers to such living readers as they may find, they require some preliminary notice.

The *Vita Nuova* (or Autobiography of Dante's youth till about his twenty-seventh year) is already well known to many in the original, or by means of essays and of English versions partial or entire;

though I believe there is not one of the latter which has been published in any full sense of the word. It is, therefore, and on all accounts, unnecessary to say much more of it here than it says for itself. Wedded to its exquisite and intimate beauties are personal peculiarities which excite wonder and conjecture, best replied to in the words which Beatrice herself is made to utter in the *Commedia:* "Questi *fù tal* nella sua vita nuova."* Thus then young Dante *was*. All that seemed possible to be done here for the work was to translate it in as free and clear a form as was consistent with fidelity to its meaning; to ease it, as far as possible, from notes and encumbrances; and to accompany it for the first time with those poems from Dante's own lyrical series which have reference to its events, as well as with such native commentary (so to speak) as might be afforded by the writings of those with whom its author was at that time in familiar intercourse. Not chiefly to Dante, then, of whom so much is known to all or may readily be found written, but to the various other members of his circle, these few pages should be devoted.

It may be noted here, however, how necessary a knowledge of the Vita Nuova is to the full comprehension of the part borne by Beatrice in the *Commedia*. Moreover, it is only from the perusal of its earliest and then undivulged self-communings that we can divine the whole bitterness of wrong to such a soul as Dante's, its poignant sense of abandonment, or its deep and jealous refuge in memory. Above all, it is here that we find the first manifestations of that wisdom of obedience, that natural breath of duty, which afterwards, in the

* Purgatorio, C. xxx.

Commedia, lifted up a mighty voice for warning and testimony. Throughout the Vita Nuova there is a strain like the first falling murmur which reaches the ear in some remote meadow, and prepares us to look upon the sea.

Boccaccio, in his Life of Dante, tells us that the great poet, in later life, was ashamed of this work of his youth. Such a statement hardly seems reconcilable with the allusions to it made or implied in the Commedia; but it is true that the Vita Nuova is a book which only youth could have produced, and which must chiefly remain sacred to the young; to each of whom the figure of Beatrice, less lifelike than lovelike, will seem the friend of his own heart. Nor is this, perhaps, its least praise. To tax its author with effeminacy on account of the extreme sensitiveness evinced by this narrative of his love, would be manifestly unjust, when we find that, though love alone is the theme of the Vita Nuova, war already ranked among its author's experiences at the period to which it relates. In the year 1289, the one preceding the death of Beatrice, Dante served with the foremost cavalry in the great battle of Campaldino, on the eleventh of June, when the Florentines defeated the people of Arezzo. In the autumn of the next year, 1290, when for him, by the death of Beatrice, the city as he says " sat solitary," such refuge as he might find from his grief was sought in action and danger : for we learn from the Commedia (*Hell*, C. xxi.) that he served in the war then waged by Florence upon Pisa, and was present at the surrender of Caprona. He says, using the reminiscence to give life to a description, in his great way :—

"I've seen the troops out of Caprona go
On terms, affrighted thus, when on the spot
They found themselves with foemen compass'd so."
(CAYLEY's *Translation.*)

A word should be said here of the title of Dante's autobiography. The adjective *Nuovo, nuova,* or *Novello, novella,* literally *New,* is often used by Dante and other early writers in the sense of *young.* This has induced some editors of the Vita Nuova to explain the title as meaning *Early Life.* I should be glad on some accounts to adopt this supposition, as everything is a gain which increases clearness to the modern reader; but on consideration I think the more mystical interpretation of the words, as *New Life,* (in reference to that revulsion of his being which Dante so minutely describes as having occurred simultaneously with his first sight of Beatrice,) appears the primary one, and therefore the most necessary to be given in a translation. The probability may be that both were meant, but this I cannot convey.*

---

* I must hazard here (to relieve the first page of my translation from a long note) a suggestion as to the meaning of the most puzzling passage in the whole *Vita Nuova*,—that sentence just at the outset which says, " La gloriosa donna della mia mente, la quale fu chiamata da molti Beatrice, i quali non sapeano che si chiamare." On this passage all the commentators seem helpless, turning it about and sometimes adopting alterations not to be found in any ancient manuscript of the work. The words mean literally, " The glorious lady of my mind who was called Beatrice by many who knew not how she was called." This presents the obvious difficulty that the lady's name really *was* Beatrice, and that Dante throughout uses that name himself. In the text of my version I have adopted, as a rendering, the one of the various compromises which seemed to give the most beauty to the meaning. But it occurs to me that a less irrational escape out of the difficulty than any I have seen suggested may possibly be found by linking

PART II. 193

Among the poets of Dante's circle, the first in order, the first in power, and the one whom Dante has styled his " first friend," is GUIDO CAVALCANTI, born about 1250, and thus Dante's senior by some fifteen years. It is therefore probable that there is some inaccuracy about the statement, often repeated, that he was Dante's fellow-pupil under Brunetto Latini; though it seems certain that they both studied, probably Guido before Dante, with the same teacher. The Cavalcanti family was among the most ancient in Florence; and its importance may be judged by the fact that in 1280, on the occasion of one of the various missions sent from Rome with the view of pacifying the Florentine factions, the name of " Guido the son of Messer Cavalcante de' Cavalcanti" appears as one of the sureties offered by the city, for the quarter of San Piero Scheraggio. His father must have been notoriously a sceptic in matters of religion, since we find him placed by Dante in the sixth circle of Hell, in one of the fiery tombs of the

---

this passage with the close of the sonnet at page 275 of the Vita Nuova, beginning, "I felt a spirit of Love begin to stir," in the last line of which sonnet Love is made to assert that the name of Beatrice is *Love*. Dante appears to have dwelt on this fancy with some pleasure, from what is said in an earlier sonnet (page 233) about " Love in his proper form" (by which Beatrice seems to be meant) bending over a dead lady. And it is in connection with the sonnet where the name of Beatrice is said to be Love, that Dante, as if to show us that the Love he speaks of is only his own emotion, enters into an argument as to Love being merely an accident in substance,— in other words, " Amòre e il cor gentil son una cosa." This conjecture may be pronounced extravagant; but the Vita Nuova, when examined, proves so full of intricate and fantastic analogies, even in the mere arrangement of its parts, (much more than appears on any but the closest scrutiny,) that it seems admissible to suggest even a whimsical solution of a difficulty which remains unconquered.

unbelievers. That Guido shared this heresy was the popular belief, as is plain from an anecdote in Boccaccio which I shall give; and some corroboration of such reports, at any rate as applied to Guido's youth, seems capable of being gathered from an extremely obscure poem which I have translated on that account (at page 373) as clearly as I found possible. It must be admitted, however, that there is to the full as much devotional as sceptical tendency implied here and there in his writings; while the presence of either is very rare. We may also set against such a charge the fact that Dino Compagni refers, as will be seen, to his having undertaken a religious pilgrimage. But indeed he seems to have been in all things of that fitful and vehement nature which would impress others always strongly, but often in opposite ways. Self-reliant pride gave its colour to all his moods; making his exploits as a soldier frequently abortive through the headstrong ardour of partisanship, and causing the perversity of a logician to prevail in much of his amorous poetry. The writings of his contemporaries, as well as his own, tend to show him rash in war, fickle in love, and presumptuous in belief; but also, by the same concurrent testimony, he was distinguished by great personal beauty, high accomplishments of all kinds, and daring nobility of soul. Not unworthy, for all the weakness of his strength, to have been the object of Dante's early emulation, the first friend of his youth, and his precursor and fellow-labourer in the creation of Italian Poetry.

In the year 1267, when Guido cannot have been much more than seventeen years of age, a last attempt was made in Florence to reconcile the Guelfs and

Ghibellines. With this view several alliances were formed between the leading families of the two factions; and among others, the Guelf Cavalcante de' Cavalcanti wedded his son Guido to a daughter of the Ghibelline Farinata degli Uberti. The peace was of short duration; the utter expulsion of the Ghibellines (through French intervention solicited by the Guelfs) following almost immediately. In the subdivision, which afterwards took place, of the victorious Guelfs into so-called " Blacks " and " Whites," Guido embraced the White party, which tended strongly to Ghibellinism, and whose chief was Vieri de' Cerchi, while Corso Donati headed the opposite faction. Whether his wife was still living at the time when the events of the Vita Nuova occurred, is probably not ascertainable; but about that time Dante tells us that Guido was enamoured of a lady named *Giovanna* or Joan, and whose Christian name is absolutely all that we know of her. However, on the occasion of his pilgrimage to Thoulouse, recorded by Dino Compagni, he seems to have conceived a fresh passion for a lady of that city named Mandetta, who first attracted him by a striking resemblance to his Florentine mistress. Thoulouse had become a place of pilgrimage from its laying claim to the possession of the body, or part of the body, of Saint James the Apostle; though the same supposed distinction had already made the shrine of Compostella in Gallicia one of the most famous throughout all Christendom. That this devout journey of Guido's had other results besides a new love, will be seen by the passage from Compagni's Chronicle. He says:—

" A young and noble knight named Guido, son of Messer

Cavalcante Cavalcanti,—full of courage and courtesy, but disdainful, solitary, and devoted to study,—was a foe to Messer Corso (Donati) and had many times cast about to do him hurt. Messer Corso feared him exceedingly, as knowing him to be of a great spirit, and sought to assassinate him on a pilgrimage which Guido made to the shrine of St. James; but he might not compass it. Wherefore, having returned to Florence and being made aware of this, Guido incited many youths against Messer Corso, and these promised to stand by him. Who being one day on horseback with certain of the house of the Cerchi, and having a javelin in his hand, spurred his horse against Messer Corso, thinking to be followed by the Cerchi that so their companies might engage each other; and he running in on his horse cast the javelin, which missed its aim. And with Messer Corso were Simon his son, a strong and daring youth, and Cecchino de' Bardi, who with many others pursued Guido with drawn swords; but not overtaking him they threw stones after him, and also others were thrown at him from the windows, whereby he was wounded in the hand. And by this matter hate was increased. And Messer Corso spoke great scorn of Messer Vieri, calling him the Ass of the Gate; because, albeit a very handsome man, he was but of blunt wit and no great speaker. And therefore Messer Corso would say often, ' To-day the Ass of the Gate has brayed,' and so greatly disparage him; and Guido he called *Cavicchia*.* And thus it was spread abroad of the *jongleurs*; and especially one named Scampolino reported worse things than were said, that so the Cerchi might be provoked to engage the Donati."

* A nickname chiefly chosen, no doubt, for its resemblance to *Cavalcanti*. The word *cavicchia, cavicchio,* or *caviglia* means a wooden peg or pin. A passage in Boccaccio says, "He had tied his ass to a strong wooden pin," (*caviglia*.) Thus Guido, from his mental superiority, might be said to be the Pin to which the Ass, Messer Vieri, was tethered at the Gate, (that is, the Gate of San Pietro, near which he lived.) However, it seems quite as likely that the nickname was founded on a popular phrase by which one who fails in any undertaking is said " to run his rear on a peg," (*dare del culo in un cavicchio*.) The haughty Corso Donati himself went by the name of *Malefammi* or " Do-me-harm." For an account of his death in 1307, which proved in keeping with his turbulent life, see Dino Compagni's *Chronicle*, or the *Pecorone* of Giovanni Fiorentino (Gior. XXIV. Nov. 2.)

The praise which Compagni, his contemporary, awards to Guido at the commencement of the foregoing extract, receives additional value when viewed in connection with the sonnet addressed to him by the same writer (see page 355), where we find that he could tell him of his faults.

Such scenes as the one related above had become common things in Florence, which kept on its course from bad to worse till Pope Boniface VIII resolved on sending a legate to propose certain amendments in its scheme of government by *Priori* or representatives of the various arts and companies. These proposals, however, were so ill received, that the legate, who arrived in Florence in the month of June, 1300, departed shortly afterwards greatly incensed, leaving the city under a papal interdict. In the ill-considered tumults which ensued we again hear of Guido Cavalcanti.

"It happened (says Giovanni Villani in his History of Florence) that in the month of December (1300) Messer Corso Donati with his followers, and also those of the house of the Cerchi and their followers, going armed to the funeral of a lady of the Frescobaldi family, this party defying that by their looks would have assailed one another; whereby all those who were at the funeral having risen up tumultuously and fled each to his house, the whole city got under arms, both factions assembling in great numbers, at their respective houses. Messer Gentile de' Cerchi, Guido Cavalcanti, Baldinuccio' and Corso Adimari, Baschiero della Tosa and Naido Gherardini, with their comrades and adherents on horse and on foot, hastened to St. Peter's Gate to the house of the Donati. Not finding them there they went on to San Pier Maggiore, where Messer Corso was with his friends and followers; by whom they were encountered and put to flight, with many wounds and with much shame to the party of the Cerchi and to their adherents."

By this time we may conjecture as probable that

Dante, in the arduous position which he then filled as chief of the nine *Priori* on whom the government of Florence devolved, had resigned for far other cares the sweet intercourse of thought and poetry which he once held with that first friend of his who had now become so factious a citizen. Yet it is impossible to say how much of the old feeling may still have survived in Dante's mind when, at the close of the year 1300 or beginning of 1301, it became his duty, as a faithful magistrate of the republic, to add his voice to those of his colleagues in pronouncing a sentence of banishment on the heads of both the Black and White factions, Guido Cavalcanti being included among the latter. The Florentines had been at last provoked almost to demand this course from their governors, by the discovery of a conspiracy, at the head of which was Corso Donati, (while among its leading members was Simone de' Bardi, once the husband of Beatrice Portinari), for the purpose of inducing the Pope to subject the republic to a French peace-maker (*Paciere*) and so shamefully free it from its intestine broils. It appears therefore that the immediate cause of the exile to which both sides were subjected lay entirely with the "Black" party, the leaders of which were banished to the Castello della Pieve in the wild district of Massa Trabœria, while those of the "White" faction were sent to Sarzana, probably (for more than one place bears the name) in the Genovesato. "But this party" (writes Villani) "remained a less time in exile, being recalled on account of the unhealthiness of the place, which made that Guido Cavalcanti returned with a sickness, whereof he died. And of him was a great loss ; seeing that he was a man, as in philosophy, so in many things deeply versed; but therewithal too fastidious and prone to take offence." His death apparently took place in 1301.

When the discords of Florence ceased, for Guido, in death, Dante also had seen their native city for the last time. Before Guido's return he had undertaken that embassy to Rome which bore him the bitter fruit of unjust and perpetual exile: and it will be remembered that a chief accusation against him was that of favour shown to the White party on the banishment of the factions.

Besides the various affectionate allusions to Guido in the *Vita Nuova*, Dante has unmistakeably referred to him in at least two passages of the *Commedia*. One of these references is to be found in those famous lines of the Purgatory (C. xi.) where he awards him the palm of poetry over Guido Guinicelli (though also of the latter he speaks elsewhere with high praise,) and implies at the same time, it would seem, a consciousness of his own supremacy over both.

" Lo, Cimabue thought alone to tread
   The lists of painting; now doth Giotto gain
The praise, and darkness on his glory shed.
   Thus hath one Guido from another ta'en
The praise of speech, and haply one hath pass'd
   Through birth, who from their nest will chase the
      twain."—CAYLEY'S *Translation*.

The other mention of Guido is in that pathetic passage of the Hell (C. x.) where Dante meets among the lost souls Cavalcante de' Cavalcanti:—

" All roundabout he look'd, as though he had
Desire to see if one was with me else.
But after his surmise was all extinct,

> He weeping said : ' If through this dungeon blind
> Thou goest by loftiness of intellect,—
> Where is my son, and wherefore not with thee ?'
> And I to him : ' Of myself come I not :
> He who there waiteth leads me thoro' here,
> Whom haply in disdain your Guido had.'*
>
>   * * * *
>
> Raised upright of a sudden, cried he : ' How
> Did'st say *He had?* Is he not living still ?
> Doth not the sweet light strike upon his eyes ?'
> When he perceived a certain hesitance
> Which I was making ere I should reply,
> He fell supine, and forth appear'd no more."

Dante, however, conveys his answer afterwards to the spirit of Guido's father, through another of the condemned also related to Guido, Farinata degli Uberti, with whom he has been speaking meanwhile :—

> " Then I, as in compunction for my fault,
> Said : ' Now then shall ye tell that fallen one
> His son is still united with the quick.
> And, if I erst was dumb to the response,
> I did it, make him know, because I thought
> Yet on the error you have solved for me.' "
>   (*Translated by* W. M. ROSSETTI.)†

---

* Virgil, Dante's guide through Hell. Any prejudice which Guido entertained against Virgil depended, no doubt, only on his strong desire to see the Latin language give place, in poetry and literature, to a perfected Italian idiom.

† These passages are extracted from a literal blank verse translation of the *Inferno* made by my brother, which is as yet in MS., but which I trust may before long see the light ; as I believe such a work not to be superfluous even now, notwithstanding the many existing versions of the *Commedia*. It is long since Mr. Cary led the way with a good but rather free rendering, more perhaps in the spirit of that day than of this, and accompanied by notes and other editorial matter which are among the clearest and most complete that Dante's work has ever received. Mr. Cayley's version, of much more recent date, seems to me to have now occupied (and that without much likelihood of its being superseded) the post which is the first in all such cases,—that of a fine English poem rendering a great foreign one in its own metre, with all essential

PART II. 201

The date which Dante fixes for his vision is Good Friday of the year 1300. A year later, his answer must have been different. The love and friendship of his Vita Nuova had then both left him. For ten years Beatrice Portinari had been dead, or (as Dante says in the *Convito*) " lived in heaven with the angels and on earth with his soul." And now, distant and probably estranged from him, Guido Cavalcanti was gone too.

Among the Tales of Franco Sacchetti, and in the Decameron of Boccaccio, are two anecdotes relating to Guido. Sacchetti tells us how, one day that he was intent on a game at chess, Guido (who is described as " one who perhaps had not his equal in Florence") was disturbed by a child playing about, and threatened punishment if the noise continued. The child, however, managed slily to nail Guido's coat to the chair on which he sat, and so had the laugh against him when he rose soon afterwards to fulfil his threat. This may serve as an amusing instance of Guido's hasty temper, but is rather a disappointment after its magniloquent

---

fidelity, for the use of English readers who read for the sake of poetry. Dr. Carlyle's prose translation takes other ground, that of word-for-word literality, for which it presupposes prose to be indispensable. I will venture to assert that my brother's work yields nothing to his, however, in minute precision of this kind; and if so, it can hardly be doubtful that its being in blank verse is a great gain, even as adding the last refinement to exactness by showing the division of the lines; but of course also on the higher poetic ground. I do not forget that a version already exists, by Mr. Pollock, professing a like aim with my brother's; and must again express a hope that publicity will shortly afford to all an opportunity of judging the claims of the new attempt. I may here also acknowledge my obligations to my brother for valuable suggestions and assistance in the course of my present work.

heading, which sets forth how " Guido Cavalcanti, being a man of great valour and a philosopher, is defeated by the cunning of a child."

The ninth Tale of the sixth Day of the Decameron relates a repartee of Guido's, which has all the profound platitude of mediæval wit. As the anecdote, however, is interesting on other grounds, I translate it here.

" You must know that in past times there were in our city certain goodly and praiseworthy customs no one of which is now left, thanks to avarice which has so increased with riches that it has driven them all away. Among the which was one whereby the gentlemen of the outskirts were wont to assemble together in divers places throughout Florence, and to limit their fellowships to a certain number, having heed to compose them of such as could fitly discharge the expense. Of whom to-day one, and to-morrow another, and so all in turn, laid tables each on his own day for all the fellowship. And in such wise often they did honour to strangers of worship and also to citizens. They all dressed alike at least once in the year, and the most notable among them rode together through the city; also at seasons they held passages of arms, and specially on the principal feast-days, or whenever any news of victory or other glad tidings had reached the city. And among these fellowships was one headed by Messer Betto Brunelleschi, into the which Messer Betto and his companions had often intrigued to draw Guido di Messer Cavalcante de' Cavalcanti; and this not without cause, seeing that not only he was one of the best logicians that the world held, and a surpassing natural philosopher, (for the which things the fellowship cared little,) but also he exceeded in beauty and courtesy, and was of great gifts as a speaker; and everything that it pleased him to do, and that best became a gentleman, he did better than any other; and was exceeding rich and knew well to solicit with honourable words whomsoever he deemed worthy. But Messer Betto had never been able to succeed in enlisting him; and he and his companions believed that this was through Guido's much pondering which divided him from other men. Also because he held somewhat of the opinion of the Epicureans, it was said among the vulgar sort, that his speculations were only to cast about whether he might find that there was no God. Now on a certain day Guido having left Or San Michele, and held along the Corso degli Adimari as far as San Giovanni (which oftentimes was his walk); and coming to the great marble tombs which now are in the Church of Santa Reparata, but were then with many others in San Giovanni; he being between the porphyry columns which are there among those tombs, and the gate of San Giovanni which was locked;—it so chanced that Messer Betto and his fellowship came riding up by the Piazza di Santa Reparata, and seeing Guido among the sepulchres, said, ' Let us go and engage him.' Whereupon, spurring their horses in the fashion of a pleasant assault, they were on him almost before he was aware, and began to say to him, ' Thou, Guido, wilt none of our fellowship; but lo now! when thou shalt have found that there is no God, what wilt thou have done?' To whom Guido, seeing himself hemmed in among then, readily replied, ' Gentlemen, ye are at home here, and may say what ye please to me.' Wherewith, setting his hand on one of those high tombs, being very light of his person, he took a leap and was over on the other side; and so having freed himself from them, went his way. And they all remained bewildered, looking on one another; and began to say that he was but a shallow-witted fellow, and that the answer he had made was as though one should say nothing; seeing that where they were, they had not more to do than other citizens, and Guido not less than they. To whom Messer Betto turned and said thus : ' Ye yourselves are shallow-witted if ye have not understood him. He has civilly and in few words said to us the most uncivil thing in the world; for if ye look well to it, these tombs are the homes of the dead, seeing that in them the dead are set to dwell; and here he says that we are at home; giving us to know that we and all other simple unlettered men, in comparison of him and the learned, are even as dead men; wherefore, being here, we are at home.' Thereupon each of them understood what Guido had meant, and was ashamed; nor ever again did they set themselves to engage him. Also from that day forth they held Messer Betto to be a subtle and understanding knight."

In the above story mention is made of Guido Cavalcanti's wealth, and there seems no doubt that at that time the family was very rich and powerful. On this account I am disposed to question whether the Canzone at page 370 (where the author speaks of his poverty) can really be Guido's work, though I have included it as being interesting if rightly attributed to him; and it is possible that, when exiled, he may have suffered for the time in purse as well as person. About three years after his death, on the 10th June, 1304, the Black party plotted together and set fire to the quarter of Florence chiefly held by their adversaries. In this conflagration the houses and possessions of the Cavalcanti were almost entirely destroyed; the flames in that neighbourhood (as Dino Compagni records) gaining rapidly in consequence of the great number of waxen images in the Virgin's shrine at Or San Michele; one of which, no doubt, was the very image resembling his lady to which Guido refers in a sonnet (see page 333.) After this, their enemies succeeded in finally expelling from Florence the Cavalcanti family,* greatly impoverished by this monstrous fire in which nearly two thousand houses were consumed.

Guido appears, by various evidence, to have written, besides his poems, a treatise on Philosophy and another on Oratory, but his poems only have survived to our day. As a poet, he has more individual life of his own than belongs to any of his predecessors; by far

---

* With them were expelled the still more powerful Gherardini, also great sufferers by the conflagration; who, on being driven from their own country, became the founders of the ancient Geraldine family in Ireland. The Cavalcanti reappear now and then in later European history; and especially we hear of a second Guido Cavalcanti, who also cultivated poetry, and travelled to collect books for the Ambrosian Library; and who, in 1563, visited England as Ambassador to the court of Elizabeth from Charles IX. of France.

the best of his pieces being those which relate to himself, his loves and hates. The best known, however, and perhaps the one for whose sake the rest have been preserved, is the metaphysical canzone on the Nature of Love, beginning, " Donna mi priega," and intended, it is said, as an answer to a sonnet by Guido Orlandi, written as though coming from a lady, and beginning, " Onde si muove e donde nasce Amore?" On this canzone of Guido's there are known to exist no fewer than eight commentaries, some of them very elaborate and written by prominent learned men of the middle ages and *renaissance ;* the earliest being that by Egidio Colonna, a beatified churchman who died in 1316; while most of the too numerous Academic writers on Italian literature speak of this performance with great admiration as Guido's crowning work. A love-song which acts as such a fly-catcher for priests and pedants looks very suspicious; and accordingly, on examination, it proves to be a poem beside the purpose of poetry, filled with metaphysical jargon, and perhaps the very worst of Guido's productions. Its having been written by a man whose life and works include so much that is impulsive and real, is easily accounted for by scholastic pride in those early days of learning. I have not translated it, as being of little true interest; but was pleased lately, nevertheless, to meet with a remarkably complete translation of it by the Rev. Charles T. Brooks of Cambridge, United States.* The stiffness and cold conceits which prevail in this poem may be found

* This translation occurs in the Appendix to an Essay on the Vita Nuova of Dante, including extracts, by my friend Mr. Charles E. Norton, of Cambridge, U. S.,—a work of high delicacy and appreciation which originally appeared by por-

disfiguring much of what Guido Cavalcanti has left, while much besides is blunt, obscure, and abrupt: nevertheless, if it need hardly be said how far he falls short of Dante in variety and personal directness, it may be admitted that he worked worthily at his side, and perhaps before him, in adding those qualities to Italian poetry. That Guido's poems dwelt in the mind of Dante is evident by his having appropriated lines from them, (as well as from those of Guinicelli,) with little alteration, more than once, in the *Commedia*. I should not forget to state in conclusion that a portrait of Guido (of which there is an engraving, I should think badly rendered) exists in the gallery of Florence.

Towards the close of his life, Dante, in his Latin treatise *De Vulgari Eloquio*, again speaks of himself as the friend of a poet,—this time of CINO DA PISTOIA. In an early passage of that work he says that " those who have most sweetly and subtly written poems in modern Italian are Cino da Pistoia and a friend of his." This friend we afterwards find to be Dante himself; as among the various poetical examples quoted are several by Cino followed in three instances by lines from Dante's own lyrics, the author of the latter being again described merely as "Amicus ejus." In immediate proximity to these, or coupled in two instances with examples from Dante alone, are various quotations taken from Guido Cavalcanti; but in none of these cases is anything said to connect Dante with him who was once " the first of his friends."*

tions in the *Atlantic Monthly*, but has since been augmented by the author and privately printed in a volume which is a beautiful specimen of American typography.

* It is also noticeable that in this treatise Dante speaks of Guido Guinicelli on one occasion as *Guido Maximus*, thus

As commonly between old and new, the change of Guido's friendship for Cino's seems doubtful gain. Cino's poetry, like his career, is for the most part smoother than that of Guido, and in some instances it rises into truth and warmth of expression; but it conveys no idea of such powers, for life or for work, as seem to have distinguished the "Cavicchia" of Messer Corso Donati. However, his one talent (reversing the parable) appears generally to be made the most of, while Guido's two or three remain uncertain through the manner of their use.

Cino's Canzone addressed to Dante on the death of Beatrice, as well as his answer to the first sonnet of the Vita Nuova, indicate that the two poets must have become acquainted in youth, though there is no earlier mention of Cino in Dante's writings than those which occur in his treatise on the Vulgar Tongue. To their younger days also we may pro-

seeming to contradict the preference of Cavalcanti which is usually supposed to be implied in the passage I have quoted from the Purgatory. It has been sometimes surmised (perhaps for this reason) that the two Guidos there spoken of may be Guittone d'Arezzo and Guido Guinicelli, the latter being said to surpass the former, of whom Dante elsewhere in the Purgatory has expressed a low opinion. But I should think it doubtful whether the name Guittone, which (if not a nickname, as some say) is substantially the same as Guido, could be so absolutely identified with it: at that rate Cino da Pistoia even might be classed as one Guido, his full name, Guittoncino, being the diminutive of Guittone. I believe it more probable that Guinicelli and Cavalcanti were then really meant, and that Dante afterwards either altered his opinion, or may (conjecturably) have chosen to imply a change of preference in order to gratify Cino da Pistoia whom he so markedly distinguishes as his friend throughout the treatise, and between whom and Cavalcanti some jealousy appears to have existed, as we may gather from one of Cino's sonnets (at page 393); nor is Guido mentioned anywhere with praise by Cino, as other poets are.

bably ascribe the two sonnets translated at pages 319-20 of this volume. It might perhaps be inferred with some plausibility that their acquaintance was revived after an interruption by the sonnet and answer at pages 321-22, and that they afterwards corresponded as friends till the period of Dante's death when Cino wrote his elegy. Of the two sonnets in which Cino expresses disapprobation of what he thinks the partial judgments of Dante's *Commedia*, the first seems written before the great poet's death, but I should think that the second dated after that event, as the *Paradise*, to which it refers, cannot have become fully known in its author's lifetime. Another sonnet sent to Dante elicited a Latin epistle in reply, where we find Cino addressed as " frater carissime." Among Cino's lyrical poems are a few more written in correspondence with Dante, which I have not translated as being of little personal interest.

Guittoncino de' Sinibuldi (for such was Cino's full name) was born in Pistoia, of a distinguished family, in the year 1270. He devoted himself early to the study of law, and in 1307 was Assessor of Civil Causes in his native city. In this year, and in Pistoia, the endless contest of the " Black " and " White " factions first sprang into activity; the " Blacks " and Guelfs of Florence and Lucca driving out the " Whites " and Ghibellines, who had ruled in the city since 1300. With their accession to power came many iniquitous laws in favour of their own party; so that Cino, as a lawyer of Ghibelline opinions, soon found it necessary or advisable to leave Pistoia, for it seems uncertain whether his removal was voluntary or by proscription. He directed his course towards Lombardy, on whose confines the chief of the "White" party in Pistoia, Filippo Vergiolesi, still held the fortress of Pitecchio. Hither Vergiolesi had retreated with his family and adherents when resistance in the city became no longer possible; and it may be supposed that Cino came to join him not on account of political sympathy alone; as Selvaggia Vergiolesi, his daughter, is the lady celebrated throughout the poet's compositions. Three years later, the Vergiolesi and their followers, finding Pitecchio untenable, fortified themselves on the Monte della Sambuca, a lofty peak of the Apennines; which again they were finally obliged to abandon, yielding it to the Guelfs of Pistoia at the price of eleven thousand *lire*. Meanwhile the bleak air of the Sambuca had proved fatal to the lady Selvaggia, who remained buried there, or, as Cino expresses it in one of his poems,

"Cast out upon the steep path of the mountains,
Where Death had shut her in between hard stones."

Over her cheerless tomb Cino bent and mourned, as he has told us, when, after a prolonged absence spent partly in France, he returned through Tuscany on his way to Rome. He had not been with Selvaggia's family at the time of her death; and it is probable that, on his return to the Sambuca, the fortress was already surrendered, and her grave almost the only record left there of the Vergiolesi.

Cino's journey to Rome was on account of his having received a high office under Louis of Savoy, who preceded the Emperor Henry VII. when he went thither to be crowned in 1310. In another three years the last blow was dealt to the hopes of the exiled and persecuted Ghibellines, by the death of the Emperor, attributed sometimes to poison.

P

This death Cino has lamented in a Canzone. It probably determined him to abandon a cause which seemed dead, and return, when possible, to his native city. This he succeeded in doing before 1319, as in that year we find him deputed together with six other citizens, by the Government of Pistoia, to take possession of a stronghold recently yielded to them. He had now been for some time married to Margherita degli Ughi, of a very noble Pistoiese family, who bore him a son named Mino, and four daughters, Diamante, Beatrice, Giovanna, and Lombarduccia. Indeed, this marriage must have taken place before the death of Selvaggia in 1310, as in 1325-26, his son Mino was one of those by whose aid from within, the Ghibelline Castruccio Antelminelli obtained possession of Pistoia, which he held in spite of revolts till his death some two or three years afterwards, when it again reverted to the Guelfs.

After returning to Pistoia, Cino's whole life was devoted to the attainment of legal and literary fame. In these pursuits he reaped the highest honours, and taught at the universities of Siena, Perugia, and Florence; having for his disciples men who afterwards became celebrated, among whom rumour has placed Petrarch, though on examination this seems very doubtful. A sonnet by Petrarch exists, however, commencing " Piangete donne e con voi pianga Amore," written as a lament on Cino's death and bestowing the highest praise on him. He and his Selvaggia are also coupled with Dante and Beatrice in the same poet's *Trionfi d'Amore*, (cap. 4.)

Though established again in Pistoia, Cino resided there but little till about the time of his death, which occurred in 1336-7. His monument, where he is represented as a professor among his disciples, still exists in the Cathedral of Pistoia, and is a mediæval work of great interest. Messer Cino de' Sinibuldi was a prosperous man, of whom we have ample records, from the details of his examinations as a student, to the inventory of his effects after death, and the curious items of his funeral expenses. Of his claims as a poet it may be said that he filled creditably the interval which elapsed between the death of Dante and the full blaze of Petrarch's success. Most of his poems in honour of Selvaggia are full of an elaborate and mechanical tone of complaint which hardly reads like the expression of a real love; nevertheless there are some, and especially the sonnet on her tomb (at page 390), which display feeling and power. The finest, as well as the most interesting, of all his pieces, is the very beautiful canzone in which he attempts to console Dante for the death of Beatrice. Though I have found much fewer among Cino's poems than among Guido's which seemed to call for translation, the collection of the former is a larger one. Cino produced legal writings also, of which the chief one that has survived is a Commentary on the Statutes of Pistoia, said to have great merit, and whose production in the short space of two years was accounted an extraordinary achievement.

Having now spoken of the chief poets of this division, it remains to notice the others of whom less is known.

DANTE DA MAIANO (Dante being, as with Alighieri, the short of Durante, and Maiano in the neighbourhood of Fiesole) had attained some reputation as a poet before the career of his great namesake began; his lady Nina going by the then unequivocal title of " La Nina di Dante." This also appears to have been the case from the contemptuous answer sent by him to Dante Alighieri's dream-sonnet in the *Vita Nuova* (see page 396). All the writers on early Italian poetry seem to agree in specially censuring this poet's rhymes as coarse and trivial in manner; nevertheless, they are sometimes distinguished by a careless force not to be despised, and even by snatches of real beauty. Of Dante da Maiano's life no record whatever has come down to us.

Most literary circles have their prodigal, or what in modern phrase might be called their " scamp;" and among our Danteans, this place is indisputably filled by CECCO ANGIOLIERI, of Siena. Nearly all his sonnets (and no other pieces by him have been preserved) relate either to an unnatural hatred of his father, or to an infatuated love for the daughter of a shoemaker, a certain married Becchina. It would appear that Cecco was probably enamoured of her before her marriage as well as afterwards, and we may surmise that his rancour against his father may have been partly dependent, in the first instance, on the disagreements arising from such a connection. However, from an amusing and lifelike story in the Decameron (Gior. IX. Nov. 4.) we learn that on one occasion Cecco's father paid him six months' allowance in advance, in order that he might proceed to the Marca d'Ancona and join the suite of a Papal Legate who was his patron; which looks, after all, as if the father had some care of his graceless son. The story goes on to relate how Cecco (whom Boc-

PART II. 213

caccio describes as a handsome and well-bred man) was induced to take with him as his servant a fellow-gamester with whom he had formed an intimacy purely on account of the hatred which each of the two bore his own father, though in other respects they had little in common. The result was that this fellow, during the journey, while Cecco was asleep at Buonconvento, took all his money and lost it at the gaming-table, and afterwards managed by an adroit trick to get possession of his horse and clothes, leaving him nothing but his shirt. Cecco then, ashamed to return to Siena, made his way, in a borrowed suit and mounted on his servant's sorry hack, to Corsignano where he had relations; and there he stayed till his father once more (surely much to his credit) made him a remittance of money. Boccaccio seems to say in conclusion that Cecco ultimately had his revenge on the thief.

Many both of Cecco's love-sonnets and hate-sonnets are very repulsive from their display of powers perverted often to base uses; while it is impossible not to feel some pity for the indications they contain of self-sought poverty, unhappiness, and natural bent to ruin. Altogether they have too much curious individuality to allow of their being omitted here. Their humour is sometimes strong, if not well chosen; their passion always forcible from its evident reality: nor indeed is the sonnet which stands fourth among my translations devoid of a certain delicacy. This quality is also to be discerned in other pieces which I have not included as having less personal interest; but it must be confessed that for the most part the sentiments expressed in Cecco's poetry are either impious or licentious. Most of the sonnets of his which are in print are here given;* the selections concluding with an extraordinary one in which he proposes a sort of murderous crusade against all those who hate their fathers. This I have placed last (exclusive of the sonnet to Dante in exile) in order to give the writer the benefit of the possibility that it was written last, and really expressed a still rather blood-thirsty contrition; belonging at best, I fear, to the content of self-indulgence when he came to enjoy his father's inheritance. But most likely it is to be received as the expression of impudence alone, unless perhaps of hypocrisy.

Cecco Angiolieri seems to have had poetical intercourse with Dante early as well as later in life; but even from the little that remains, we may gather that Dante soon put an end to any intimacy which may have existed between them. That Cecco already poetized at the time to which the *Vita Nuova* relates is evident from a date given in one of his sonnets,— the 20th June, 1291, and from his sonnet raising objections to the one at the close of Dante's autobiography. When the latter was written he was probably on good terms with the young Alighieri; but within no great while afterwards they had discovered that they could not agree, as is shown by a sonnet in which Cecco can find no words bad enough for Dante, who has remonstrated with him about

---

* It may be mentioned (as proving how much of the poetry of this period still remains in MS.) that Ubaldini, in his Glossary to Barberino, published in 1640, cites as grammatical examples no fewer than twenty-two short fragments from Cecco Angiolieri, one of which alone is to be found among the sonnets which I have seen, and which I believe are the only ones in print. Ubaldini quotes them from the Strozzi MSS.

Becchina.* Much later, as we may judge, he again addresses Dante in an insulting tone, apparently while the latter was living in exile at the court of Can Grande della Scala. No other reason can well be assigned for saying that he had " turned Lombard;" while some of the insolent allusions seem also to point to the time when Dante learnt by experience " how bitter is another's bread and how steep the stairs of his house."

Why Cecco in this sonnet should describe himself as having become a Roman, is more puzzling. Boccaccio certainly speaks of his luckless journey to join a papal legate, but does not tell us whether fresh clothes and the wisdom of experience served him in the end to become so far identified with the Church of Rome. However, from the sonnet on his father's death he appears (though the allusion is desperately obscure) to have been then living at an abbey; and also, from the one mentioned above, we may infer that he himself, as well as Dante, was forced to sit at the tables of others: coincidences which almost seem to afford a glimpse of the phenomenal fact that the bosom of the church was indeed for a time the refuge of this shorn lamb. If so, we may further conjecture that the wonderful crusade-sonnet was an *amende honorable* then imposed on him, accompanied probably with more fleshly penance.

It must be remarked, however, that if Guido Cavalcanti's sonnet at page 362, should happen really to have been addressed to Cecco, (a possibility there

---

* Of this sonnet I have seen two printed versions, in both of which the text is so corrupt as to make them very contradictory in important points; but I believe that by comparing the two I have given its meaning correctly. (See page 411.)

suggested in a foot-note,) he must have become a rich man before the period of Dante's exile, as the death of Guido immediately preceded that event. At the same time, there is of course nothing likelier than that he may have found himself poor again before long, and may then (who knows?) have fled to Rome for good, whether with sacred or profane views.

Though nothing indicates the time of Cecco Angiolieri's death, I will venture to surmise that he outlived the writing and revision of Dante's *Inferno*, if only by the token that he is not found lodged in one of its meaner circles. It is easy to feel sure that no sympathy can ever have existed for long between Dante and a man like Cecco; however arrogantly the latter, in his verses, might attempt to establish a likeness and even an equality. We may accept the testimony of so reverent a biographer as Boccaccio, that the Dante of later years was far other than the silent and awe-struck lover of the *Vita Nuova*; but he was still (as he proudly called himself) " the singer of Rectitude," and his that " disdainful soul" which made blessed the mother who had borne him.*

Leaving to his fate (whatever that may have been) the Scamp of Dante's Circle, I must risk the charge of a confirmed taste for slang by describing GUIDO ORLANDI as its Bore. No other word could present him so fully. Very few pieces of his exist besides the five I have given. In one of these,† he rails against his political adversaries; in three,‡ falls foul of his brother poets; and in the remaining one,§

" Alma sdegnosa,
Benedetta colei che in te s' incinse!"
(*Inferno*, C. VIII.)
† Page 423. ‡ Pages 334, 351, 398. § Page 357.

seems somewhat appeased (I think) by a judicious morsel of flattery. I have already referred to a sonnet of his which is said to have led to the composition of Guido Cavalcanti's Canzone on the Nature of Love. He has another sonnet beginning, " Per troppa sottiglianza il fil si rompe,"* in which he is certainly enjoying a fling at somebody, and I suspect at Cavalcanti in rejoinder to the very poem which he himself had instigated. If so, this stamps him a master-critic of the deepest initiation. Of his life nothing is recorded; but no wish perhaps need be felt to know much of him, as one would probably have dropped his acquaintance. We may be obliged to him, however, for his character of Guido Cavalcanti (at page 351) which is boldly and vividly drawn.

Next follow three poets of whom I have given one specimen apiece. By BERNARDO DA BOLOGNA (page 353) no other is known to exist, nor can anything be learnt of his career. GIANNI ALFANI was a noble and distinguished Florentine, a much graver man, it would seem, than one could judge from this sonnet of his (page 352), which belongs rather to the school of Sir Pandarus of Troy.

DINO COMPAGNI, the chronicler of Florence, is represented here by a sonnet addressed to Guido Cavalcanti,† which is all the more interesting, as the same writer's historical work furnishes so much of the little known about Guido. Dino, though one

---

* This sonnet, as printed, has a gap in the middle; let us hope (in so immaculate a censor) from unfitness for publication.

† Crescimbeni (*Ist. d. Volg. Poes.*) gives this sonnet from a MS., where it is headed, " To Guido Guinicelli;" but he surmises, and I have no doubt correctly, that Cavalcanti is really the person addressed in it.

of the noblest citizens of Florence, was devoted to the popular cause, and held successively various high offices in the state. The date of his birth is not fixed, but he must have been at least thirty in 1289, as he was one of the *Priori* in that year, a post which could not be held by a younger man. He died at Florence in 1323. Dino has rather lately assumed for the modern reader a much more important position than he occupied before among the early Italian poets. I allude to the valuable discovery, in the Magliabecchian Library at Florence, of a poem by him in *nona rima* containing 309 stanzas. It is entitled " L' Intelligenza," and is of an allegorical nature with romantic episodes.*

I have placed LAPO GIANNI in this second division on account of the sonnet by Dante (page 340) in which he seems undoubtedly to be the Lapo referred to. It has been supposed by some that Lapo degli Uberti (father of Fazio, and brother-in-law of Guido Cavalcanti) is meant; but this is hardly possible. Dante and Guido seem to have been in familiar intercourse with the Lapo of the sonnet at the time when it and others were written; whereas no Uberti can have been in Florence after the year 1267, when the Ghibellines were expelled; the Uberti family (as I have mentioned elsewhere) being the one of all others which was most jealously kept afar and excluded from every amnesty. The only information which I can find respecting Lapo Gianni is the statement that he was a notary by profession. I have also seen it somewhere asserted (though where

---

* See *Documents inédits pour servir à l'histoire littéraire de l'Italie, &c. par A. F. Ozanam*, (Paris, 1850,) where the poem is printed entire.

I cannot recollect, and am sure no authority was given) that he was a cousin of Dante. We may equally infer him to have been the Lapo mentioned by Dante in his treatise on the Vulgar Tongue, as being one of the few who up to that time had written verses in pure Italian.

Dino Frescobaldi's claim to the place given him here will not be disputed when it is remembered that by his pious care the seven first cantos of Dante's Hell were restored to him in exile, after the Casa Alighieri in Florence had been given up to pillage; by which restoration Dante was enabled to resume his work. This sounds strange when we reflect that a world without Dante would almost be a poorer planet. But for Dino Frescobaldi, too, what labour might not have been spared to how many generations of the bonders and bottlers of Dante, the dealers in foreign wind and words!* Meanwhile, beyond this great fact of Dino's life, which perhaps hardly occupied a day of it, there is no news to be gleaned of him.

Giotto falls by right into Dante's circle, as one great man comes naturally to know another. But he is said actually to have lived in great intimacy with Dante, who was about twelve years older than himself; Giotto having been born in or near the year 1276, at Vespignano, fourteen miles from Florence. He died in 1336, fifteen years after Dante. On the authority of Benvenuto da Imola, (an early commentator on the Commedia,) of Vasari, and others, it is said

* Of course the allusion is only to the floods of empty eloquence and philological acumen which have been lavished upon Dante: no historical labours connected with him can ever be deemed useless.

that Dante visited Giotto while he was painting at Padua; that the great poet furnished the great painter with the conceptions of a series of subjects from the Apocalypse, which he painted at Naples; and that Giotto, finally, passed some time with Dante in the exile's last refuge at Ravenna. There is a tradition that Dante also studied drawing with Giotto's master Cimabue; and that he practised it in some degree is evident from the passage in the *Vita Nuova*, where he speaks of his drawing an angel. The reader will not need to be reminded of Giotto's portrait of the youthful Dante, painted in the Bargello at Florence, then the chapel of the Podestà. This is the author of the Vita Nuova. That other portrait shown us in the posthumous mask,—a face dead in exile after the death of hope,—should front the first page of the Sacred Poem to which Heaven and earth had set their hands; but which might never bring him back to Florence, though it had made him haggard for many years.*

Giotto's Canzone on the doctrine of voluntary poverty,—the only poem we have of his,—is a protest against a perversion of gospel teaching which had gained ground in his day to the extent of becoming a popular frenzy. People went literally mad upon it; and to the reaction against this madness may also be assigned (at any rate partly) Cavalcanti's poem on Poverty, which, as we have seen, is otherwise not easily explained, if authentic. Giotto's canzone is all the more curious when we re-

---

* " Se mai continga che il poema sacro
   Al quale ha posto mano e cielo e terra,
   Sì che m' ha fatto per più anni macro,
   Vinca la crudeltà che fuor mi serra," &c.
             (*Parad.* C. xxv.)

member his noble fresco at Assisi, of Saint Francis wedded to Poverty.* It would really almost seem as if the poem had been written as a sort of safety-valve for the painter's true feelings, during the composition of the picture. At any rate, it affords another proof of the strong common sense and turn for humour which all accounts attribute to Giotto.

I have next introduced, as not inappropriate to the series of poems connected with Dante, SIMONE DALL' ANTELLA's fine sonnet relating to the last enterprises of Henry of Luxembourg, and to his then approaching end,—that death-blow to the Ghibelline hopes which Dante so deeply shared. This one sonnet is all we know of its author, besides his name.

GIOVANNI QUIRINO is another name which stands forlorn of any personal history. Fraticelli (in his well-known and valuable edition of Dante's Minor Works) says that there lived about 1250 a bishop of that name, belonging to a Venetian family. But the tone of the sonnet which I give (and which is the only one attributed to this author) seems foreign at least to the confessions of bishops. It might seem credibly thus ascribed, however, from the fact that Dante's sonnet probably dates from Ravenna, and that his correspondent writes from some distance; while the poet might well have formed a friendship with a Venetian bishop at the court of Verona.

For me Quirino's sonnet has great value; as Dante's answer† to it enables me to wind up this

---

* See Dante's reverential treatment of this subject, (*Parad.* C. XI.)

† In the case of the above two sonnets, and of all others interchanged between two poets, I have thought it best to

INTRODUCTION TO PART II.

series with the name of its great chief; and, indeed, with what would almost seem to have been his last utterance in poetry, at that supreme juncture when he

" Slaked in his heart the fervour of desire,"

as at last he neared the very home

" Of Love which sways the sun and all the stars."*

I am sorry to see that this necessary introduction to my second division is longer than I could have wished. Among the severely-edited books which had to be consulted in forming this collection, I have often suffered keenly from the buttonholders of learned Italy who will not let one go on one's way; and have contracted a horror of those editions where the text, hampered with numerals for reference, struggles through a few lines at the top of the page, only to stick fast at the bottom in a slough of verbal analysis. It would seem unpardonable to make a book which should be even as these; and I have thus found myself led on to what I fear forms, by its length, an awkward *intermezzo* to the volume, in the hope of saying at once the most of what was to say; that so the reader may not find himself perpetually worried with footnotes during the consideration of something which may require a little peace. The glare of too many tapers is apt to render a picture confused and inharmonious, even when their smoke does not obscure or deface it.

place them together among the poems of one or the other correspondent, wherever they seemed to have most biographical value; and the same with several epistolary sonnets which have no answer.

* The last line of the *Paradise* (CAYLEY'S *Translation*).

BRIEF COMMENTARY.

EVERY Preface, or introductory commentary, has a certain number of readers, who may be described as the natural friends of Prefaces, or their natural enemies. Let me hope to mitigate the animosity of the latter (being one of the number myself) by informing them, that, although this Poem has passed through six editions in England, and several more in foreign countries, the present Commentary—a portion of which was, in a manner, forced from me in Australia, some sixteen years ago—is the only one that has been written for it,—that the remarks will be as concise as possible,—and that, in my own opinion, there really is no great need that anybody should read them. They are offered, however, in deference to the judgment of others.

The poem of 'Orion' was intended to work out a special design, applicable to all times, by means of antique or classical imagery and associations; and this design, with the hero and the several characters who appear on the scene, as well as the general structure and distribution of the action, were long considered before a line was written. A sort of cartoon of the whole was then made, and submitted to my friend Dr. Leonhard Schmitz, long since recognised as one of the most learned men of the day, and equally possessed of a profound philosophical spirit. To his kind and thoughtful revision I have great pleasure in acknowledging my obligations.

Orion, the hero of my fable, is meant to present a type of the struggle of man with himself, *i. e.* the contest between the intellect and the senses, when powerful energies are equally balanced. *Orion* is man standing naked before Heaven and Destiny, resolved to work as a really free agent to the utmost pitch of his powers for the good of his race. He is a truly practical believer in his gods, and in his own conscience; a child with the strength of a giant; innocently wise; with a heart expanding towards the largeness and warmth of Nature, and a spirit unconsciously aspiring to the stars. He is a dreamer of noble dreams, and a hunter of grand shadows (in accordance with the ancient symbolic mythos), all tending to healthy thought, or to practical action and structure. He is the type of a Worker and a Builder for his fellow-men. He presents the picture (well or ill painted, the author cannot certainly know) of a great and simple nature, struggling to develope all its loftiest energies—determined to be, and to do, to obtain knowledge, and to use it—to live up to its faculties—feeling and acting nobly and powerfully for the service of the world, and seeking its own reward and happiness in the consciousness of a well-worked life, and the possession of a perfect sympathy enshrined in some lovely object.*

With regard to this intense sympathy with some lovely object of personal passion and affection, a witty authoress once said to me,—'But why should it require three goddesses to perfect one giant?' The question, though put playfully, is too profound to be answered in the

---

* On the first appearance of this poem, two young poets, who have since become eminent in various ways (Edmund Ollier and George Meredith), wrote to me their several views of the design and character of *Orion*, each of which was far better said than the above, and in less than half the space. I am ashamed to say that I cannot recollect their words, or they would have stood in the place of mine.

same vein. It may be briefly said, however, that the three great phases of the ordeal of the passion of love, which most strong natures pass through, are fairly portrayed in the story of 'Orion.' He might have been represented as finding perfection at the outset; but since the lot of humanity is seldom (if ever) so fortunate, it seemed best that he should pass through the several gradations of disappointment and suffering, in order to arrive at the highest refinements of sympathy and happiness. If the happiness was short-lived, and met with destruction at the selfish hands of a limited nature (an imperfect sympathy), who resented the bliss it was itself incapable of attaining or conferring, that also is the type of a melancholy truth. The law of progress forbids man to rest in happiness: in his misery he will not, cannot rest; but this law generally cuts short the work of a man, not merely when he has done his best, or perhaps before, but even when he has done as much as his age is capable of using. He must go away, and make room for a different greatness. The needs of a future age must be supplied by future genius, because to see too far in advance is just so much intellectual activity projected into the air. Nothing can be done with it. And the only result is the ridicule, persecution, or utter neglect of the day.

Mr. G. H. Lewes, at the time this poem was first published, being specially occupied with the German metaphysicians, among whom the business of a long life has often been that of abstract speculation, and a kind of illustration of the Hegelian subjectivity and objectivity interpenetrating each other, endeavoured one day to show me that the real hero of my poem was not *Orion*, but *Akinetos*. Now, I had studiously drawn the character of the giant *Akinetos*—the Great Unmoved—in contradis-

Brief Commentary.

tinction to that of *Orion*—a Great Mover of the world—the one all action, the other all thought leading to no action. Had *Akinetos* heard the remark, he would have scorned to be called a hero of any kind: he would have asked what was the good of building houses on the sands of the sea-shore? The amusement of fools incapable of sitting still. The philosophy of *Akinetos* may be difficult to refute in the abstract, but since human life is a mixture of hard realities, with perfect illusions, *Akinetos* was no hero, nor a good model for any one to follow, and therefore I finally set him in stone, while *Orion* shines for ever.

The other characters speak for themselves. My friend Mr. Tennyson smilingly accused me about the same period, of intending the plausible giant *Encolyon* as a largely outlined portrait of a certain eminent statesman of the day. There was, perhaps, an amusing resemblance in some respects; but I had no such intention. Besides, it would have been unbecoming the dignity of Epic story. For a similar reason some objection has been taken to the corn-dealing episode of the inhabitants of stony Ithaca during a famine, in Canto ii. B. i. But while I believe the principles there set forth in fable, are simple and universal—applicable in all ages—I trust the form and picture are sufficiently idealized to be in perfect harmony with the rest of the story, its imagery, local scenery, and characteristics. The reader, therefore, ought not, I think, to reproach me for this, especially as it is not certain that many people would have found it out, if I had not told them.

Of the design and structure of this poem, as a work of imagination, and also of its execution, it does not become me to speak; but as various complimentary remarks on its philosophy were made in England and America (more especially in the *Times*, and in the critical essays of so accomplished a genius as Edgar Allan Poe)—remarks to which I never offered any due acknowledgment or reply—a few words may now be permitted me in explanation.

The philosophy of 'Orion' gives the widest scope to nature, natural action, and genius; it advocates the broadest views, and most energetic progress, with a belief in the constant advancement of mankind, here and hereafter. It may be said that the converse of all this can be shown by the quotation of certain passages; and the words of the starving man gathering gum from the lentisk-trees have been cited:—

'Like the hot springs
That boil themselves away, and serve for nought,
Which yet must have some office, rightly used,
Man hath a secret source for some great end,
Which by delay seems wasted. Ignorance
Chokes us, and Time outwits us.'—B. i. canto iii.

This is admitted; nor need I be ashamed to confess that, like many others, I have myself had hours, even days, of extreme despondency (never of despair), during which the foregoing lines were realized to a degree that, had I then been dying, might have induced me to choose those words for my epitaph. But garbled extracts are no proof of a desponding philosophy, nor of anything else in most cases. The morbid is burnt up in the sanguine. With all vigorous natures these periods of gloom and hopelessness are very brief; and for every single passage of such tendency in 'Orion,' a dozen may be found of the opposite: and this belief in the pre-arranged and constant progress of man is expressly developed in the opening of Book iii. Canto i. Although it may be true, in some rare instances, that—

> 'The man, who for his race might supersede
> The work of ages, dies worn out—not used!'

Yet it is shown that his influence continues :—

> 'The circle widens as the world spins round—
> The earth hath tough rind, but a subtle heart—
> His soul works on, while he sleeps 'neath the grass.'

The opening of the last Canto, and the concluding Song of Orion, after death, while taking his station among the constellated thrones, certainly place the philosophy of the poem beyond question as a whole, whatever speeches or remarks may be cited from *Akinetos*.

With similar design, the Intellectual and the Sensuous have each been given a fair and open field. Detached passages might be found equally forcible on each side; and in order to render this equi-vocal philosophy *not* equivocal in the dishonest sense of the word, a certain sage, in opposition to the courtiers of *Oinopion's* palace, hazards an opinion on this all-important point,—

> 'That human nerves,
> And what they wrought, were wondrous as the mind,
> And in the eye of Zeus none could decide
> Which held the higher place.'—B. ii. canto i.

If the temeritous sage, by promulgating the above opinion, became a martyr to the hypocritical mind of society (*i. e.* the outward pretences of minds that know better), nobody can find anything unusual in such a result, down to this very day of our self-deluding civilization. The early ages in their philosophies, their 'loves and wars,' only display the same generic characteristics as at present—the American Civil War, and the late Franco-Prussian ferocities being a perfect settlement of the question of Christian authorities and influence;—and those who have seen savage life as well as the highest modern refinements, can but have observed that the savage man and the civilized man are identical in first principles. There is only a sheet of papyrus between them. When the great sanitary reformer, the late Dr. Southwood Smith, wrote his *Philosophy of Health,* and his work on *The Divine Govern-*

ment, one may clearly see that opinions on the right estimation of our corporeal conditions must have passed through his mind, which, had he given them a more palpable enunciation, with a practical bearing, would have caused the loss of all his private practice as a physician. But as it is, 'his soul works on, while he sleeps 'neath the grass;' and we may also say with the author of the *Songs before Sunrise*,—

> ' Thou art not dead, as these are dead who live
> Full of blind years, a sorrow-shaken kind :
> *   *   *   *
> The savour of heroic lives that were,
> Is it not mixed into thy common air?
> The sense of them is shed about thee now!'

Whether the hypocrisies of a fundamental part of the present social scheme be unwise or wise, with a view to keeping ‧the born-savage in order, a great change in our so-called 'science of ethics,' as far as relates both to 'frail' and forcible animal nature, will have to accompany, if it does not precede, the Church of the Future. And it is clear to me, that instead of resisting the idea of our Darwinian 'promotion,' we should gratefully and hopefully regard it as promissory of a series of higher grades for ever-aspiring humanity.

From time immemorial, though this monomania of superstition seemed to reach its height in the cruel self-martyrdom of old monastic devotees and their deluded victims, the system of 'mortifying the flesh,' and the general view taken of the human body, with all its immutable laws and functions, has continued down to the present day. Notwithstanding all the knowledge of physiology, and the psychology inextricably involved in our corporeal fabric and conditions, the same dead-set against man's body is constantly made. Man seems determined to know better than his Maker, and not merely to regulate dogmatically, but altogether to check, if not expunge, some of the Divine ordinations. Among the latest signs of this asceticism, we may point to an article that has just appeared—and in one of the most intellectual of our periodicals—entitled *The Fleshly School of Poetry.* Supposing there were such a school, why should it not exist as well as schools that preach exclusively of the spirit? Are we gravely to be told, at this day, that 'the flesh, and the devil,' are almost cognate terms, and that the spirit and the devil never cause men to commit evil deeds?

The direct tendency of my fable, as far as it relates to the passion of love, is clearly shown to advocate that combination of the intellectual and the sensuous which is most conducive to the noble progress and happiness of special natures.

Thus, when a critique which appeared in the *Athenæum* (written by the greatest poetess of the age—of any age—need I say, Mrs. Elizabeth Barrett Browning?) designated 'Orion' as a 'spiritual epic,' it might with equal truth have been termed a corporeal epic, or one of mere external action. It is both. The life of *Orion* begins amidst 'ponderous substance,' and is continually employed in physical action, when not absorbed with the converse. The poem is intended equally to advocate the real and the ideal, the precursive dream, theory, or shadow —and the substance and action which originate therefrom. The opinion that it was a 'spiritual epic' is a remarkable illustration of the tone which a highly-refined spirit can give to all that it contemplates; and how it can touch what the world calls 'pitch' without soiling the pearl and coral of the fairy fingers. Howbeit, the writer of this poem having been a sailor in many a stormy sea, intends to stick fast by the timbers of our mortal vessel.

Brief Commentary. xix

After the allusions to 'ponderous substance' and other bodily forces, the reader, if he has duly observed my design, ought not to be surprised on reverting to a passage in the first Canto, commencing with —

' " Hunter of Shadows, thou thyself a Shade,"
Be comforted in this,— that substance holds
No higher attributes,' &c.

The elucidatory justification which follows may not, by everybody, be considered as satisfactory; suffice it for the writer that he honestly thought, and thinks, it was so.

I have been very frequently requested, particularly by letters from total strangers, to make some explanations of this kind concerning the design of 'Orion,' and have always resisted, simply because it seemed to me that it was plain enough, or at least open to such study as any epic poem, at all worthy of the name, might fairly ask of all lovers of poetry. I trust, however, that my tardy consent will not have made any of my old readers, in various parts of the world, angry or indifferent, since I have ever regarded an intellectual sympathy as the highest treasure an author can obtain,—the only heartfelt reward of all his labours.

As for the allegorical vein running through the poem, transparently enough, no one need be in the least troubled about that matter, if the underworking be not sufficiently obvious. A child may read the story. And here let me borrow Hazlitt's excellent and graphic settlement of the question. 'Some people,' he remarks, in his Lecture on the English Poets, 'will say that all this may be very fine, but that they cannot understand it on account of the allegory. They are afraid of the allegory, as if they thought it would bite them. They look at it as a child looks at a painted dragon, and think that it will strangle them in its shining folds. This is very idle. If they do not meddle with the allegory, the allegory will not meddle with them. Without minding it at all, the whole is as plain as a pike-staff. It might as well be pretended that we cannot see Poussin's pictures for the allegory.'

In a few instances, it is admitted, a certain fabulous aureola may render a passage not so clear to the understanding as if it had been ela borated in prose. There are occasions in imaginative compositions in which it is best not to strive to be too definite, because some designs are destroyed by a hard outline; and also because poems often suggest one thing to one person, and another thing to another person, by the variety of our memories and special natures, —and, in certain cases, poems suggest things differing in some degree from the poet's meaning and intention.

I must add one remark to this, which of course will be regarded by most persons as heretical; viz. that in many instances, the moment a poetical passage is 'laid upon the table' for analysis, the soul vanishes! The moving principle, the partner for life, is gone. This opinion obviously does not refer to philosophical, didactic, or what are called 'practical poems,' but only to those which depend, like most first impressions, upon sympathy. In like manner, the silly fellow who pauses in reading a beautiful lyric in order to *examine* if the rhymes suit his eye or his ear, need not read any more, for the essence of that beauty has evaporated for ever. In fine, it is quite certain, that what has been so constantly said about poets being born poets, applies in a similar sense to their readers. Many people, and of very great understanding in other respects, are born with the impossibility of understanding

Brief Commentary. xxiii

poetry in its highest essence, or even perhaps in its humblest, if it be true poetry. The Elephant who was introduced to Pegasus, said there must be a mistake somewhere!

The reader may smile to hear, or to remember, that in the preliminary Note to the early editions of 'Orion' it was said that the poem was, in several respects, 'an experiment upon the mind of a nation.' But considering that about that period the far-sweeping tide of broad-farce literature, caricature, and burlesque, had set in, and that it has continued with accumulating and desecrating influence during the last twenty years and more, my 'experiment' has been a success in the main. If the superstitious asceticism of ancient dogmas and legends still holds out in its old stone fortresses, 'Orion' has nevertheless starred the rock, and let in some clear rays of healthy light.

' But because,' writes Thomas Hobbes,

'there be many men called Criticks, and Wits, and Virtuosi, that are accustomed to censure the Poets, and most of them of divers Judgments: how is it possible (you'll say) to please them all? Yes, very well; if the Poem be as it should be. For, men can judge what's Good that know not what is Best. For he that can judge what is best must have considered all these things (though they be almost innumerable) that concur to make the reading of an Heroick Poem pleasant. Whereof I'll name as many as shall come into my mind.'* Now, while it will be obvious that no writer can be so purblind and rash in self-opinion as to assume that even the majority must regard his work as good, there is one of the conditions set down by Hobbes as fourth in his list, to which I do make claim, viz. 'The Justice

---

* Preface to the Translation of the *Iliads* and *Odysses*, by Thomas Hobbes of Malmesbury. 1686.

and Impartiality of the Poet.' The last he mentions is, 'Amplitude of the Subject;'—but this, of course, is in the nature of things, and the 'servant of Nature' can only lay claim to a profound and reverent sympathy.

In the early editions of 'Orion,' a sort of explanatory apology was offered for employing the old Greek names in a Greek fable, on the grounds that 'the Gods and Goddesses of ancient Italy were perfectly distinct from those of the ancient Hellenic races;' and that I had also adopted the latter 'with a view to getting rid of commonizing associations.' The Bacchus and Neptune, for instance, of the present day, are singularly vulgar and technical non-representatives of the beautiful Iacchus and the grand Poseidon,—while Phoibos, Aphrodité, and Artemis may be truly said to be utterly burlesqued, and only worthy of the places in which they are most commonly found. The present Poem of elaborate design was the first that ventured to give, with one or two discretionary variations, the old Greek names: but there is no need to apologize for this at the present time.

It only remains to offer a word concerning several amusing speculations and idle fancies that have been extensively promulgated, and which have enabled those who know nothing of the poem to seem to say something. I allude to the unusual circumstance (which *ought* to be common enough with all those authors who could so much better afford it) of the book having been given away in the first instance. As there was scarcely any instance of an Epic Poem attaining any reasonable circulation during its author's lifetime (certainly not up to *that* period, with the exception of Voltaire's 'Henriade'), the first, second, and third editions of 'Orion' were published gratuitously,—that is, they were published at a nominal price, the least coin of the realm, to avoid the trouble and greatly additional expense of forwarding presentation copies; which, moreover, are not always particularly desired by those who receive them. After the third edition, there were several editions at a price which amply remunerated the publisher, and left the author no great loser. There has also been an Australian edition, and, I believe, more than one in America; but all have long been out of print.

The present is the first Library Edition, and has the author's latest, and probably his final corrections. Two lines have been erased from the poem as previously published, and some forty lines have been added to the last Canto. Hail! and farewell!

R. H. H.

London, November 1871.

PREFACE.

THE author, in preparing, on the fiftieth anniversary of its publication, a final revision of this poem, has been advised by friends whose opinions he much esteems, to foresay to a rising generation of students, a few words indicative briefly of certain leading features which have, more or less from the beginning, (as illustrating the ultimate triumph of good over evil), distinguished the work, from others conversant with a like class of topics; and to make some alterations in the current issue which, it is believed, will recommend themselves to the judgment of the observant reader.

The poem has been taken to be a sketch of world-life, and is a summary of its combined moral and physical conditions, estimated on a theory of spiritual things, opposed as far as possible to that of the partialist, pessimist and despairing sceptic, the belief of the misbeliever, so prevalent in our time; not only in regard to the creation, government and administration of the world by divine providence, but in its views as to the origin of the so-called mystery of moral evil; and in its general positions known as universalist, illustrative of the highest aspirations and the happiest future, here and hereafter of humanity. Here, however, it may be as well to premise that, substantially, the poem stands now, and indeed in most of its chief respects remains, unchanged; and it does so for the reason more especially, that very soon after its first appearance, the author perceived the original outline to be sufficiently extensive and elastic to admit almost every variety of classifiable thought, and reasonable enlargement of purpose upon such matters as human faith, morals and progress could not fail to present to the ripening experiences of life. In the course, however, of years, it becomes almost inevitable, in the case of a living writer, that some things shall have been added, some things, for sundry reasons, varied, and some things taken away.

To begin, for instance, with what has been varied; it may be stated that in compliance with the representations already made public, of more than one notable writer and fully competent critic, and in accord with conclusions of the author's more matured thought, all the utterances ascribed in previous editions of the poem to various divine interlocutors are now assigned solely to one uni-personal Deity, being more suitable, we are led to believe, to the purpose and position of poetry generally, among the arts, in modern monotheistic times, during which the expansion of the horizon of the moral universe has at least equalled that of the material; and certainly as being more congruous with the philosophic tendencies, at the present day, of religious thought, in which the unity and infinity, alike inseparable from each other, and in themselves indivisible even in conception, of the Divine Nature, is unquestionably, and for ever established.

The parts that have been taken away are several passages of an almost exclusively theological cast that bore but a distant relation to the ruling motives of the invention, as a whole, and a few songs and lyrical effusions, some of them pretty general favourites, which though missing from their accustomed place will be found comprised more appropriately it is thought in a collection of minor miscellaneous verse intended presently to see the light.

In regard to additional matter admitted into the text; the Angel-world, the Star-flight of Luniel and Festus, and considerable portions of the Spiritual Legend, the first for sometime withdrawn, have now been all re-adjusted and brought more palpably into parallel with the progressive action of the story ; while, along with the closing war of good and ill, in which the souls of that generation are represented as determining by their own free choice of sides, their future spiritual destiny ; the blending of sacred millennial aspirations forenoted of old to be ultimately verified, as well as the conjecturally realized triumphs of humanitary theories, secular but not irrational ; and the happy results of pious and inspired charity in the treatment of subdued evilhood, takes each its place as an integral segment of the circle to which all belong.

Certain changes less or more organic, in the constitution of the poem as at this moment it presents itself, being thus accounted for, the writer far from seeking to apply to it any formal or minute analysis, but being desirous merely to supply the unaccustomed reader with a brief prescript, regarding its primary and more prominent objects and aspects, trusts confidently that upon a few such heads as construction, characterization, main scope or tendency, and special note of difference from other works occupied with similar, if not equally comprehensive, schemes, and which not many of the criticisms likely to fall into a stranger's hands have grasped very effectively, the following remarks may suffice to prepossess the reader with a serviceable summary of the work now in his hands.

Viewed structurally then, the poem will be found through all its semi-century or so of scenes, one continuous whole ; resolving itself, upon examination, not into books, or acts, but into twelve or more groups, celestial, astral, interstellar and terrestrial, solar, planetary, and one other, the sphere of the Infernals ; that is to say, into so many clusters of sections subordinated into seven classes, finally reducible into three, Heavenly, firmamental, earthly ; throughout variously distributed.

With regard, for example, to the celestial scenes, three in number, with two of which the poem opens and terminates ; the first shadowing forth predictively the forewarnings and decrees of divine providence, afterwards to be embodied in the action of the story ; the last, which is completive, showing wherein the main issues are summed up and justified ; while both are seen to be divided centrally by a mid heavenly section, judicial and punitive in character, of the same elevation as the others, and which, while securing a symmetrical arrangement of the interjacent portions, reflects equally upon the preceding and succeeding developments of the narrative.

Of the terrestrial scenes, more numerous, as might be expected, than those of any other class, devoted to the earthly experiences of the hero, his loves, his friends, his companions, his adventures, the temptations and trials by which he is tested, and the offences of pride and passion by which he is temporarily overcome, his aspirations and shortcomings, his penitences and griefs, his voluntary self-demission of the surpassing and so to speak miraculous gifts and privileges with which he has been endowed, and his gradual advance morally and spiritually from the world chaos of conflicting partialist and imperfect beliefs to the sufficing system of simple and philosophic truth to which he at last attains, it is at this time unnecessary to speak. The story, which as a whole more regards the future than the passed or the present, comprises and connects all these particulars, having, besides a plan overt, what may be called an under plan; the latter mainly concerned with the initiation and perfection of a social but secret agency of the world's wisest well-wishers, who are supposed in every state and country throughout the globe to be actively engaged in the removal of every cause of national animosity in men's hearts, preparatory to such a condition of things as can only morally issue in the establishment of universal peace among all peoples; the culmination of which imaginary policy proving precisely coincident, in point of time, with the openly announced impending end of the world as told in the very first scene, and towards the conclusion shown realized; and coincident, in point of fact, with the covert but philanthropic action of the sages of all lands in elevating to a throne of universal peace, a single sovereign soul, both are shown ultimately to convene, and make one.

Interspersed with these, the several clusters of the supramundane scenes will be found to be occupied chiefly with the assertion and illustration of the unity of God's moral law, in analogy with that of the physical, as alike universal, eternal and all sufficient, in contrast with the views of a late eminent but eccentric metaphysician, which amount, it cannot be denied, to hypothetical polytheism. Here and there, and among the interspaces between star and star, where almost nothing more is brought forward scenically than what the simple ideas of duration, extension, distance and magnitude abstractedly imply; and not all inaptly therefore perhaps dedicated to legendary narrative, with divers moral and metaphysical speculations will be found, such as those connected with spiritual pre-existence, soul discipline throughout all spheres, the efficacy of prayer, and the everlasting validity of the prophet-preached principle of penitence; topics in themselves neither uninteresting nor unimportant, nor in their high and comprehensive scope, inappropriate to those rare and rarely reachable regions in which they are represented to occur.

Further, in relation with matters such as those pertaining to that mysterious spiritual future, which, dependent as it is upon action, may be said to be in a certain sense, always with us, the enlargement, will possibly be noted, since its first appearance, of The Starflight of Festus and the angel Luniel, which traversing the astral signs of the sun's annual course, present a fair field for the indulgence of conjecture upon those theories of preparatory ghostly purification proper to brighter spheres, with which such bards and seers as have elected or aspired to present in their works any passable rationale of the moral universe, have from time to time familiarized the world, before the divinely conceded entrance of human spirits even those of the great and good, patriots and sages of old, as recorded for us by some of their "least earthly minds," upon the full fruition of their predestined heritage. These may be taken, though in ever so inadequate a degree, not only to typify to the ardent aspirant after eternal perfections the many glorious species of possible felicity in a future state so, figuratively, conveyed; but also, a novelty in serious verse, to indicate a boundless variety of directions in which, besides the soul-exalting worship of Deity, the highest hopes, the largest life, the broadest extension of faculties, and the noblest exercise of human duties, not less than spiritual prerogatives, may be looked forward to, and enjoyed.

Turning, in the meantime, in order to complete and conclude our brief inspection of this class of scenes, the supernatural, which forms an essential element of the fiction, to the instance, exceptional in its nature, of the sphere of the Infernals, or Hell Purgatorial, answering morally to that antichthonal and hypothetical sphere, though invisible in the physical order of things, which early Greek philosophy found herself at the very outset of her career constrained to demand as a necessary counterpoise to the insoluble difficulties and rampant anomalies sensible throughout the actual system of things, and in default of which exemplification of God's severe but rational equity, the teaching as a whole embodied in the work were manifestly imperfect, it will be seen, nevertheless, that this judicial section has designedly features of a remedial and ameliorative quality, analogous to those shown during the current period, by civilized society, in the treatment of its criminal law-breakers; which strongly and pointedly differentiate the story from all preceding poetical adumbrations of the place of so-called endless and hopeless torment. In this condition or position, place or state, necessarily abides the obstinate and unrepentant sinner of all worlds; but whence, by ministry of the angelic and compassionate sons of God, divine clemency has provided, as in more than one instance exampled, a means, if availed of duly, of self-deliverance; and it is in the collation and adaptation of these two sections just passed under notice, in which soul is represented as undergoing in due order, the just judgment of heaven, because of offence, and the self imposed penalties of penitent conscience, prior to that loftier and happier course of self emendative discipline, and spiritual advancement symbolized by the varied experiences recounted in The Star-flight; and which enure according to the poet's creation, and his conception of the moral world, until, consistently with its plan, final felicity is universally won; and the character of Deity vindicated, as one who having righteously made man responsible for his deeds will still not render a creature of finite faculties, whether as regards active forces or powers of passion, amenable to fines, infinite, and out of all proportion possible to their causes. Thus his nature and essence, as a Being of unassailable sovereignty and consequently imperturbable equity is demonstrated; and one of the implicit but cardinal purports of the poem plenarily achieved.

Passing on therefore from these and like aboriginal rudiments of a fable not indebted for its peculiarities to the somewhat newly-rationalized divinity of the day, to the next head, that of characterization which appears naturally to express itself in a few primary and typical conceptions, such as, first, that of Deity which has already been touched upon as above, reverently; and which will be found represented, and in opposition to the pantheism, the nature-worship, and the man-worship, all equally idolatrous, of our times, as a personal Infinite; one whose infinitude, if personality signifies, in any sense, those attributes or qualities which distinguish one individual entity from all others, constitutes his personality; an affirmation which may doubtless surprise certain censors who ignorantly or unfairly have accused of Pantheism a work that from its first page to its last, abounds with witness to the existence of the one and sole Infinite, the eternal, almighty, and voluntary creator of the world, who containing in himself, and pervading, the universe, and existing in a manner which to us incomprehensible, is still not wholly by finite intelligence inapprehensible; but, in a like sense to that which Pauline. Pantheism, as it has been called, presents to us, namely that of the Great Spirit in whom we live and move and have our being, as an Infinite, always and everywhere present to us; a universal conscience cognizant of our every act, perfectly and convincingly knowable; we, in the meantime seeing and knowing that all the acts of a finite being, along with the being itself, are alike commensurables; but that the eternity which pertains only to Deity, is with aught, or with all, created, incommensurable and incommunicable; and that whatever dogma or decree is metaphysically inconsistent with reason's demonstrable conclusions, can never be theologically, nor scientifically, tenable.

Next, in accord with all sacred traditions, ancient and orient, that of angelhood in its double capacity, on the one hand of a mighty hierarchy, loyal naturally and by all-sufficient reason, to its bounteous Creator, a world of holy ministrant intelligences, guardians of orbs, of nations, of souls, shown in vital and beneficent relations with various personages of the poem, the main events connected with which, such as the destruction and re-creation of the earth, the visitations extended to other spheres, the Initiations, the foundation of a world-wide empire, and many other instances of the marvellous, being, it is taken for granted, of sufficient dignity to justify, æsthetically, the invoked presence or aid of superior powers;—and, on the other, of that false, fallen, and as yet impenitent host, of whom the head, the tempter, the flatterer, the deluder of men, the Lucifer of the story, stands intended to represent our generalized or abstract idea of evil as a principle, if we may so speak, temporally impersonate; endowed with certain almost spatial dignities that serve, at least from a poetical point of view, to individualize a character, which in its prospective rehabilitation yields only in the interest it attracts to that inspired by the position of the protagonist.

And lastly, of Humanity generally, under its twofold aspect, primarily, spiritual, exemplified in two instances; one recently released from bodily bonds, and passing through the process of probational purification; another, rejoicing in assured beatitude; secondarily, as outlined in the person and career of the hero and his companion characters, with such peculiarities and qualifications of gift and temperament as pertain to their chief, and the various members of the poetical circle alluded to, as suffice to vitalize the framework of the pageant, and demark it from the range of simple allegory.

Of the general scope and nature of the story, the reader, even if it be his first essay, keeping in mind what he may have already gathered from the foregoing remarks; from the spirit of the teachings they convey indirectly, or more directly illustrate, from the general reputation of the work, such as that expressed in the words of one of its critics intimating the aim of the poem to be the exhibition of "a soul gifted, tried, buffeted, beguiled, stricken, purified, redeemed, pardoned and triumphant;" of a soul, it may be added, passing through and from knowledge, to wisdom; from passion and worldly and frivolous pleasures, to heart purity and spiritual happiness, a philosophic creed and a comprehensive calm of mind; from the tyranny of doubt and the benumbing influence of contradictory and incredible beliefs, to the certainty of assured faith in simplest and amplest truth ; from voluntary humiliation and self-denudation of all temporal and extrinsic gifts and privileges, to the enjoyment of perfect and unlimited power, accomplished on the appointed day, when mankind, by enlightened self-development, and the prevenient will of God, shall have arrived at absolute and universal sovereignty over the powers of nature, and have rendered subservient to common use, all the conquests and the treasures of science, all the best institutions and safeguards of civil society ;—the reader, being thus informed, it is the author's impression, will scarcely require any further details before commencing his perusal of the pages before him.

Upon the execution of the poem, which has been called by some of its censors an epic drama, and which certainly belongs rather to the order of the many-stringed harp than to the lyre, it does not become the author to speak. Criticism, which has not been lacking either in the old world or the new, may be said, with a few minor exceptions, to have fairly enough and even generously discharged its always honourable functions. And if not any poem,—agreeably with the somewhat denunciatory decree of one of the mediæval councils, *omnia poëmata hæretica sunt*,—precisely satisfies a rigidly orthodox pietist, it is some consolation to a delinquent of this class if, in his choice of heresies, he thinks he has done his best to favour a simple creed which comprises in its consecrated elements a belief in the benignant providence of God, in the immortality of the soul, in the harmonized gospel of reason and faith combined, in the just, discriminative and equitable judgment of the spirit after death by Deity, and in the delightsome duty of aiding upon earth the peaceful, morally progressive and voluntary self-evolution of Humanity as one brotherhood—an eclectic and philosophic symbol anticipated towards the end of the work as destined eventually to be everywhere on earth welcomed and established, and one which, however much in some quarters misunderstood, yet in its original inception and design spaciously and presciently conceived, has since been not inconsistently nor immethodically carried out, to the ultimate achievement of all that from the first was promised or predicted.

BLACKHEATH,
May, 1889.

THE AUTHOR OF "FESTUS" AND THE SPASMODIC SCHOOL.

Mr. Philip James Bailey, the author of *Festus*, has often been called the father of the Spasmodic School. He energetically repudiates the title and was induced in 1893 to set forth his views in the following letter :—

"As regards the especial school of poetry to which you refer, I am only so far interested or concerned with the members of it as to acknowledge, along with both public and publicist, the generally bright colouring, pure morality, happy imagery, and exquisite similitudes manifest in one or two of their poems; but I have no sympathy with their works specially, nor with their ways: as indicated also by such of them as still continue with us, for I look upon them as a permanent class in literature; any more than with the startling or awful titles which are blazoned forth in the advertisements of their works.

"Given a crude and hasty treatment by an aspirant after poetical 'fame,' of what sounds as a lofty or ambitious topic; the world being never so full as now of a respectably educated mass of litterateurs; and without waiting to discover by self-examination whether their mental calibre and culture as a whole be adequate to the handling of such matters as are not seldom selected by them, they hasten to complete their periodical rotation round themselves or the idol of their imitation, with almost mechanical regularity; and are suitably applauded and rewarded. But as showing any true mark of real study in the construction and elaboration of a well-considered and elevated theme, there is a plentiful lack in the great majority of them.

"On the other hand, to one early trained to metaphysical and poetical studies, in their highest school, as regards the former; and as to the latter, accustomed to view and to discuss such studies according to well-known æsthetic rules, and the best classical exemplars both ancient and modern, a young receptive and imaginative mind might very easily be supposed to be imbued with tastes and tendencies of a character that might under favourable circumstances readily develop into a life-long pursuit, and a persistent purpose which nothing could shake nor divert.

"When therefore is shown, as is obvious to any one who has only read even the preface to the recent Jubilee edition of *Festus*, that no more orderly and methodical poem is to be found in the whole range of English literature; no vaster nor more comprehensive theme; no poetical scheme embracing spiritual, ethical, physical and metaphysical bearings more consistently wrought together in relation to inter-dependent parts; nor, considering the extent of its compass, more fitly compacted as a whole; and when now in supplement to what is there written in regard to the simple entirety of the work, its original constitution and construction; its design and scope, characterisation and machinery; its solutions of such vexed questions as the nature, origin, end, and endurance of evil; transitional, not eternal; phenomenal, not essential; the necessary imperfection of all created Being; the ontological identity of unity and infinity; and many other illustrations of pure and mixed theology; of terrestrial ambition united with the perfectibility of civil society; and the pacification of the world in the interests of a spiritually minded humanity; we may suppose added under the final heading of the prefatory analysis above alluded to, a special differentiation of the work which follows, in its spiritual teachings and conclusions, from those insisted upon by the majority of writers who have advisedly chosen the illustration of such themes as are implied in the outline of a religio-philosophic faith—and poetry can in no instance aspire to any higher position—by Milton, for instance, not to go further back, in his confused Arianism, and, through Satan's success, his virtual Dualism; by Byron, in his intermittent scepticism and reiterated Manicheism; by Shelley, in his rapid and irrational atheism: in the infuriated predictions of everlasting torments to be inflicted upon all sinners, angelical or human, dilated on with horrible ingenuity by Young both in his *Night Thoughts* and in *Judgment Day*; and by the author of *The Course of Time* (the writer's contemporary and almost class-fellow) in his frequently sublime, but too often gloomy and somewhat bigoted literalness as regards his conceptions of Divine and morally equitable retribution in the world to come; there is a feeling of deep dissatisfaction should occupy the mind of a student of Poetical Divinity.

"But, if extending our view beyond our own English poetical cycle of bards and divines, we include, through translation, that vast jumble of Greek and Gothic fable laid before the world by Goethe in his divisional, and therefore æsthetically unsatisfactory production, *Faust*; the author of which, abandoning altogether the motive and purport of the original national legend he had set himself to handle the very core of which was the hard and harsh ecclesiastical dogma of the inefficacy of repentance, after any supposed compact with the powers of evil, opposed to the prophetic teachings of the Bible; and after showing the learned Doctor, in company with Mephistopheles, an evil imp it appears of a mean and subordinate class, teaching and preaching a sensuous and impure Pantheism to the victim of their united attentions; she, after such undermining of her moral nature, beguiled into the commission of parricide, constructive fratricide, and finally of infanticide, only it is painfully evident over-conscious of a somewhat too voluntary sacrifice; and concluding the first section of the story with the death in jail, and the announcement by a divine voice from heaven of the unconditional salvation of the interesting heroine, commences the second segments of the story (not the shadow of a trace being visible from first to last of the circumstances attending the close of the hero's mortal career, and of his pitiful compunction and repentance, made so much of by Marlowe and in the primitive tradition) with the resuscitation of the amiable and ever-fascinating Faust, in an Elysium or fairyland sort of scene, where he endeavours to while away the time by a double adultery with Helen of Troy, and other repulsive incidents as the results of such a brilliant invention; until after the smothering of Mephistopheles by the celestial saints beneath showers of roses, and the separation of Faust's humanity into elements partly perishable and partly divine; the whole terminates in the worshipful glorification of eternal wifelihood; a fact, of which in the respective cases of Margaret and Helen of Troy he had shown such a keen and delicate appreciation.

"From considerations and reflections connected with studies of this nature, and the dissatisfaction and disappointment necessarily attendant upon the conclusions to be drawn from them, the author of *Festus* may, he trusts, be regarded as not altogether unjustified in his desire to illustrate an alternative theory, not only of Divinity, but Humanity, in a future spiritual condition, purificatory and progressive, both of them more in accord with our present day beliefs as to the nature and perfections of Deity, and His more probable mode of dealing by providential and remedial process with all His rational creation, if erring still amenable to the gracious influences of Divine omnipotence and benevolence; an alternative, at all events, unique among works of imagination; and neither in itself, be it allowable to hope, incredible, nor unworthy of celebration.

"In this light, and as completive of what may be called a synoptic view of the moral evangels of various poetical messengers (some of them named above), the work may now be regarded, and will repay the study of any reader interested in serious and elevated thought. It is not criticism of it that is wanted. There are volumes of it, several of the writers of which, from the cheery and voluminous balladist of his day to the literary Caliban of the current hour, have endeavoured to perpetuate, with an eye to their own renown, their self-inflicted stigmata of ignorance and incompetence.

"Of our two chief contemporaries in verse recently passed away, they neither of them said anything about myself as a friend or writer but what was good in itself or kind and just; one of them, beside that tribute of high admiration of my work with which the world has for many years been familiar, gave me some advice which he was fully qualified to give; and the other said he had himself written too much, but that I had not written enough. I did not grudge them their approval by the million; they did not grudge me theirs.

"I am, very sincerely yours,
"PH. JAS. BAILEY.

"*The Elms, The Ropewalk, Nottingham.*
"*March 10th, 1893.*"

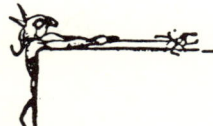

PREFACE.

A FURTHER edition of this book—the sixteenth—having been called for, I have been asked by the publishers to furnish a preface to it. For prefaces I have no love. Books should speak for themselves. Prefaces can scarcely be otherwise than egotistic, and one would not willingly add to the too numerous illustrations of this tendency with which the literature of the day abounds. I would much rather leave the volume with the simple "Envoy" which I wrote for it when the Bon Gaultier Ballads were first gathered into a volume. There the products of the dual authorship of Aytoun and myself were ascribed to the Bon Gaultier under whose editorial auspices they had for the most part seen the light. But my publishers tell me that people want to know why, and how, and by which of us these poems were written,—a curiosity, complimentary, no doubt, but which it is by no means easy for the surviving bard to satisfy. It is sixty years since most of these verses were written with the light heart and fluent pen of youth, and with no thought of their surviving beyond the natural life of ephemeral magazine pieces of humour. After a long and very crowded life, of which literature has occupied the smallest part, it is difficult for me to live back into the circumstances and conditions under which they were written, or to mark, except to a very limited extent, how far to Aytoun, and how far to myself, separately, the contents of the volume are to be assigned. I found this difficult when I wrote Aytoun's Life in 1867, and it is necessarily a matter of greater difficulty now in 1903.

I can but endeavour to show how Aytoun and I came together, and how for two or three years we worked together in literature. Aytoun (born 21st June 1813) was three years older than myself, and he was known already as a writer in 'Blackwood's Magazine' when I made his acquaintance in 1841. For

PREFACE.

some years I had been writing in Tait's and Fraser's Magazines, and elsewhere, articles and verses, chiefly humorous, both in prose and verse, under the *nom de guerre* of Bon Gaultier. This name, which seemed a good one for the author of playful and occasionally satirical papers, had caught my fancy in Rabelais,[1] where he says of himself, "A moy n'est que honneur et gloire d'estre dict et reputé Bon Gaultier et bon Compaignon; en ce nom, suis bien venue en toutes bonnes compaignees de Pantagruelistes."

It was to one of these papers that I owed my introduction to Aytoun. What its nature was may be inferred from its title—" Flowers of Hemp; or, The Newgate Garland. By One of the Family." Like most of the papers on which we subsequently worked together, the object was not merely to amuse, but also to strike at some prevailing literary craze or vitiation of taste. I have lived to see many such crazes since. Every decade seems to produce one. But the particular craze against which this paper was directed was the popularity of novels and songs, of which the ruffians

[1] Prologue de première livre.

of the Newgate Calendar were the accepted heroes. If my memory does not deceive me, it began with Harrison Ainsworth's 'Rookwood,' in which the gallantries of Dick Turpin, and the brilliant description of his famous Ride to York, caught the public fancy. Encouraged by the success of this book, Ainsworth next wooed the sympathies of the public for Jack Sheppard and his associates in his novel of that name. The novel was turned into a melodrama, in which Mrs Keeley's clever embodiment of that "marvellous boy" made for months and months the fortunes of the Adelphi Theatre; while the sonorous musical voice of John Reeve as Blueskin in the same play brought into vogue a song with the refrain,

"Nix my dolly, pals, fake away!"

which travelled everywhere, and made the patter of thieves and burglars "familiar in our mouths as household words." It deafened us in the streets, where it was as popular with the organ-grinders and German bands as Sullivan's brightest melodies ever were in a later day. It clanged at midday from the

steeple of St Giles, the Edinburgh cathedral;[1] it was whistled by every dirty "gutter-snipe," and chanted in drawing-rooms by fair lips, that, little knowing the meaning of the words they sang, proclaimed to their admiring friends—

> "In a box of the stone jug I was born,
> Of a hempen widow the kid forlorn;
> My noble father, as I've heard say,
> Was a famous marchant of capers gay;"

ending with the inevitable and insufferable chorus,

> "Nix my dolly, pals, fake away!"

Soon after the Newgate Calendar was appealed to for a hero by the author of 'Pelham,' who had already won no small distinction, and who in his 'Paul Clifford' did his best to throw a halo of romance around the highwayman's career. Not satisfied with this, Bulwer next claimed the sympathies of his readers for Eugene Aram, and exalted a very common type of murderer into a nobly minded and highly sentimental scholar. Crime and criminals became the favourite theme of a multi-

---

[1] A fact. That such a subject for cathedral chimes, and in Scotland, too, could ever have been chosen, will scarcely be believed. But my astonished ears often heard it.

tude of novelists of a lower class. They even formed the central interest of the 'Oliver Twist' of Charles Dickens, whose Fagin and his pupil "the Artful Dodger," Bill Sykes and Nancy, were simultaneously presented to us in their habits as they lived by the genius of George Cruikshank, with a power that gave a double interest to Dickens's masterly delineation of these worthies.

The time seemed—in 1841—to have come to open people's eyes to the dangerous and degrading taste of the hour, and it struck me that this might be done by pushing to still further extravagance the praises which had been lavishly bestowed upon the gentlemen whose career generally terminated in Newgate or on the Tyburn Tree, and by giving "the accomplishment of verse" to the sentiments and the language which formed the staple of the popular thieves' literature of the circulating libraries. The medium chosen was the review of a manuscript, supposed to be sent to the writer by a man who had lived so fully up to his own convictions as to the noble vocation of those who set law at defiance, and lived by picking pockets, burglary, and highway robbery, diversified by an occasional murder, that, with the finisher of the law's assistance, he had ended his exploits in what the slang of his class called "a breakfast of hartichoke with caper sauce." How hateful the phrase! But it was one of many such popularly current in those days.

The author of my "Thieves' Anthology" was described in my paper as a well-born man of good education, who, having ruined himself by his bad habits, had fallen into the criminal ranks, but had not forgotten the *literæ humaniores* which he had learned at the Heidelberg University. Of the purpose with which he had written he spoke thus in what I described as the fragments of a preface to his Miscellany:—

"To rescue from oblivion the martyrs of independence, to throw around the mighty names that flash upon us from the squalor of the Chronicles of Newgate the radiance of a storied imagination, to clothe the gibbet and the hulks 'in golden exhalations of the dawn,' and secure for the boozing-ken and the gin-palace that hold upon the general sympathies which has too long been monopolised by the cottage and the drawing-room, has been the aim and the achievement of many recent authors of distinction. How they have succeeded, let the populous state of the public jails attest. The office of 'dubsman' [hangman] has ceased to be a sinecure, and the public and Mr Joseph Hume have the satisfaction of knowing that these useful functionaries have now got something to do for their salaries. The number of their pupils has increased, is increasing, and is not likely to be diminished. But much remains to be done. Many an untenanted cell still echoes only to the sighs of its own loneliness. New jails are rising around us, which require to be filled. The Penitentiary presently erecting at Perth is of the most commodious description.

"In this state of things I have bethought myself of throwing, in the words of Goethe, 'my corn into the great seed-field of time,' in the hope that it may blossom to purposes of great public utility. The aid of poetry has hitherto been but partially employed in the spread of a taste for Conveyancing, especially in its higher branches. Or where the Muse has shown herself, it has been but in the evanescent glimpses of a song. She has plumed her wings for no sustained flight. . . .

"The power of poetry over the heart and impulses of man has been recognised by all writers from Aristotle down to Serjeant Talfourd. In dexterous hands it has been known to subvert a severe chastity by the insinuations of a holy flame, to clothe impurity in vestments 'bright with something of an angel light,' to exalt spleen into elevation of soul, and selfishness into a noble scorn of the world, and, with the ringing cadences of an enthusiastic style, to ennoble the vulgar and to sanctify the low. How much may be done, with an engine of such power, in increasing the numbers of 'The Family' may be conceived. The Muse of Faking, fair daughter of the herald Mercury, claims her place among 'The Mystic Nine.' Her language, erewhile slumbering in the pages of the Flash Dictionary, now lives upon the lips of all, even in the most fashionable circles. Ladies accost crossing-sweepers as 'dubsmen'; whist-players are generally spoken of in gambling families as '*dummy*-hunters'; children in their nursery sports are accustomed to 'nix their dolls'; and the all but universal summons to exertion of every description is 'Fake away!'

"'Words are things,' says Apollonius of Tyana. We cannot be long familiar with a symbol without becoming intimate with that which it expresses. Let the public mind, then, be in the habit of associating these and similar expressions with passages of poetical power, let the ideas they import be imbedded in their hearts and glorified in their imaginations, and the fairest results may with confidence be anticipated."

In song and sonnet and ballad these views were illustrated and enforced. They served

the purpose of the ridicule which it was hoped might operate to cure people of the prevailing toleration for the romance of the slums and the thieves' kitchen. Naturally parody was freely used. Wordsworth did not escape. His

"Milton, thou shouldst be living at this hour,"

found its echo in

"Turpin, thou shouldst be living at this hour,
England hath need of thee," &c.

And his "Great men have been among us," &c., was perverted into

"Great men have been among us,—Names that lend
  A lustre to our calling ; better none ;
  Maclaine, Duval, Dick Turpin, Barrington,
Blueskin and others, who called Sheppard friend.
  .   .   .   .
       . . . Now, 'tis strange,
We never see such souls as we had then ;
  Perpetual larcenies and such small change !
No single cracksman paramount, no code,
No master spirit, that will take the road,
But equal dearth of pluck and highwaymen !"

Nor did even Shelley's magnificent sonnet "Ozymandias" escape the profane hand of the burglar poet. He wrote,—

"I met a cracksman coming down the Strand,
   Who said, 'A huge Cathedral, piled of stone,
Stands in a churchyard, near St Martin's Le Grand,
   Where keeps Saint Paul his sacerdotal throne.
A street runs by it to the northward. There
For cab and bus is writ 'No Thoroughfare,'
   The Mayor and Councilmen do so command.
And in that street a shop, with many a box,
   Upon whose sign these fateful words I scanned:
'My name is Chubb, who makes the Patent Locks;
   Look on my works, ye burglars, and despair!'
Here made he pause, like one that sees a blight
   Mar all his hopes, and sighed with drooping air,
'Our game is up, my covies, blow me tight!'"

The versatile genius of the poet was equally at home in the simpler lyric region of the Haynes Bayley school. Taking for his model the favourite drawing-room ballad of the period, "She wore a wreath of roses the night that first we met," he made a parody of its rhythmical cadence the medium for presenting some leading incidents in the career of a Circe of "the boozing ken," as thus,—

"She wore a rouge like roses the night that first we met;
Her lovely mug was smiling o'er mugs of heavy wet;
Her red lips had the fulness, her voice the husky tone,
That told her drink was of a kind where water was unknown."

Then after a few more glimpses of this charming creature in her downward progress, the bard wound up with this characteristic close to her public life,—

"I saw her but a moment, but methinks I see her now,
As she dropped the judge a curtsey, and he made her a bow."

But it would be out of place to dwell longer upon those reckless imitations. The only poem which ultimately found a place in the Bon Gaultier volume was "The Death of Duval."

The paper was a success. Aytoun was taken by it, and sought an introduction to me by our common friend Edward Forbes the eminent Naturalist, then a leading spirit among the students of the Edinburgh University, beloved and honoured by all who knew him. Aytoun's name was familiar to me from his contributions to 'Blackwood's Magazine,' and I was well pleased to make his acquaintance, which rapidly grew into intimate friendship, as it could not fail to do with a man of a nature so manly and genial, and so full of spontaneous humour, as well as of marked literary ability.

His fancy had been caught by some of the things I had written in this and other papers under the name of Bon Gaultier, and when I proposed to go on with articles in a similar vein, he fell readily into the plan and agreed to assist in it. Thus a kind of Beaumont and Fletcher partnership was formed, which commenced in a series of humorous papers that were published in Tait's and Fraser's Magazines during the years 1842, 1843, and 1844. In these papers appeared, with a few exceptions, the verses which form the present volume. They were only a portion, but no doubt the best portion, of a great number of poems and parodies which made the chief attraction of papers under such headings as " Puffs and Poetry," " My Wife's Album," " The Poets of the Day," and " Cracknels for Christmas."

In the last of these the parody appeared under the name of " The Jilted Gent, by Theodore Smifzer," which, as " The Lay of the Lovelorn," has become perhaps the most popular of the series. I remember well Aytoun bringing to me some ten or a dozen lines of admirable parody of " Locksley Hall." That poem had been published about two years before, and was

at the time by no means widely known, but was enthusiastically admired by both Aytoun and myself. What these lines were I cannot now be sure, but certainly they were some of the best in the poem. They were too good to appear as a fragment in the paper I was engaged upon, and I set to work to mould them into the form of a complete poem, in which it is now known. It was introduced in the paper thus:—

"There is a peculiar atrocity in the circumstances which gave rise to the following poem, that stirs even the Dead Sea of our sensibilities. The lady appears to have carried on a furious flirtation with the bard—a cousin of her own—which she, naturally perhaps, but certainly cruelly, terminated by marrying an old East Indian nabob, with a complexion like curry powder, innumerable lacs of rupees, and a woful lack of liver. A refusal by one's cousin is a domestic treason of the most ruthless kind; and, assuming the author's statement to be substantially correct, we must say that the lady's conduct was disgraceful. What her sensations must be on reading the following passionate appeal we cannot of course divine; but if one spark of feeling lingers in her bosom, she must, for four-and-twenty hours at least, have little appetite for mulligatawny."

The reviewer then quotes the poem down to the general commination, ending with

"Cursed be the clerk and parson,—cursed be the whole concern!"

He then resumes his commentary:—

"This sweeping system of anathema may be consonant to what the philosophers call a high and imaginative mood of passion, but it is surely as unjust as any fulminations that ever emanated from the Papal Chair. No doubt Cousin Amy behaved shockingly; but why, on that account, should the Bank of England, incorporated by Royal Charter, or the most respectable practitioner who prepared the settlements, along with his innocent clerk, be handed over to the uncovenanted mercies of the foul fiend? No, no, Smifzer, this will never do! In a more manly strain is what follows."

The remainder of the poem is then given, ending with,

"Rest thee with thy yellow nabob, spider-hearted Cousin Amy!"

and the critic resumes:—

"Bravo, Smifzer! This is the right sort of thing— no wishy-washy snivelling about a wounded heart and all that kind of stuff, but savage sarcasm, the lava of a volcanic spirit. In a fine prophetic strain is that vision of Amy's feelings as the inebriated nawaub stumbles hazily into the drawing-room, steaming fulsomely of chilma! And that picture of the African jungle, with Smifzer *in puris* mounted on a high-trotting giraffe, with his twelve dusky brides around him,—Cruikshank alone could do it justice. But the triumph of the poem is in the high-toned sentiment of civilisation and moral duty, which, esteeming 'the grey barbarian' lower than the 'Christian cad,'—and that is low enough in all conscience,—tears the captivating delusions of freedom and polygamy from the poet's eyes, even when his pulse is throbbing at the wildest, and sends him from the shades of the palm and the orange tree to the advertising columns of the 'Morning Post.' This is indeed a great poem, and we need only add that the reader will find something like it in Mr Alfred Tennyson's 'Locksley Hall.' There has been pilfering somewhere; but Messieurs Smifzer and Tennyson must settle it between them."

How little did I dream, when writing this, that I should hear the parody quoted through the years up till now almost as often as the original poem! Smifzer was wiser than Tennyson, for he never spoiled the effect of his poem by admitting, like Tennyson in his "Locksley Hall, Sixty Years After," that it was a good thing that "spider-hearted" Amy threw him over as she did.

Luckily for us, not a few poets were then living whose style and manner of thought were sufficiently marked to make imitation easy, and sufficiently popular for a parody of their characteristics to be readily recognised. Lockhart's "Spanish Ballads" were as familiar in the drawing-room as in the study. Macaulay's "Lays of Ancient Rome," and his two other fine ballads, were still in the freshness of their fame. Tennyson and Mrs Browning were opening up new veins. These, with Moore, Leigh Hunt, Uhland, and others of minor note, lay ready to our hands, as Scott, Byron, Crabbe, Coleridge, Moore, Wordsworth, and Southey had done to James and Horace Smith in 1812, when writing the "Rejected Addresses." Never, probably, were verses thrown off with a keener sense of enjoyment, and assuredly the poets parodied had no warmer admirers than ourselves. Very pleasant were the hours when we met, and now Aytoun and now myself would suggest the subjects for each successive article, and the verses with which they were to be illustrated. Most commonly this

was done in our rambles to favourite spots in the suburbs of "our own romantic town," on Arthur Seat, or by the shores of the Forth, and at other times as we sat together of an evening, when the duties of the day were over, and joined in putting line after line together until the poem was completed. In writing thus for our own amusement we never dreamed that these "nugæ literariæ" would live beyond the hour. It was, therefore, a pleasant surprise when we found to what an extent they became popular, not only in England, but also in America, which had come in for no small share of severe though well-meant ridicule. In those days who could say what fate might have awaited us had we visited the States, and Aytoun been known to be the author of "The Lay of Mr Colt" and "The Fight with the Snapping Turtle," or myself as the chronicler of "The Death of Jabez Dollar" and "The Alabama Duel"? As it was, our transatlantic friends took a liberal revenge by instantly pirating the volume, and selling it by thousands with a contemptuous disregard of author's copyright.

For Aytoun the extravagances of melodrama

and the feats and eccentricities of the arena at Astley's amphitheatre had always a peculiar charm. "The terrible Fitzball," the English Dumas, in quantity, not quality, of melodrama, Gomersal, one of the chief equestrians, and Widdicomb, the master of the ring at Astley's, were three of his favourite heroes. Ducrow, manager of Astley's, the most daring and graceful of equestrians, and the fair Miss Woolford, the star of his troupe, had charms irresistible for all lovers of the circus. In Aytoun's enthusiasm I fully shared. Mine found expression in "The Courtship of our Cid," Aytoun's in "Don Fernando Gomersalez," in which I recognise many of my own lines, but of which the conception and the best part of the verses were his. Years afterwards his delight in the glories of the ring broke out in the following passage in a too-good-to-be-forgotten article in 'Blackwood,' which, to those who may never hope to see in any circus anything so inspiring, so full of an imaginative glamour, may give some idea of the nightly scenes in the halcyon days of Astley's:—

"We delight to see, at never-failing Astley's, the revived glories of British prowess—Wellington in the midst of his staff, smiling benignantly on the facetious pleasantries of a Fitzroy Somerset — Sergeant M'Craw of the Forty-Second delighting the *élite* of Brussels by the performance of the reel of Tullochgorum at the Duchess of Richmond's ball — the charge of the Scots Greys — the single-handed combat of Marshal Ney and the infuriated Life-Guardsman Shaw — and the final retreat of Napoleon amidst a volley of Roman candles and the flames of an arsenicated Hougomont. Nor is our gratification less to discern, after the subsiding of the showers of sawdust so gracefully scattered by that groom in the doeskin integuments, the stately form of Widdicomb, cased in martial apparel, advancing towards the centre of the ring, and commanding — with imperious gesture, and some slight flagellation in return for dubious compliment — the double-jointed clown to assist the Signora Cavalcanti to her seat upon the celebrated Arabian. How lovely looks the lady, as she vaults to her feet upon the breadth of the yielding saddle! With what inimitable grace does she whirl these tiny banners around her head, as winningly as a Titania performing the sword exercise! How coyly does she dispose her garments and floating drapery to hide the too-maddening symmetry of her limbs! Gods! She is transformed all at once into an Amazon — the fawn-like timidity of her first demeanour is gone. Bold and beautiful flushes her cheek with animated crimson — her full voluptuous lip is more compressed and firm — the deep passion

of the huntress flashing in her lustrous eyes! Widdicomb becomes excited—he moves with quicker step around the periphery of his central circle—incessant is the smacking of his whip—not this time directed against Mr Merriman, who at his ease is enjoying a swim upon the sawdust—and lo! the grooms rush in, six bars are elevated in a trice, and over them all bounds the volatile Signora like a panther, nor pauses until with airy somersets she has passed twice through the purgatory of the blazing hoop, and then, drooping and exhausted, sinks like a Sabine into the arms of the Herculean master, who —a second Romulus—bears away his lovely burden to the stables, amid such a whirlwind of applause as Kemble might have been proud to earn."

Astley's has long been levelled with the dust; it is many years since Widdicomb, Gomersal, Ducrow, and the Woolford passed into the Silent Land. May their memory be preserved for yet a few years to come in the mirthful strains of two of their most ardent and grateful admirers!

Of the longer poems in this volume the following were exclusively Aytoun's: "The Broken Pitcher," "The Massacre of the Macpherson," "The Rhyme of Sir Launcelot Bogle," "Little John and the Red Friar," "A Midnight Meditation," and that admirable imitation

of the Scottish ballad, "The Queen in France." Some of the shorter poems were also his— "The Lay of the Levite," "Tarquin and the Augur," "La Mort d'Arthur," "The Husband's Petition," and the "Sonnet to Britain." The rest were either wholly mine or produced by us jointly.

After 1844 the Bon Gaultier co-operation ceased. My profession and removal from Edinburgh to London left no leisure or opportunity for work of that kind, and Aytoun became busy with the Professorship of Belles Lettres in the University and with his work at the Bar and on 'Blackwood's Magazine.' We had also during the Bon Gaultier period worked together in a series of translations of Goethe's Poems and Ballads for 'Blackwood's Magazine,' which, like the Bon Gaultier Ballads, were collected, added to, and published in a volume a year or two afterwards. In 1845 I left Edinburgh for London, and only met Aytoun at intervals there or at Homburg in the future years; but our friendship was kept alive by active correspondence. Literature was naturally his vocation, and he wrote much and well, with exemplary industry, enlivening his papers in

'Blackwood,' till his death in August 1865, with the same manly sense, the same playfulness of fancy and flow of spontaneous humour, which made his society and his letters always delightful to his friends.

> "Multis ille bonis flebilis occidit,
> Nulli flebilior quam mihi!"

The first edition of this book, now very rare, appeared in 1845. It was illustrated by Alfred Henry Forrester (Alfred Crowquill). In the subsequent editions drawings by Richard Doyle and John Leech, in a kindred spirit of fanciful extravagance, were added, and helped materially towards the attractions of the volume. Its popularity surpassed the utmost expectations of the authors. To them not the least pleasant feature of its success was that it was widely read both in the Navy and the Army, and was nowhere more in demand than in the trenches before Sebastopol in 1854.

THEODORE MARTIN.

31 Onslow Square,
October 1903.

MEMOIR OF JOHN KEATS.

BY

RICHARD MONCKTON MILNES.

The "Life, Letters, and Literary Remains of John Keats," published in 1848, contain the biography of the Poet, mainly conveyed in the language of his own correspondence. The Editor had little more to do than to arrange and connect the letters freely supplied to him by kinsmen and friends, and leave them to tell as sad, and, at the same time, as ennobling a tale of life as ever engaged the pen of poetic fiction. But these volumes can scarcely be in the hands of all to whose hours of study or enjoyment the Poems of Keats may find ready access; and thus it has been desired that the Editor should transcribe into a few pages the characteristics of an existence in itself so short, but radiant with genius and rich in virtue.

The publication of three small volumes of verse, some earnest friendships, one profound passion, and a premature death, are the main incidents here to be recorded—ordinary indeed, and common to many men whose names have passed, and are passing, away, and here only notable, as illustrating the wonderful nature and progress of certain mental faculties, and as exhibiting a character which inspires the deepest human sympathy amidst all its demands on our admiration.

John Keats was born on the 29th of October, 1795, in the upper rank of the middle-class, his mother possessing sufficient means to give her children an excellent education, when left a widow in 1804. She is reputed to have been a woman of saturnine demeanour, but on an occasion of illness, John, then a child between four and five years old, remained for hours as a sentinel at her door, with a drawn sword, that she might not be disturbed: and at her death, which occurred when he was at Mr. Clarke's school at Enfield, he hid himself for several days in a nook under the master's desk, passionately inconsolable—traits of disposition that illustrate his character as a boy, energetic, ardent, and popular. "He combined," writes one of his school-fellows," a terrier-like resoluteness with the most noble placability;" and another mentions that his singular animation and ability in all exercises of skill and courage, impressed them with a conviction of his future greatness, " but rather in a military or some such active sphere of life, than in the peaceful arena of literature."* This impression was assisted by the rare vivacity of his countenance and much beauty of feature: his eyes were large and sensitive, flashing with strong emotion or suffused with tender sympathies; his hair hung in thick brown ringlets round a head diminutive for the breadth of the shoulders below, while the smallness of the lower limbs, which in later life marred the proportion of his person was not then apparent, any more than the undue prominence of the lower lip, which afterwards gave his face too pugnacious a character to be entirely pleasing, but at that time only completed such an image as the ancients had of Achilles—of joyous and glorious youth everlastingly striving.

Careless of an ordinary school-reputation, his zeal for the studies themselves led him frequently to spend his holidays over Virgil or Fenelon, and when his master forced him into the open air for his health, he would be found walking with a book in his hand. The scholarship of the establishment had no peculiar pretensions, and the boy's learning was limited to the elements of a liberal education. He was never taught Greek, and he took his mythology from Tooke's Pantheon and Lemprière's Dictionary, making the affiliation of his mind with the old Hellenic world the more marvellous and interesting. It is doubtful whether

* Mr. E. Holmes, author of the "Life of Mozart," &c.

at any time his information exceeded these scanty limits, and it is a curious speculation whether deeper and more regular classical studies would have checked or encouraged the natural consanguinity, so to say, of his fancy with the ideal life of ancient Greece, and whether a more distinct knowledge of what the old mythology really meant, would, or would not, have hindered that reconstruction of forms

> "Not yet dead,
> But in old marbles ever beautiful,"

which is now not the less agreeable from being the evolution of his unlearned and unaided imagination.

Mr. Charles Cowden Clarke, the son of his preceptor, remained the friend of Keats, when removed from school in 1810, and apprenticed for five years to a surgeon of some eminence at Edmonton. This intelligent companion supplied him with books, which he eagerly perused, but so little expectation was formed of the direction in which his talents lay, that when in 1812, he asked for the loan of Spenser's Fairy Queen, Mr. Clarke remembers that the family were amused at the ambitious desires of their former pupil. He must indeed have known something of Shakspeare, for he had told a young school-fellow that "he thought no one would dare to read Macbeth alone at two o'clock in the morning;" but it was Spenser that struck the secret spring and opened the flood-gates of his fancy. "He ramped through the scenes of the romance," writes Mr. Clarke, "like a young horse turned into a spring meadow:" he could talk of nothing else: his countenance would light up at each rich expression, and his strong frame would tremble with emotion as he read. The lines " in imitation of Spenser " are the earliest known verses of his composition, and to the very last the traces of this main impulse of his poetic life are visible. But few memorials remain of his other studies: there is a " Sonnet to Byron " of little merit, dated 1814; one of much grace and juvenile conceit on Chaucer's Tale of the " Flower and the Leaf," written on the blank leaf, while his friend was asleep over the book; and one of most clear thought and noble diction, " On first looking into Chapman's Homer." It was to Mr. Clarke again that he owed his introduction to this fine interpretation, which preserves so much of the heroic simplicity and the metre of which, after all various attempts, including that of the hexameter, still appears the best adapted, from its length and its powers, to represent in English the Greek epic verse. Unable to read the original, Keats had long stood by Homer as a great dumb name, and now he read it all night long, with intense delight, even shouting aloud, when some especial passage struck his imagination.

The " Epistles " to his friends and his brother George, then a clerk in London, indicate a rapid development of the poetic faculty, especially free from the formalism and imitation which encumber the early writings even of distinguished poets, and full of an easy gaiety, which at times runs into conversational common-place, or helps itself out of difficulties by quaintnesses that look like affectations. But, even in these first efforts, the peculiarity of making the rhymes to rest on the most picturesque and varied words, instead of the conventional resonance of unimportant syllables, is distinctive, and an effect is produced which from its very novelty often mars the force and beauty of the expression, and lowers the sense of poetic harmony into an ingenious concurrence of sounds. It is also a palpable consequence of this mode of composition, that the sense appears too often made for the rhyme, and, while most poets would be loth to allow how frequently the necessity of the rhyme suggests the corresponding thought, here the uncommon prominence of the rhyme keeps this effect constantly before the reader. Yet, when approached with sympathetic feeling and good will, this impression soon vanishes before the astonishing affluence of thought and imagination, which at once explains and excuses the defect, if it be one. Picture after picture seems to rise before the poet's eye in a succession so rapid as to embarrass judgment and limit choice, and fancies and expressions that elsewhere would be strange and far-fetched are here felt to have been the first suggested.

When Keats's apprenticeship was over, and he removed to London to "walk the hospitals," he soon became acquainted with men capable of appreciating and cultivating his genius. Among the foremost Leigh Hunt welcomed him with a sympathy that ripened into friendship, and the sonnet "on the day Leigh Hunt left prison," attests the earnestness of reciprocal affection. They read and walked much together, and wrote in competition on subjects proposed. Much has been said of the influence of this connection on the writings of Keats, and much of their mannerism has been traced to this source. The justice of this supposition is more than doubtful, and the stupid malevolence of the criticisms which mainly sustained it is now too well exposed to require refutation. It is indeed probable that the fresh mind of Keats was directed by Hunt into many of the channels which had delighted his own, and that peculiarities that had taken the fancy of the one were easily pressed on the imagination of the other. But Keats always defended himself energetically against the notion that he belonged to Leigh Hunt's or any other school. "I refused" he wrote "to visit Shelley, that I might have my own unfettered scope," and he never ceased to desire to bear all the defects of his own originality. It is no contradiction to this to infer, that if the talents of Keats had been subjected to the discipline of a complete and regular classical education, and a self-distrust inculcated by the continual presence of the highest original models of thought and form, he would have escaped very much of the mannerism which accompanied his early efforts; but it may be doubted whether the well-trained plant would have thrown out such luxurious shoots and expanded into such rare and delightful foliage. The most that can be said of the influence of Leigh Hunt and his friends on Keats was that he became obnoxious to those evils which inevitably beset every literary *coterie*, that he learned rather to encourage than to restrain individual peculiarities, and to demand a public and permanent attention for matters that could only justly claim a private and personal interest. But on the other hand it is impossible to deny that in this genial atmosphere the faculty of the young poet ripened with incredible facility, and advantages of literary culture were afforded which no just critic can disparage or conceal. Chatterton eating out his heart in his desolate lodging and ignoble service to low magazines, or Burns drinking down thought in country taverns and town society little more refined, afford mournful contrasts to the pleasant and elevating associations enjoyed by Keats during his residence in London, which he would have been the last to undervalue. Hazlitt, Haydon, Godwin, Basil Montague and his remarkable family, and many other persons of literary and artistic reputation received him with kindness: Mr. Reynolds, whose poems written under feigned names are full of merit, Mr. Dilke, whose intelligent criticism, large information, and manly sense, have had so beneficial an effect on the modern history of English letters, Archdeacon Bailey, and Severn the poetical painter, became his devoted friends: while in Mr. Ollier, himself a poet, and afterwards in Messrs. Taylor and Hessey, he found considerate and liberal publishers.

It soon became apparent that the profession for which young Keats was destined was too unsuitable to be maintained There remain careful annotations on the lectures he attended, but when he had once entered on the practical part of his business, although successful in all his operations, he found his mind so oppressed with an over-wrought apprehension of doing harm, that he determined on abandoning the course of life to which he had devoted a considerable portion of his small fortune. "My dexterity" he said, "used to seem to me a miracle, and I resolved never to take up a surgical instrument again." The little volume of poems, the beloved first-born, scarcely touched the public attention: it was not even observed as a sign of the existence of a new Cockney poet, whom the critic was bound to silence or to convert, or as the production of a new member of the revolutionary propaganda, to be hunted down with ridicule or obloquy. These honours were reserved for maturer labours. The characteristic lines,

"Glory and loveliness have passed away, &c.,"

were written in the midst of a merry circle of friends, who happened to be present when the printer sent to say that if there was to be a dedication he must send it directly; and he did so,—for the main thought, the regeneration of the images of Pagan beauty, was ever present with him. His health at this time was far from good, and in the spring of 1817, he returned to the quiet of the Isle of Wight to write "Endymion," a subject long germinating in his fancy, and thus shadowed out in the first poem of his early volume:—

"He was a poet, sure a lover too,
Who stood on Latmus' top, what time there blew
Soft breezes from the myrtle vale below;

> And brought, in faintness solemn, sweet, and slow,
> A hymn from Dian's temple; while upswelling,
> The incense rose to her own starry dwelling.
> But tho' her face was clear as infants' eyes,
> Tho' she stood smiling o'er the sacrifice,
> The poet wept at her so piteous fate,
> Wept that such beauty should be desolate:
> So in fine wrath some golden sounds he won,
> And gave meek Cynthia her Endymion."

The solitude was not very propitious to his work, but he composed some other good verses, such as the sonnet "On the Sea," and others illustrative of his thoughts and feelings at the time. In a letter to Haydon he thus expressed himself with a noble humility: "I must think that difficulties nerve the spirit of a man; they make our prime objects a refuge as well as a passion; the trumpet of Fame is as a tower of strength, the ambitious bloweth it, and is safe." * * * "There is no greater sin, after the seven deadly, than to flatter oneself into the idea of being a great poet, or one of those beings who are privileged to wear out their lives in the pursuit of honour. How comfortable a thing it is to feel that such a crime must bring its heavy penalty, that if one be a self-deluder, accounts must be balanced." Again to Hunt: "I have asked myself so often why I should be a Poet more than other men, seeing how great a thing it is, how great things are to be gained by it, that at last the idea has grown so monstrously beyond my seeming power of attainment, that the other day I nearly consented with myself to drop into a Phaethon. Yet 'tis a disgrace to fail even in a huge attempt, and at this moment

I drive the thought from me. I began my poem about a fortnight since, and have done some every day, except travelling ones."

In September he visited his friend Bailey, at Oxford, and wrote thence as follows:—" Believe me, my dear——, it is a great happiness to me that you are, in this finest part of the year, winning a little enjoyment from the hard world. In truth, the great Elements we know of, are no mean comforters: the open sky sits upon our senses like a sapphire-crown; the air is our robe of state; the earth is our throne; and the sea a mighty minstrel playing before it—able, like David's harp, to make such a one as you forget almost the tempest-cares of life. * * * * I shall ever feel grateful to you for having made known to me so real a fellow as Bailey. He delights me in the selfish, and, please God, the disinterested part of my disposition. If the old Poets have any pleasure in looking down at the enjoyers of their works, their eyes must bend with double satisfaction upon him. I sit as at a feast when he is over them, and pray that if, after my death, any of my labours should be worth saving, they may have as 'honest a chronicler' as Bailey. Out of this, his enthusiasm in his own pursuit and for all good things is of an exalted kind, worthy a more healthful frame and an untorn spirit. He must have happy years to come; 'he shall not die—by God.' "*

---

* In p. 62 of the "Life and Letters of Keats," the biographer spoke of the decease of Mr. Bailey: he had been erroneously informed as to that

Some later extracts from letters to this excellent friend are interesting; they were part of the occupation of the winter of 1817-18, which Keats passed at Hampstead among his friends, perhaps the happiest period of his life.—" I have heard Hunt say, 'Why endeavour after a long poem?' to which I should answer, 'Do not the lovers of poetry like to have a little region to wander in, where they may pick and choose, and in which the images are so numerous that many are forgotten and found new in a second reading,— which may be food for a week's stroll in the summer. * * * Besides, a long poem is a test of Invention, which I take to be the polar-star of poetry, as Fancy is the sails, and Imagination the rudder. Did our great Poets ever write short pieces? I mean, in the shape of tales. This same Invention seems indeed of late years to have been forgotten as a poetical excellence.' But enough of this, I put on no laurels till I shall have finished Endymion."

" One thing has pressed upon me lately and increased my humility and capability of submission, and that is this truth: men of genius are great as certain ethereal chemicals operating on the mass of neutral intellect, but they have not any individuality, any determined character. I would call the top and head of those who have a proper self, Men of Power." * * * * * "I wish I was

event, but he regrets to add that the newspapers, within the last ew weeks, record the death of Archdeacon Bailey, lately returned from Ceylon, where he had long resided.

as certain of the end of all your troubles as that of your momentary start about the authenticity of the Imagination. I am certain of nothing but of the holiness of the heart's affections, and the truth of Imagination. What the Imagination seizes as Beauty must be Truth, whether it existed before or not;—for I have the same idea of all our passions as of Love; they are all, in their sublime, creative of essential Beauty. The Imagination may be compared to Adam's dream: he awoke and found it Truth. I am more zealous in this affair, because I have never yet been able to perceive how anything can be known for Truth by consecutive reasoning, and yet it must be so. Can it be that even the greatest philosopher ever arrived at his goal without putting aside numerous objections? However it may be, O for a life of sensations rather than of thoughts! It is 'a vision in the form of youth,'—a shadow of reality to come,—and this consideration has further convinced me,—for it has come as auxiliary to another speculation of mine,—that we shall enjoy ourselves hereafter by having what we call happiness on earth repeated in a finer tone. And yet such a fate can only befall those who delight in Sensation, rather than hunger, as you do, after Truth. Adam's dream will do here, and seems to be a conviction that Imagination and its empyreal reflection is the same as human life and its spiritual repetition. But, as I was saying, the simple imaginative mind may have its rewards in the repetition of its own silent working coming continually on the spirit with a fine suddenness. To compare great things with small, have you never, by being surprised with an old melody, in a delicious place, by a delicious voice, *felt* over again your very speculations and surmises at the time it first operated on your soul? Do you not remember forming to yourself the singer's face—more beautiful than it was possible, and yet, with the elevation of the moment, you did not think so? Even then you were mounted on the wings of Imagination, so high that the prototype must be hereafter: that delicious face you will see.—Sure this cannot be exactly the case with a complex mind—one that is imaginative and, at the same time, careful of its fruits,—who would exist partly on sensation, partly on thought,—to whom it is necessary that 'years should bring the philosophic mind?' Such an one I consider yours, and therefore it is necessary to your eternal happiness that you not only drink this old wine of Heaven, which I shall call the redigestion of our most ethereal musings on earth, but also increase in knowledge, and know all things."

This self-drawn picture of the mind, or rather the temperament, of Keats might well inspire painful reflections. If this were a completely true representation, it is evident that those sensuous appetites, and that yearning for enjoyment which has made his poetry the wail and remonstrance of a disinherited Paganism, must ere long have worn away all manliness of character and degenerated into a peevish sentimentalism. But he was preserved from this destiny by the strong presence of counteracting qualities,—unselfish benevolence, a sturdy love of right, and that main security and test of moral earnestness, a deep sense of honour. In this spirit he wrote about the same time to his brothers—after asserting that works of genius are the finest things in this world—"No! for that sort of probity and disinterestedness which such men as Bailey possess does hold and grasp the tip-top of any spiritual honours that can be paid to anything in this world. And, moreover, having this feeling at this present come over me in its full force, I sat down to write to you with a grateful heart, in that I had not a brother who did not feel and credit me for a deeper feeling and devotion for his uprightness, than for any marks of genius, however splendid."

With a great work on hand and in improved health he seems at this time to have enjoyed himself thoroughly. His bodily vigour must have been considerable, for he signalised himself one day by giving a severe drubbing to a butcher whom he caught beating a little boy, to the enthusiastic admiration of a crowd of bystanders. His society was much sought after from the agreeable combination of earnestness and pleasantry, which distinguished him both from graver and gayer men. The good and fine things he said gained much by his happy transitions of manner. His habitual gentleness gave effect to his occasional bursts of indignation, and at the mention of oppression or wrong, or at any calumny against those he loved, he rose into grave manliness at once and seemed like a tall man. On one occasion when a falsehood respecting the young artist Severn was repeated and dwelt upon, he left the room, saying, "he should be ashamed to sit with men who could utter and believe such things." Another time, hearing of some base conduct, he exclaimed, "Is there no human dust-hole into which we can sweep such fellows?" He used to complain of the usual character of conversation, and said, "If Lord Bacon were alive, and to make a remark in the present day in company, the conversation would stop on a sudden."

To the production of Endymion, Keats added some charming compositions in a lighter style, such as the "Lines on the Mermaid Tavern," "Robin Hood," and "Fancy," showing a perfect mastery over the more ordinary and fluent rhythm. His sense of the poetic function evidently grew with his task. He wrote to Mr. Reynolds, "We hate Poetry that has a palpable design upon us, and, if we do not agree, seems to put its hand into its breeches pocket. Poetry should be great and unobtrusive, a thing which enters into one's soul, and does not startle it or amaze it with itself, but with its subject. How beautiful are the retired flowers! How would they lose their beauty, were they to throng into the highway, crying out, 'Admire me, I am a violet! Dote upon me, I am a primrose!'"

Again, "When man has arrived at a certain ripeness of intellect, any one grand and spiritual passage serves him as a starting-post towards all 'the two-and-thirty palaces.' How happy is such a voyage of conception, what delicious diligent indolence! A doze upon a sofa does not hinder it, and a nap upon clover engenders ethereal finger-pointings; the prattle of a child gives it wings, and the converse of middle-age a strength to beat them; a strain of music conducts to 'an odd angle of the Isle,' and when the leaves whisper, it 'puts a girdle round the earth.' Nor will this sparing touch of noble books be any irreverence to these writers; for, perhaps, the honours paid by man to man are trifles in comparison to the benefit done by great works to the 'spirit and pulse of good' by their mere passive existence. Memory should not be called knowledge. Many have original minds who do not think it: they are led away by custom. Now it appears to me that almost any man may, like the spider, spin from his own inwards, his own airy citadel. The points of leaves and twigs on which the spider begins her work are few, and she fills the air with a beautiful circuiting. Man should be content with as few points to tip with the fine web of his soul, and weave a tapestry empyrean—full of symbols for his spiritual eye, of softness for his spiritual touch, of space for his wandering, of distinctness ,for his luxury. But the minds of mortals are so different and bent on such diverse journeys, that it may at first appear impossible for any common taste and fellowship to exist between two or three, under those suppositions. It is however quite the contrary. Minds would lead each other in contrary directions, traverse each other in numberless points, and at last greet each other at the journey's end. An old man and a child would talk together, and the old man be led on his path and the child left thinking. Man should not dispute or assert, but whisper results to his neighbour, and thus by every germ of spirit sucking the sap from mould ethereal, every human being might become great, and humanity, instead of being a wide heath of furze and briars, with here and there a remote oak or pine, would become a grand democracy of forest-trees."

A lady whose feminine acuteness of perception is only equalled by the vigour of her understanding, thus describes Keats as he appeared about this time at Hazlitt's lectures:— "His eyes were large and blue, his hair auburn; he wore it divided down the centre, and it fell in rich masses on each side his face; his mouth was full and less intellectual than his other features. His countenance lives in my mind as one of singular beauty and brightness; it had the expression as if he had been looking on some glorious sight. The shape of his face had not the squareness of a man's, but more like some women's faces I have seen—it was so wide over the forehead and so small at the chin. He seemed in perfect health, and with life offering all things that were precious to him."

The increased ill-health of his brother Tom and the determination of George to emigrate to America cast much gloom over the completion of "Endymion," which was, however, dispersed by a pedestrian tour through Scotland, in the company of Mr. Brown, a retired merchant, who had been Keats's neighbour during the preceding summer, and whose sympathetic and congenial disposition he had much enjoyed. Mr. Reynolds' objection to a projected Preface provoked the following spirited remonstrance:—

"I have not the slightest feeling of humility towards the public or to anything in existence but the Eternal Being, the Principle of Beauty, and the Memory of great Men. When I am writing for myself, for the mere sake of the moment's enjoyment, perhaps nature has its course with me; but a Preface is written to the public—a thing I cannot help looking upon as an enemy, and which I cannot address without feelings of hostility. If I write a Preface in a supple or subdued style, it will not be in character with me as a public speaker. I would be subdued before my friends, and thank them for subduing me, but among multitudes of men I have no feel of stooping: I hate the idea of humility to them. I never wrote one single line of poetry with the least shadow of public thought. Forgive me for vexing you, and making a Trojan horse of such a trifle, both with respect to the matter in question, and myself; but it eases me to tell you: I could not live without the love of my friends; I would jump down Etna for any great public good, but I hate a mawkish popularity."

In a fine fragment too, written about this time, he spoke of

"Bards who died content on pleasant sward,
Leaving great verse unto a little clan.
O give me their old vigour, and unheard,
Save of the quiet Primrose, and the span

> Of Heaven and few ears,
> Rounded by thee, my song should die away
> Content as theirs,
> *Rich in the simple worship of a day."*

And yet, after all, the Preface which did appear was in the main deprecatory and with no "undersong of disrespect for the public;" and when the Poet looked back on his labour he found it "a feverish attempt rather than a deed accomplished." He said; "the imagination of a boy is healthy, and the mature imagination of a man is healthy, but there is a space of life between, in which the soul is in a ferment, the character undecided, the way of life uncertain, the ambition thick-sighted."

Surely, there was much in this to disarm the violence of the criticism which was levelled at the Poem at its first birth into literary existence. The articles themselves, both in the "Quarterly" and in "Blackwood," were so superficial and coarse, so thoroughly uncritical, that, whatever sensations of disgust and anger they may have aroused at the time, there could hardly have been a question of their permanent influence on the mind and destiny of Keats, but for the belief of many of his friends that they inflicted on his susceptible nature a shock which he never recovered. This notion was confirmed in public estimation by the well-known stanza of the eleventh canto of Don Juan; concluding—

> "'Tis strange the mind, that very fiery particle,
> Should let itself be snuffed out by an article."

It is perhaps bold to say in opposition to the testimony of many near and dear friends of Keats, that these effects had no existence, but it is certain they have been greatly exaggerated. The sublime curse hurled at the brutal critic in the "Adonais" of Shelley has its due place in that lofty elegy, but with such means as we have to judge from, with the letters and acts of Keats, immediately after the reviews appeared, before us, his feelings seem to have had much more of indignation and contempt in them than of wounded pride and mortified vanity. I should incline to believe that the little public interest which "Endymion" excited, and the growing sense of his own deficiencies, weighed far more on his mind than those shallow ribaldries, which Jeffrey's article in the Edinburgh Review, if it had appeared somewhat sooner, would have so completely counterbalanced. When told "to go back to his gallipots," just as Simon Peter might have been told to go back to his nets, and when reminded that "a starved apothecary was better than a starved poet," his inclination certainly was rather to call the satirist to account, "if he appears in squares and theatres where we might possibly meet," than to let the scoffing visibly affect his health and spirits. Indeed in a letter to his publisher, after thanking some writer who had vindicated him, he says:—

"As for the rest, I begin to get a little acquainted with my own strength and weakness. Praise or blame has but a momentary effect on the man whose love of beauty in the abstract makes him a severe critic on his own works. My own domestic criticism has given me pain without comparison beyond what 'Blackwood' or the 'Quarterly' could possibly inflict; and also when I feel I am right, no external praise can give me such a glow as my own solitary reperception and ratification of what is fine. * * * I will write independently. I have written independently *without judgment*, I may write independently, and *with judgment*, hereafter. The genius of poetry must work out its own salvation in a man. It cannot be matured by law and precept, but by sensation and watchfulness in itself. That which is creative must create itself. In 'Endymion' I leaped headlong into the sea, and thereby have become better acquainted with the soundings, the quicksands, and the rocks than if I had stayed upon the green shore, and piped a silly pipe, and taken tea and comfortable advice." He also wrote to his brother:— "This is a mere matter of the moment. I think I shall be among the English poets after my death. Even as a matter of present interest, the attempt to crush me in the Quarterly has only brought me more into notice. * * It does me not the least harm in society to make me appear little and ridiculous. I know when a man is superior to me, and give him all due respect; he will be the last to laugh at me." And again on his birthday:—" The only thing that can ever affect me personally for more than one short passing day, is any doubt about my powers for poetry: I seldom have any; and I look with hope to the nighing time when I shall have none."

After reading these passages it is difficult to see in what

spirit more wise or manly an author could receive unseemly and insolent criticism. When Lord Byron boasts that, after the article on his early poems, "instead of breaking a blood-vessel," he drank three bottles of claret and began an answer, "finding that there was nothing in it for which he could, lawfully, knock Jeffrey on the head, in an honourable way," one is glad of the indignation that produced the "English Bards and Scotch Reviewers," but the use which Keats made of the annoyance in elevating and purifying his self-judgment is surely far more estimable. The letters show that no morbid feelings prevented him from most heartily enjoying his Scotch tour, where the sublimities of nature met him for the first time. He went to the country of Burns as on a pilgrimage, and notwithstanding that he was shown the cottage of Kirk Alloway "by a mahogany-faced old jackass who knew Burns, and who ought to have been kicked for having spoken to him," he says, "one of the pleasantest means of annulling self is approaching such a shrine: we need not think of his misery—that is all gone, bad luck to it! I shall look upon it hereafter with unmixed pleasure, as I do on my Stratford-on-Avon day with Bailey."

It gave some colour to the belief of the mental injury inflicted on Keats by the reviewers, that after this time his spirits and health began to decline, and the short remainder of his life was exposed to continual troubles and anxieties. His brother Tom, whom he loved most devotedly, and who much resembled himself in temperament and appearance, died in the autumn, and shortly before this event he met the lady who inspired him with the profound passion which under other circumstances might have combined all his dreams of happiness, but which was destined to increase tenfold the bitterness of his premature decay.* Up to this period he had been singularly shy of women's society, and frequently expressed himself freely on the subject, as for instance:—

" I am certain I have not a right feeling towards women; at this moment I am striving to be just to them, but I cannot. Is it because they fall so far beneath my boyish imagination? When I was a schoolboy, I thought a fair woman a pure goddess; my mind was a soft nest in which some one of them slept, though she knew it not. I thought them ethereal, above men. I find them perhaps equal—great by comparison is very small. * * When among men, I have no evil thoughts, no malice, no spleen; I feel free to speak or to be silent. I can listen, and from every one I can learn. When I am among women, I have evil thoughts, malice, spleen; I cannot speak or be silent; I am full of suspicions, and therefore listen to nothing; I am in a hurry to be gone. You must be charitable, and put all this perversity to my being disappointed since my boyhood."

But now his time had come. At a house where he was very intimate, he met a cousin of the family, a lady of East

* In Keats's copy of Shakspeare, the words *Poor Tom*, in "King Lear," are pathetically underlined.

Indian connections, who had there found an asylum from some domestic discomfort. He first heard much in her praise, which did not interest him, then something in her dispraise, which took his fancy. He wrote: "She is not a Cleopatra, but is, at least, a Charmian: she has a rich Eastern look: she has fine eyes, and fine manners. When she comes into the room, she makes the same impression as the beauty of a leopardess. She is too fine and too conscious of herself to repulse any man who may address her: from habit she thinks that nothing particular. I always find myself more at ease with such a woman: the picture before me always gives me a life and animation, which I cannot possibly feel with anything inferior. I am, at such times, too much occupied in admiring to be awkward or in a tremble: I forget myself entirely, because I live in her." He then protests that he is not in love with her, but that she kept him awake one night, "as a tune of Mozart's might do." He "won't cry to take the moon home with him in his pocket, nor fret to leave her behind him." And then reverting to his love to his brothers and sisters: "As a man of the world, I love the rich talk of a Charmian; as an eternal being, I love the thought of you. I should like her to ruin me, and I should like you to save me."

Residing in the house of his friend Mr. Brown, and in daily intercourse with this lady, the path of life would have lain out before him brightly indeed, had it not soon appeared that his circumstances were such as to render their union very difficult, if not impossible. The radiant imagination and the redundant heart now came into fierce conflict with poverty and disease. Hope was there, with Genius his everlasting sustainer, and Fear never approached but as the companion of Necessity: but the intensity of passion helped to wear away a physical frame originally feeble, and he might have lived longer if he had loved less.

Several of the Tales and Odes, which are contained in the volume of miscellaneous poetry, had been written by this time: the "Pot of Basil" before his highland tour, and the "Eve of St. Agnes," and the Odes "to Psyche" and "on Melancholy," in the winter; "Lamia" and the "Ode to Autumn" in the advancing year. In most of these the Spenserian influence is still strongly predominant, augmented no doubt by the study of the Italian Poets, to which, during these months, Keats sedulously applied himself. The fragment of "Hyperion" which Lord Byron, with an exaggeration akin to his former depreciation, declared to "seem actually inspired by the Titans and as sublime as Æschylus," was written so sensibly under another inspiration as to be distasteful to its author. "I have given up Hyperion," he writes, "there were too many Miltonic inversions in it. Miltonic verse cannot be written but in an artful, or rather, artist's humour." In all these Poems, in their different styles, the progress in purity and grace of diction was manifest. The simplicity of language which had been inaugurated by Goldsmith and Cowper, formalised into a theory by Wordsworth, and by him and other writers both of the Lake and the London schools carried to extravagance, had been adapted by Keats to a class of subjects to which, according to literary taste and habit, it was especially inappropriate, and where it produced on many minds almost the sensation of a classical burlesque. Such of the Gods as had spoken English up to this time had done so in formal and courtly language, and the familiarity of poetic diction which in any case was novel, here appeared extravagant. Now that Endymion has taken its place as a great English Poem, and is in truth become a region of delight in which the youth of every generation finds " a week's stroll in the summer," we can hardly feel the force of those objections, which, if they had been temperately urged by critics who in other matters recognised the genius of Keats, would have had due weight not only with the public but with the Poet himself. But while he owed nothing to the sledge-hammer censure he had endured, his own refined judgment and enlarged knowledge induced him to throw off, as puerilities and conceits, much that had before presented itself to his fancy as invention and simplicity, and to send out his noble thoughts and images so worthily arrayed, that if he had lived to maturity, he would probably have had less of peculiarity and mannerism than any other Poet of his time.

An experiment of double authorship between Keats and his friend Brown was not equally successful: the tragedy of

"Otho the Great" was thus written—Brown supplying the fable, characters, and dramatic conduct; Keats, the diction and the verse. The two composers sat opposite, Brown sketching all the incidents of each scene, and Keats translating them into his rich and ready language. As a literary diversion the process may have been instructive and amusing, but a work of art thus created could be hardly worthy of the name. As the play advanced, Keats thought the events too melodramatic, and concluded the fifth act alone. The tragedy was offered to, and accepted by, Elliston, Kean having expressed a desire to act the principal part; but it is unlikely that even his representation would have carried through a performance so unsuited for the stage. As a literary curiosity it remains interesting, and abounds with fine phrases and passages marred by the poverty of the construction. It is doubtful whether at this time Keats alone could have produced a much better play: he might have written a Midsummer Night's Dream, as Coleridge might have written a Hamlet, but in both the great human element would have been wanting, which Shakspeare combines with high philosophy or with fairy-land.

George Keats paid a short visit to England in the early part of this year and received his share of the property of the youngest brother. He probably repaid himself for moneys advanced for John's education or liabilities, and thus the share which John received was not above 200*l*. By this time little, if anything, remained of John's original fortune, and it is deeply to be regretted that the more enterprising brother did not come to some distinct understanding with the other, before he finally quitted England, as to John's future means of support. Keats's friends believed that George took with him some remnants of John's fortune to speculate with, but no proof of this remains in any of the letters on either side; and, after John's death, when the legal administration of his effects showed that no debts were owing to the estate, George offered, without any obligation, to do his utmost to discharge his brother's engagements.

At the time when these embarrassments began to press most heavily on Keats, he returned one night late to Hampstead in a state of strange physical excitement, like violent intoxication: he told his friend he had been outside the stage-coach and received a severe chill, but added, "I don't feel it now." Getting into bed, he slightly coughed, and said, "That is blood—bring me the candle," and after gazing on the pillow, turning round with an expression of sudden and solemn calm, said, "I know the colour of that blood, it is arterial blood,—I cannot be deceived in that colour; that drop is my death-warrant. I must die." He was bled, fell asleep, and, after some weeks, apparently recovered. During his illness he told Mr. Brown, "If you would have me recover, flatter me with a hope of happiness when I shall be well; for I am now so weak that I can be flattered into hope." When he said one day, "Look at my hand, it is that of a man of fifty," it was remembered that years before, Coleridge meeting Keats in a lane near Highgate, and shaking hands with him, had turned round to Mr. Hunt and whispered, 'There is death in that hand.'"

This illness seemed at the time not to be without its compensations: he wrote to Mr. Rice in Feb. (1820):—

"For six months before I was taken ill, I had not passed a tranquil day. Either that gloom overspread me, or I was suffering under some passionate feeling, or, if I turned to versify, that acerbated the poison of either sensation. The beauties of nature had lost their power over me. How astonishingly (here I must premise that illness, as far as I can judge in so short a time, has relieved my mind of a load of deceptive thoughts and images, and makes me perceive things in a truer light),—how astonishingly does the chance of leaving the world impress a sense of its natural beauties upon us! Like poor Falstaff, though I do not 'babble,' I think of green fields; I muse with the greatest affection on every flower I have known from my infancy; their shapes and colours are as new to me as if I had just created them with a superhuman fancy. It is because they are connected with the most thoughtless and happiest moments of our lives. I have seen foreign flowers in hothouses, of the most beautiful nature, but I do not care a straw for them. The simple flowers of our Spring are what I want to see again."

And he saw them—for towards the end of the spring his

health was apparently so much better that the physician recommended another tour in Scotland. Mr. Brown, however thought him unfit for the exertion and went alone: the two friends parted in May and never met again. In the previous autumn Keats had removed to a lodging in Westminster, when he was trying to make some money by contributing to periodical works, but soon found he had miscalculated his own powers of endurance. She, whose name

> "Was ever on his lip
> But never on his tongue,"

exercised too mighty a restraint over his being for him to remain at a distance which was neither absence nor presence, and he soon returned to where at least he could rest his eyes on her habitation, and enjoy each chance opportunity of her society. After Mr. Brown's departure, he seems to have been all but domesticated with her family for a short time, but with the sad consciousness of the absolute necessity of some great change of life to ward off absolute destitution. "My mind," he writes, "has been at work all over the world to find out what to do. I have my choice of three things or, at least, two—South America, or surgeon to an Indiaman, which last, I think, will be my fate. I shall resolve in a few days."

It was probably this pressure which forced him, against his will, to publish the volume of Tales and Poems, which seemed at last to move even the literary world to some consciousness of his merits. It had no great sale, but it was received respectfully, and, even without the catastrophe that soon invested it with so solemn an interest, it would have gone far to establish him as a poet even in vulgar fame. During its completion he had spent much time on an Ariosto-like Poem, which he called the "Cap and Bells," exhibiting his play of fancy to great advantage, and getting away as it were, as far as possible, from the gross realities that occupied and tormented his existence. His main passion finds no place in his verse; a few, and not eminent, fragments betray the haunting thought, but the careful exclusion of the topic from his literature adds one more testimony to the truth that the highest poetry exhibits itself in objective forms, moulded and coloured by the feelings and experiences of the writer, and not in subjective representations of his immediate and perhaps temporary sensations.

Keats thought himself to be slowly but surely recovering, when a spitting of blood came on, followed by tightness of the chest and other symptoms, which made it apparent that nothing but a winter in a milder climate would have a chance of saving his life. It is sad to contemplate with what delight, under other auspices, he would have undertaken a visit to those southern lands, the favourites of nature, still tenanted by those mythologic presences of beauty which he had so peculiarly made his own. Now he writes, "the journey to Italy wakes me at daylight every morning, and haunts me horribly. I shall endeavour to go, though it be with the sensation of marching up against a battery." He felt he had a "core of disease in him not easy to pull out," and he had no sufficient hope of ultimate good to remedy the pangs of present separation. He had been tended for a few weeks by the one hand that could soothe him, and that he must leave, perhaps for ever. And he would have had to go alone but for the affection of Mr. Severn, the young artist, who had just won the gold medal given by the Royal Academy for historical painting which had not been adjudged for the last twelve years. Regardless of personal and professional advantages the painter devoted himself to the afflicted poet, and they started in the middle of September by sea. When scarcely embarked, Keats wrote despondingly to Mr. Brown, taking that opportunity of ease, "for time seems to press." He wishes to write on subjects that would not agitate him, and yet he is ever recurring to that which wears his heart away.

"If my body would recover of itself, this would prevent it; the very thing which I want to live most for will be a great occasion of my death. * * I wish for death every day and night to deliver me from these pains, and then I wish death away, for death would destroy even those pains, which are better than nothing. Land and sea, weakness and decline, are great separators, but death is the great divorcer for ever. When the pang of this thought has passed through my mind, I may say the bitterness of death is passed. * * I am in a state at present in which woman, merely as woman, can have no more power over me than stocks and stones, and yet the difference of my sensations with respect to Miss —— and my sister is amazing: the one seems to absorb the other to a degree incredible. I seldom think of my brother and sister in America; the thought of leaving Miss —— is beyond everything horrible—the sense of darkness coming over me —I eternally see her figure eternally vanishing."

At Naples the gloom grows still darker, and we feel that the night is at hand.

" The fresh air revived me a little, and I hope I am well enough this morning to write you a short calm letter—if that can be called one, in which I am afraid to speak of what I would fainest dwell upon. As I have gone thus far into it, I must go on a little—perhaps it may relieve the load of *wretchedness* which presses upon me. The persuasion that I shall see her no more will kill me. My dear Brown, I should have had her when I was in health, and I should have remained well. I can bear to die—I cannot bear to leave her. Oh, God! God! God! Everything I have in my trunks that reminds me of her goes through me like a spear. The silk lining she put in my travelling-cap scalds my head. My imagination is horribly vivid about her—I see her—I hear her. There is nothing in the world of sufficient interest to divert me from her a moment. This was the case when I was in England. I cannot recollect, without shuddering, the time that I was a prisoner at Hunt's and used to keep my eyes fixed on Hampstead all day. Then there was a good hope of seeing her again—Now!—O that I could be buried near where she lives. * * * Is there any news of George? O, that something fortunate had ever happened to me or my brothers! then I might hope, but despair is forced upon me as a habit. My dear Brown, for my sake, be her advocate for ever. I cannot say a word about Naples; I do not feel at all concerned in the thousand novelties around me. I am afraid to write to her. I should like her to know that I do not forget her. Oh! Brown, I have coals of fire in my breast. It surprises me that the human heart is capable of containing and bearing so much misery. Was I born for this end?"

He received at Naples a most affectionate letter from Mr. Shelley urging him to come to Pisa, where he would receive every comfort and attention. After the many annoyances he encountered at Rome, one almost regrets that he did not accept this offer, except that at Pisa he could not have experienced the skilful solicitude of Dr. (now Sir James) Clark, which led him through the dark passages of mortal sickness with every alleviation that medical care and knowledge could bestow. It was thus alone that his life was preserved during December and January. On the last day of November he wrote his last letter,—in a tone of mind somewhat less painful. He spoke of his real life as something passed, and as if he were leading a posthumous existence. It ends with these words:—" If I recover, I will do all in my power to correct the mistakes made during sickness, and, if I should not, all my faults will be forgiven. Write to George as soon as you receive this, and tell him how I am, as far as you can guess; and also a note to my sister—who walks about my imagination like a ghost—she is so like Tom. I can scarcely bid you good-bye, even in a letter. I always made an awkward bow. God bless you.

"JOHN KEATS."

After some weeks of acute physical suffering and of a fierce mental conflict with destiny, in which reason itself was, at times, overcome, he became calm and resigned; he talked easily and slept peacefully. To Severn, who, to use his own phrase " had been beating about so long in the tempest of his friend's mind," this change was most welcome, although conscious that it was rather owing to the increasing debility of his body, than to any real improvement of his condition. He desired a letter from his beloved, which he did not dare to read, together with a a purse and letter of his sister's * to be placed in his coffin, and that on his grave should be written these words:—

HERE LIES ONE WHOSE NAME WAS WRIT IN WATER.

* Miss Keats shortly afterwards married Señor Llaños, the author of "Don Esteban," "Sandoval the Freemason," and other works of considerable ability.

He died on the 27th of February, so quiet that Severn thought he still slept; his last words were "Thank God it has come."

Keats was buried in the Protestant cemetery at Rome, one of the most beautiful spots on which the eye and heart of man can rest. It is a grassy slope, amid verdurous ruins of the Honorian walls of the diminished city, surmounted by the pyramidal tomb which Petrarch ascribed to Remus, but which antiquarian research has attributed to the humbler name of Caius Cestius, a Tribune of the people, only remembered by his sepulchre. In one of these mental voyages into the past, which precede death, Keats had told Severn that he thought "the intensest pleasure he had received in life was in watching the growth of flowers," and another time, after lying a while quite still, he murmured, "I feel the flowers growing over me." And there they do grow even all the winter long,—violets and daisies mingling with the fresh herbage, and in the words of Shelley "making one in love with death, to think one should be buried in so sweet a place." Some years ago, when the writer of this memoir was at Rome, the thick grass had nearly overgrown the humble tomb-stone, which however few strangers of our race omit to visit; but whether this record of him escapes the wreck of years or not, there will remain, as long as the English language lasts, and be read, as far as it extends, the glorious monument, erected by the living genius of Shelley, the Elegy of Adonais. Nor will it be forgotten, how few years afterwards, in the extended burying-ground, a little above the grave of Keats, was placed another stone, recording that below rests the passionate and world-worn heart of Shelley himself—" Cor Cordium."*

The thoughtful reader will hardly consider this biographical sketch, personal as it is, without its worth in estimating the due position of these Poems in the history of British literature. By common consent, the individuality of the Poet enters more directly into the consideration of his works than that of a writer in any other mental field. That these Poems should be the productions of a young surgeon's apprentice, with no more opportunities of study and reflection than belonged to the general middle class of his time and country, is in itself a psychological wonder, only to be paralleled by the phenomenon of Chatterton. While this reflection enhances the originality and palliates the defects of the earlier works of Keats, the picture of that sympathetic temper and genial disposition, which led his imagination to a novel and unscholastic treatment of classical tradition, and made him labour to realise a world of love and beauty in which his heart found itself most at home, would induce us to ascribe to the morose nature and lonely pride of Bristol's prodigy much of the misdirection of the rarest talents, and many otherwise undeserved calamities. And, when in pursuing the course of the later Poet we find

* The words on the stone.

him too the victim of critical contempt, haunted by pressing poverty, struck with acute physical suffering, and blighted in his deepest affections, and yet, with a genius above fate, rectifying and purifying his powers to the very last, our personal interest identifies itself with our literary admiration, and we better appreciate the merit of the poet by understanding the nobility of the man. It is not indeed that he was notably one of those who "are cradled into poetry by wrong," and "learn in suffering what they teach in song," for his temperament demanded happiness for its atmosphere, and pleasure expanded without evervating his powers; but, it was perhaps required, for the vindication of his nature from the charge of sentimental sensuality and unmanly dependence, that he should be thus severely tried, and that the simple story of his life and death should be the refutation of those who knowingly calumniated, or unconsciously misapprehended him.

The works of Keats have now sustained, in some degree, the test of time; his generation, fertile in poetical ability, has passed away, and a fair comparison may be instituted among its competitors for fame. Without entering on a question of so much intricacy, it cannot be denied that these Poems are read by every accurate student of English literature. It is natural that the young should find especial delight in productions which take so much of their inspiration from the exuberant vitality of the author and of the world. But the eternal youth of antique beauty does not confine its influences to any portion of the life of man. And thus the admiration of the writings of Keats survives the hot impulses of early years, and these pages often remain open, when the clamorous sublimities of Byron and Shelley come to be unwelcome intruders on the calm of maturer age. To these and such voices the poetic sense still listens, and will listen ever, in preference to more instructive harmonies; and the fancy recognises in the unaccomplished promise of this wonderful boy, a symbol of that old world, where the perfect physical organisation of man and the perfect type of ideal beauty may seem to have been crushed and obliterated by barbarian hands, but which perished, in truth, because these very aspirations could only be realised in another and still more glorious order of the universe.

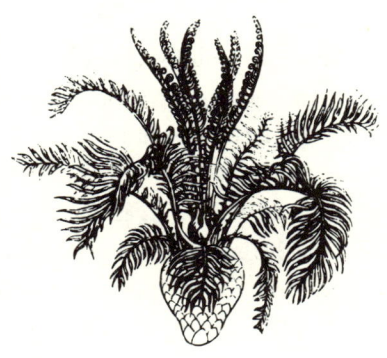

PREFATORY MEMOIR.

1.—PRELIMINARY.

IN writing a Memoir of William Blake, little or no difficulty can now arise as to the external facts—the dates, personages, and incidents. The truly valuable and so far exhaustive book of Mr. Alexander Gilchrist has settled all these points for us substantially; it barely requires to be here and there rectified or supplemented in some minor particular. Its tone moreover is as earnest and elevated as its research is true and thorough. I need hardly say that I am indebted to this book for the vast majority of my facts: any one who undertakes to write about Blake cannot be otherwise. Thus far, therefore, everything is plain: one has openly to acknowledge a genuine debt of gratitude to Mr. Gilchrist, and to run up the account freely.

The difficulty of Blake's biographers, subsequent to 1863, the date of Mr. Gilchrist's book, is of a different kind altogether. It is the difficulty of stating sufficiently high the extraordinary claims of Blake to admiration and reverence, without slurring over those other considerations which need to be plainly and fully set forth if we would obtain any real idea of the man as he was,—of his total unlikeness to his contemporaries, of his amazing genius and noble performances in two arts, of the height by which he transcended other men, and the incapacity which he always evinced for performing at all what others accomplish easily. He could do vastly more than they, but he could seldom do the like. By some unknown process, he had soared to the top of a cloud-capped Alp while they were crouching in the valley: but to reach a middle station on the mountain was what they could readily manage step by step, while Blake found that ordinary achievement impracticable. He could not and he would not do it: the want of will, or rather the utter alienation of will, the resolve to soar (which was natural to him), and not to walk (which was unnatural and repulsive), constituted, or counted in stead of, an actual want of power. *Could* Blake think, and embody his thoughts, like other men? There are instances in which he both could do so, and has done it: but certain it is, regarding him in his most characteristic moods, that mostly he would not: and, in the case of so spacious, daring, and intuitive a mind, so vivid, uncompromising, exclusive, and peremptory a character, the aversion, when it reached a certain height, amounted to incapability. For "aversion" we might perhaps substitute the word "perversity:" Blake was the most perverse of mortals, except to his own ideal, his own inspiration. To these he was loyal beyond praise, and beyond words: to aught else, equally impenetrable and contumacious. The moon partially eclipsed might be taken as no inapt image of Blake's mind: a glorious luminary, and not bedimmed or overclouded in its lucid part, but distinctly reft of light in a certain other portion. If those who urged him to do common things, or to do lofty things by common processes, were in the right, then Blake was not only in the wrong, but perverse, a "son of perdition." If Blake, on the other hand, was essentially right as to his aims and methods, then the rugged gradient of his perversity was also an ascending plane of heroism. Rapt in a passionate yearning, he realized, even on this earth and in his mortal body, a species of *nirvana*: his whole faculty, his whole personality, the very essence of his mind and mould, attained to absorption into his ideal ultimate,—into that which Dante's profound phrase designates "il Ben doll' intelletto."

Thus much may be truly and reverently said of Blake: something of the kind, indeed, cannot be left unsaid, if we would in any way appreciate, instead of merely disparaging and misconceiving, him. On certain grounds, in the totality of his intellect and aspiration, we must uphold and exalt him. So long as we consider Blake in these more general relations, to lower him would be to lower ourselves. The intrinsic greatness of the man and of his work is by this time patent and irrefutable:—clear to those persons who have examined the matter, and who are capable of entering into it with an understanding mind; contested, no doubt, by some others, and to the multitude unknown, but this goes for nothing as authority. When we proceed, however, to a more strict analysis of the operations of Blake's intellect, we shall unquestionably find much to startle and disconcert us: not now because he fails to attempt ordinary things, or to perform them well, but because he does extraordinary things in an inconceivable—not to say an often insufferable—manner. In fact, the old much-urged question "Was Blake a madman?" presents itself to us, and challenges an answer. His diligent and discerning biographer, Mr. Gilchrist, says decisively "No": so does Mr. Swinburne, in that remarkable *Critical Essay*[1] which has done more towards clearing up the darkest recesses of Blake's mind, and the most chaotic wastes of his writings, than had ever before been either achieved or attempted. This question about Blake is one on which I must necessarily have formed some kind of opinion, and ought ere I close to express it: but for the present I forbear, preferring that the reader should see something of the evidence before the deduction is presented for his consideration.

The facts to be stated regarding Blake's outer life are few, and mostly (save so far as they bear directly upon the peculiarities of his mental constitution, and the resultant works in poetry and design) are of an ordinary character. The inner life is a mine of prodigies and problems: few of these can be thoroughly explored or solved, and of many we can here take no real count at all. The works—or rather (for many others have been lost) a certain proportion of the works—which

---

[1] The books referred to are the *Life of William Blake*, by the late Alexander Gilchrist, 2 vols.: Macmillan and Co., 1863; and *William Blake, a Critical Essay*, by Algernon Charles Swinburne: Hotten, 1868.

the painter-poet produced in his incessantly laborious life, remain to us, and will, within our restricted scope and opportunities, form a principal object of our attention here.

2.—The Events of Blake's Life.

London gave birth to William Blake; and, in doing so, produced one of the strangest of all the many-millioned natives of the great city, and one moreover of the most curious and abnormal personages of the later eighteenth and earlier nineteenth centuries; a man not forestalled by predecessors, nor to be classed with contemporaries, nor to be replaced by known or readily surmisable successors. He was born on the 28th of November 1757,[1] at No. 28 Broad Street, Carnaby Market, near Golden Square; a district at that time of very respectable standing, though now fully as dingy as decorous. No. 28 is a corner-house at the narrower end of the street, which varies considerably in width. He was the second son of James and Catharine Blake, and the second child out of a family of five. The father carried on business as a hosier, and was a moderately prosperous man: in religion a Dissenter. The first child, and great favourite of the parents, was John, who turned out badly and enlisted in

---

[1] A MS. which I have seen, the production of Mr. Frederick Tatham, who knew Blake well in his latter years, gives "20" November as the date of birth. The other date, "28" November, is assigned by Mr. Gilchrist; and his accuracy in such matters leads me to adopt it, though I am not distinctly aware whether he did more than reproduce this date from Allan Cunningham's entertaining but comparatively slight memoir.

the army. Then, next after William, came James; of him, as well as of the youngest brother Robert, and of a still younger sister, William's junior by seven years, we shall hear a little more as we proceed.

William Blake's education was of the scantiest, being confined to reading and writing: arithmetic also may be guessed at, but is not recorded, and very probably his capacity for acquiring or retaining that item of knowledge was far below the average. In boyhood he was fond of little country jaunts; these were readily obtainable at that time by a resident in the Golden Square district, remote though it now is from the outskirts —themselves interminable—of the capital, ever spreading, and ever the more closely cooping up the teeming turmoil of its denizens. He began drawing very early, becoming (as Allan Cunningham has said) "at ten years of age an artist, and at twelve a poet." This last-named age is even, it would seem, too advanced by a year for the fact; for the *Poetical Sketches*, Blake's first printed volume, were stated in the prefatory words to have been begun in his "twelfth year," —and probably some other verses, still more childish in point of date, not to speak of execution, would have preceded them. He copied prints in his boyhood, and haunted sale-rooms: his parents, more especially his mother, seem to have encouraged this artistic turn. In 1767 he began attending the drawing-school of Mr. Pars in the Strand, a well-known academy, which pupils used to frequent as preparatory to the one which flourished in St. Martin's Lane. Here he had the opportunity of studying from the antique, but not from the life. At sale-rooms he bought engravings low, and selected them high; a Raphael or a Michael Angelo, a Durer or a Hemskerk. Certainly this was not the taste of the time; but the little lad Blake already moved intellectually within his own insight, as a planet within its own orbit. His own insight was always to him his epoch, his proof, and his vindication: other people—other boys in his boyhood, in his manhood other men—might shift for themselves, and live practically in a different age of the world. To him it mattered not. "I am right, and they are wrong," more or less definitely worded, was his reply. "I am happy" (he has written in certain notes upon Reynolds, not exactly squaring with the views of the British connoisseur) "I cannot say that Raphael ever was, from my earliest childhood, hidden from me. I saw and I knew immediately the difference between Raphael and Rubens."

The career of a painter would have been the natural one for Blake, with such capacities and tastes, to adopt; and he did to some considerable extent pursue it in after life. His father's means, however, were not such as to put this profession conveniently within the lad's reach: he was consequently bound to an engraver, and the engraving branch of art was that which he followed ever afterwards as his regular calling. In 1771, at the age of fourteen, he became one of the apprentices of the well-reputed engraver James Basire, who (domiciled in No. 31 Great Queen Street, Lincoln's Inn Fields) was employed on the work of the Antiquarian and the Royal Societies. For the former body he issued, in 1774, the largest engraving that had as yet been ever executed upon one plate, about forty-seven inches by twenty-seven, *The Field of the Cloth of Gold*, after the picture at Windsor. Basire's style was hard, dry, and firm: Blake naturally adopted it during his apprenticeship, and retained not a little of it in his after practice. I speak, of course, of his ordinary engravings, frequently from the works of other artists, executed in the recognized professional method; for those other engravings which he produced to illustrate many of his own writings, and in which he used processes known only to himself, are of an entirely different kind. The adoption of his instructor's style was so far well suited to Blake as that it wholly eschewed frivolity and trick: he often, in conversation or in writing, continued to uphold its superiority to the more facile and popular manner of other practitioners. It was not, however, attractive to common eyes, nor fully satisfying to those of an artist, and it must have retarded rather than promoted Blake's success with publishers and purchasers.

The master and the apprentice had reason to be mutually well-pleased during their connection: the former was upright and kind, and the latter made steady and satisfactory progress. After a while, however, some discordances arose. Two other apprentices came to the establishment towards the beginning of Blake's third year. They proved less docile than the senior pupil, and won him partly over to their side; and in consequence he was sent out of the house, from time to time, to make drawings in Westminster Abbey, and in various old churches, for the antiquary Gough. On some other subjects Blake and his fellow-apprentices were less harmonious; they wrangled over metaphysical problems, on which Blake, we may be sure, was very positive, and his opponents probably inexpert, and proportionately indisposed to be convinced. His present employment imbued Blake with a decided love of Gothic feeling and form, which (although in a very rudimentary condition) can often be traced throughout his original work. He sketched the tombs in the Abbey, engraved a selection from his studies there, and made drawings from history, and from fancy. One of his engravings, dated as early as 1773, has a peculiarity of subject foreshadowing what he did in later years. It is inscribed *Joseph of Arimathea among the Rocks of Albion*, and is founded on a design by Michael Angelo. There is also the inscription: "This is one of the Gothic artists who built the Cathedrals in what we call the Dark Ages, wandering about in sheepskins and goatskins, of whom the world was not worthy. Such were the Christians in all ages." During his apprentice days Blake's chief pleasure was in making drawings and verses, to be hung up in his mother's room. His term came to an end in 1778.

He next studied in the Antique School of the Royal Academy, under the keeper Mr. Moser—not with unmixed satisfaction. He has left us an amusing anecdote of his having been looking over prints from Raphael and Michael Angelo in the Academy library, when Moser extolled in their stead the works of Rubens and Lebrun. "These things that you call *finished*," replied Blake to Moser, "are not even begun; how then can they be finished?" He drew a great deal from the antique, and afterwards also from the living model; but he disliked the latter practice. "The life," in this condition, appeared to him "more like death," and "smelling of mortality." Another anecdote, which may appertain to this period of studentship or probably to a rather later date, is that of Blake's interview with Sir Joshua Reynolds. It may help to account for the extreme animosity which the ideal artist always showed against the consummately-gifted portrait-painter; though assuredly the deeper grounds of this feeling were matter of genuine conviction, and not of any mere personal exasperation. "Once I remember[1] his talking to me of Reynolds," writes a surviving friend; "he became furious at what the latter had dared to say of his early works. When a very young man, he had called on Reynolds, to show him some designs, and had been recommended to work with less extravagance and more simplicity, and to correct his drawing. This Blake seemed to regard as an affront never to be forgotten. He was very indignant when he spoke of it." No doubt the censure of the drawing of so severe and forcible a draughtsman as Blake, coming from one of so much loose facility as Reynolds, was peculiarly galling, notwithstanding the great difference in age and professional standing.

Blake, still domiciled with his father in Broad Street, was now beginning to paint water-colours, and also to engrave, on his own account, for publishers. He executed prints for the *Novelists' Magazine*—among others, some after Stothard—and for the *Ladies' Magazine*. An engraver named

---

[1] This passage is extracted from Mr. Gilchrist's book.

Trotter introduced him to Stothard, two years his senior; and Stothard made him known to Flaxman, who was at present subsisting on his work for Wedgwood. Flaxman professed to be—and one may fairly believe that he really was—a sincere admirer and firm friend of Blake; although the latter, at times, believed the contrary, as is amply proved by an epigram or two reproduced in the present volume, as well as by occasional passages in Blake's prose writings. Afterwards the visionary painter knew likewise Fuseli, whose life, prolonged to the age of eighty-three, ceased (in April 1825) only about two years before that of Blake himself. Him Blake always admired as an artist, and valued as a friend; indeed, if we may credit one of his own splenetic utterances in doggrel, Fuseli, being "both Turk and Jew," was "the only man who did not make him almost spue." The pithy utterance of the Swiss painter, "Blake is damned good to steal from," attested the genuinely appreciative estimate with which he repaid his friend's good opinion. The "stealing," according to Blake, was done by both Stothard and Flaxman; in other words, Blake supplied ideas, or designs more or less completely suggested, and his acquaintances availed themselves freely of these, and worked them up into materials of fame and fortune. The transparent sincerity of Blake's character does not allow of our wholly discrediting these charges. In the case of Stothard, we shall see that the accusation takes eventually a more defined form. In that of Flaxman, it does not appear that any *surreptitious* appropriation of Blake's ideas is imputed, and therefore, supposing Flaxman to have been always sincerely friendly to Blake, the charge does not bear hard on the sculptor's character—only on the grievous conditions under which the more inventive Blake had to work and live, while another received the credit. Blake, it should be remembered, was an exceedingly impulsive, and in a certain sense a violent, man—always, at the least, vehement and unmeasured. He knew and keenly felt, spite of his extreme superiority to worldly self-interest, that he was not receiving, as years passed over his head, his due of reputation from the public; and I would be quite disposed, in equity as well as in inclination, to reduce to a minimum the charge raised by him against Flaxman,[1] and in most respects against Stothard as well. Clearly, he was for years on good terms with Stothard, and still longer bore a true affection to Flaxman. If at whiles his heart burned within him, and he blurted out something that jars upon the reader's nerves and recollection, let us not suffer this to tell too severely against either Flaxman or himself; but, while not entirely exonerating Flaxman, which would amount to entirely inculpating Blake, let us think a little kindly allowance can be made for both, and lay over the infirmities or the misapprehensions of both illustrious friends one fold the closer of the veil of oblivion.

---

[1] The charge is formulated as follows in a MS. composition by Blake, never published until by Mr. Gilchrist, in his second volume, p. 156:—" Flaxman cannot deny that one of the very first monuments he did I gratuitously designed for him. At the same time he was blackening my character as an artist to Macklin, my employer [a publisher], as Macklin told me at the time, and posterity will know."

The year 1780 was that in which Blake first exhibited a picture in the Royal Academy: this was the *Death of Earl Godwin*, probably executed in water-colours. He continued exhibiting at the same institution from time to time—only five instances in all—up to the year 1808, when he sent *Christ in the Sepulchre guarded by Angels*, and *Jacob's Dream*: these were his final contributions.

About the time when he first began thus exhibiting he was "keeping company" with a lively girl, to whom the name of Clara Woods has with some likelihood been assigned: she proved indifferent, and he was jealous. At the house of Mr. Boucher, a market-gardener at Battersea (where possibly Blake was just then lodging), he was once complaining of his amorous distresses. The daughter of the house said: "I pity you from my heart." "*Do* you pity me?" asked Blake. "Yes, I do most sincerely." "Then I love you for that." "And *I* love *you*," responded the damsel. This was the beginning and the turning-point of the courtship which resulted in Blake's marriage. Catharine Sophia Boucher was one of a rather large family, a slim and graceful (or in fact, as has been said, "very pretty") brunette, with white hands, which had attracted the painter's notice, and expressive features. Belonging as she did to a very humble stock, she had received next to no education. In the marriage-register she only signed her mark, when, on the 18th of August 1782, in her twenty-first year, she became the painter's bride. He elicited the dormant powers of her mind; taught her to read and write; and trained her to the working-off of his engravings, and to colouring them now and again, and even to some skill in designing, in a class of subject-matter and general treatment closely enough resembling that which stamps his own works with so marvellous an individuality. She was, besides, a good thrifty manager, as the always narrow means of the married couple urgently required her to be; and a handy cook also in a plain unpretentious way, which was fortunate in a household where no servant was kept. In other more important respects—in short, in every sense—she was a most excellent, believing, and devoted wife. If Blake had visions, she credited them, though without professing to see the same appearances which were manifest to him, and she actually caught from him a visionary faculty of her own: if he required companionship, she was always there; help, she yielded it affectionately and efficiently; service, drudgery, she was unstinting of both. "She would get up in the night" (says Mr. John Thomas Smith, commonly called "Nollekens Smith") "when he was under his very fierce inspirations, which were as if they would tear him asunder, while he was yielding himself to the Muse, or whatever else it could be called, sketching and writing. And so terrible a task did this seem to be that she had to sit motionless and silent, only to stay him mentally, without moving hand or foot: this for hours, and night after night."

In some of the earlier years of the marriage, indeed, it is said that grave conflicts of feeling and of will arose between Blake and his wife—jealousy on her part being the essential cause, or rather something on his part which occasioned her jealousy. This will surprise no one who is cognizant of the full range of Blake's writings, and who consequently knows that his views of the sexual relation and of the marriage-tie, along with other burning questions, were of the most audacious possible kind—more conformable to the quality of an oriental patriarch or a religious and social innovator than of an English engraver of the eighteenth century. It has even been said that at one time he proposed to add a second wife to the household. This may or may not be true as fact: as an exemplification of theory, those who have more than skimmed Blake's works know that such ideas were not unfamiliar to his mind. The difference would have been not between the one startling act and the many startling words expressed or implied, but merely between the power of startling which belongs respectively to one act and to many words. Be this affair of the proposed second wife true or not, certain it is that not one of his few biographers gives any distinct intimation of *de facto* breaches of marital faith on Blake's part: he seems to have lived with regularity, and observance of the practical obligations of man in society, in this as in all other regards. Any differences between himself and his wife which may have chequered their harmony in the earlier years of wedlock seem afterwards to have subsided wholly; and we can, without either uncertainty as to the external facts, or misgiving as to the internal conditions, contemplate in the case of William and Catharine Blake—somewhat hazardously matched couple as they would appear to have been originally—a genuine marriage. Affection was truly and warmly interchanged between them; while guidance and elevating influence on the one side were requited by a tender perpetuity of service on the other.

The marriage, which proved a childless one, was not particularly pleasing to Blake's father. The young couple set up house at No. 23 Green Street, Leicester Fields. Soon afterwards Blake began to see something of literary and fashionable society, through his being introduced by Flaxman to Mrs. Mathew, the lady whose *conversazioni* at No. 27 Rathbone Place kept up at that time much of the vogue of the original "blue-stocking" meetings. Here Blake would read his poems, and also sing them; for, though he knew nothing of musical science or notation, he had set some of his verses to airs which, according to Mr. J. T. Smith, were "most singularly beautiful," and "were noted down by musical professors." His love was for simple, not elaborate, music; in his old age he would still sometimes sing when among intimate friends. These performances gave great pleasure at Mrs. Mathew's parties, where Blake was for a time a welcome guest: but his "unbending deportment," or "manly firmness of opinion," stood in the way of any such social success, and somewhere towards 1785 he ceased—or almost wholly ceased—to reappear in the house. Such a result is more than intelligible. Blake was not only a visionary and mystic, and a daring speculator in religion and morals, but he was and always continued a republican, and enemy of kings and of war, and moreover an utter nonconformist in his own special work of art and of poetry. As regards republicanism, he maintained that the very shape of his forehead, larger over the eyes than above, marked him out for that form of political opinion. And on all these debateable and exciting topics alike he was ever ready to make the most positive and exclusive affirmations, to pronounce, decree, and hear of no denial or qualification. His attitude, in short, was always that of an inspired seer: the thing was so because he saw it so, and he saw it so, not by a bodily and argumentative eye, but by a spiritual and intuitional one. Truly loveable in personal character, he conciliated a certain good-will in a number of the most unpromising quarters; but a man of this kind was plainly not destined to be of the elect in the regions of small-talk. One circumstance of some importance in his career resulted from his acquaintance with Mrs. Mathew and her husband. The latter, the Rev. Henry Mathew, combined with Flaxman in causing Blake's first volume of verse, the *Poetical Sketches,* to be printed in 1783; and the obliging clergyman wrote the few words of preface to that selection. The impression was presented to Blake—too poor now and very generally afterwards to launch out into any such expenses for himself; but it was not published in the ordinary sense.

Blake's father, dying in the summer of 1784, was succeeded in the hosiery business by his third son James, a person not wholly unlike William in a visionary (more especially a Swedenborgian) tendency, but otherwise by no means in sympathy with him. One regets to hear that, in later years, the two brothers would not speak to one another; an estrangement for which no distinct reason is on record, unless one can say that the hosier's general disapproval of the unworldliness and wilfulness of the mystic, and the mystic's scorn of the peddling and scraping habits of the hosier, furnish a not insufficient explanation. Blake set up shop next door to his brother (No. 27) as a printseller and engraver, in partnership with one of his fellow-apprentices, Mr. Parker, the firm being styled " Parker and Blake." Mrs. Blake helped in the shop. This association continued till 1787, when Blake, disagreeing with Parker, seceded. Meanwhile his favourite brother Robert, some five years younger than himself, had been with him as a gratuitous pupil in engraving; he too, like the tractable wife, took to making original designs marked by the fraternal influence. An early death closed a life of no small promise. Robert died towards the beginning of 1787: William saw his soul ascend through the ceiling, " clapping its hands for joy." After his death, and the severance of the partnership with Parker, Blake removed to the neighbouring Poland Street, No. 28. Here the spirit of Robert rendered him an essential service; directing him, in a nocturnal vision, how to proceed in bringing out poems and designs in conjunction, all of them the produce of his own hand in every executive respect, no less than of his own mind. This question—the difficulty of producing poetical works to the public when he had no money to pay for printing—had embarrassed William's mind for some while before 1787, when the *Songs of Innocence* issued forth: the spirit of Robert solved the problem. " This method," says Mr. Gilchrist, " to which Blake henceforth consistently adhered for multiplying his works, was quite an original one. It consisted in a species of engraving in relief both words and designs. The verse was written, and the designs and marginal embellishment outlined, on the copper with an impervious liquid,—probably the ordinary stopping-out varnish of engravers. Then all the white parts, or lights, (the remainder of the plate, that is) were eaten away with aquafortis or other acid, so that the outline of letter and design was left prominent, as in stereotype. From these plates he printed off in any tint— yellow, brown, blue—required to be the prevailing (or ground) colour in his facsimiles: red he used for the letterpress. The page was then coloured up by hand in imitation of the original drawing, with more or less variety of detail in the local hues." He mixed his colours with diluted glue, a process revealed to him by St. Joseph; Mrs. Blake did up the books in boards, and often assisted in tinting the designs,—sometimes, especially in the copies which she treated after her husband's death, overloading the colour: in fact, as Mr. Gilchrist points out, every item of the process was done by Blake with his wife's willing aid, save only the making of the paper.

In the same year, 1789, followed *The Book of Thel*; in 1790, *The Marriage of Heaven and Hell*; in 1791 (sole book by Blake that was both printed and published in the ordinary way), *The French Revolution, a Poem in 7 Books: Book I.* The other instalments of this rhapsodical work never appeared, nor is the value of the first Book such as to raise any grave regret for their suppression. Not one of these productions made the least way with the public at the time: but, as years rolled on, the sale, within his more or less immediate circle of acquaintance, of the *Songs of Innocence*, and some other books engraved in the same way, though often of a widely different character of writing and design (such as the *Daughters of Albion, Urizen, Jerusalem, &c.*, to be hereafter spoken of), constituted one of the least precarious and least paltry sources of income for the spiritual-minded Blake. That his income was always exiguous is attested by many incidental facts; as, for instance, that he was often compelled to work new designs on his old copper-plates. His selling price for the united *Songs of Innocence and Experience* (the latter came out in 1794) was from £1. 10s. to £2. 2s.; but occasionally, in his latter years, he received as much as £5. 5s., or, from friends who were cognizant of his necessities, yet larger sums. The highest of these amounts can be barely a third of what a good copy would now sell for.

Passing lightly over some of the work which Blake executed towards this time—such as his few designs, engraved by himself, for Mary Wollstonecraft's *Tales for Children*—we find him living on good terms with the bookseller Johnson, of St. Paul's Churchyard, and attending the dinners which the latter gave, and at which, along with Fuseli, several of the political extremists of the day were wont to gather—Price, Priestley, Miss Wollstonecraft, Godwin, Holcroft, Paine. Blake went so far as to put-on the *bonnet rouge*, and walk the streets with it; being, it is said, the only one of the set who would adventure thus patently to profess his fetterless politics. This was some little while before the prison-massacres of September 1792, which induced Blake to re-alter his head-dress. Towards the latter date, Paine, who had then been elected to the French National

Convention, was under prosecution in England for publishing his *Rights of Man*; and but for a timely warning from Blake—" You must not go home, or you are a dead man "—he might probably have delayed his departure to the land of the Republic, and would in that case have been inevitably arrested, for an order to detain him was received at Dover almost as soon as he had set sail.

In 1793 Blake quitted Poland Street for No. 13 Hercules Buildings, Lambeth; and, in May of the same year, he published his little book of symbolic designs entitled *For Children* (some copies, *For the Sexes*), *The Gates of Paradise*. This was rapidly followed by the *Visions of the Daughters of Albion*, and by *America, a Prophecy*; both still in 1793. In the ensuing year he re-engraved Flaxman's designs (which had previously been treated by Piroli) from the *Odyssey*—his style of engraving being at this time distinguished from that of most other practitioners by a much greater proportion of etching. It was not till after an interval of many years—1817—that he again engraved after Flaxman, the *Works and Days of Hesiod*. In 1794 he also issued *Europe, a Prophecy* (being a sequel to the *America*), and *The Book of Urizen, Part I.*, as well as a small quarto volume containing twenty-three engraved and coloured designs, without letter-press.

Towards the same time he made the acquaintance of Mr. Thomas Butts, of Fitzroy Square, by far the best purchasing patron whom he ever had, and one who (as testified in a letter from the grateful designer) "always left him altogether to his own judgment," which was indeed the only conceivable way for getting work out of such a man. This gentleman went on for nearly thirty years buying the paintings of Blake—ordinary water-colours, along with what the artist termed tempera-pictures or frescoes; for oil, after a few experiments (dictated, as he said, by demons such as Titian and Correggio), was a vehicle which he utterly eschewed. He would not even tolerate the historical account of the invention of oil-colours, in their modern application, by John van Eyck (or more properly by his elder brother, Hubert), but denounced this as a "silly story and known falsehood," and termed the process a "villainy" for which Rubens or Vandyck was accountable. "Oil was not used, except by blundering ignorance, till after Vandyck's time." Mr. Butts, at the end of 1805, engaged Blake, at the pay of £26. 5s. per annum, to teach drawing to his son; he would sometimes take from the artist a drawing per week, and continued his commissions, more or less, up to the year 1822 or thereabouts. At last he fell off, and almost lost sight of his old friend when age and penury were weighing heavy upon him; it appears that he found it increasingly difficult to avoid offending Blake, whose sense of independence smarted at the slightest touch of interference or advice, and found expression, at times, in very outspoken and intolerant terms. Something also may have been due to the fact that the house of Mr. Butts was then already crammed with the painter's works.[1]

---

[1] Mr. Butts (as stated in Mr. Gilchrist's book, vol. i. p. 115) was the authority for the now often-repeated story that Blake and his wife were found by the narrator sitting

The year 1795 witnessed the completion of the
"Prophetic Books" regarding the four quarters
of the globe—*Africa* and *Asia* having now been
published, under the general title of *The Song of
Los*. This name may, however, with more propriety be regarded as comprehending the *America*
and *Europe* as well; for "Los" (in Blake's
arbitrary and seldom interpretable nomenclature)
is "Time," as Mr. Swinburne, diving into the
"sunless and sonorous gulfs" of the *Jerusalem*,
has succeeded in finding out, not a little to the
advantage of the dozen or so of people who possess
some dim acquaintance with this class of Blake's
writings. *The Book of Ahania* followed, also in
1795, and may count as constituting the second
Part of the otherwise uncontinued *Urizen*. Amid
all this hurtle of amazing design, and welter of
baffling prophecy, Blake continued his plodding
work as an engraver after other artists, eminent
or undistinguished, varied occasionally by some
works of his own. One of these was issued in
1794, inscribed *Ezekiel; Take away from thee the*

---

naked in the summer-house of their Hercules Buildings home,
and that the painter called out—" Come in! It's only Adam
and Eve, you know." This practice was repeated, it is
alleged, more than once. Mr. Linnell, however, (see Mr.
Swinburne's book, p. 299) peremptorily denies that such a
transaction ever took place. It must be admitted, looking
(if nothing else) to the question of dates, that the fact might
have occurred, without Mr. Linnell's knowing, by any
possibility, anything about it, one way or the other. The
anecdote, however, has a mythic air; it has already been re-
tailed oftener than was needful for such a triviality, in the
case of so lofty a man as Blake; and, though I have not
deemed it well to pass the matter over in total silence, I
think the time has come when a foot-note, joined to a *caveat*
against too implicit credence, amply suffices for it.

desire of thine eyes (the death of the prophet's wife). Another is from *Job*—" What is man, that thou shouldst try him every moment?" The figures in these prints are the largest that Blake ever engraved. One of the most important commissions which he at any time received (though insignificant in point of remuneration, being probably only £1. 1s. per plate, design and engraving) was that for illustrating Young's *Night Thoughts*. This re-edition was undertaken in 1796 by Mr. Edwards, the publisher in New Bond Street. Part I. appeared in the Autumn of 1797, going up to the end of the Fourth Night, and containing forty-three engraved designs; an explanation of the subjects, not written by Blake himself, was published along with them. The project was not encouraged by the public, and no second part ever came out.[1]

In the first year of the nineteenth century a change came over Blake's manner of life. Flaxman had introduced him to Mr. Hayley, the author of that feeble drizzle of verse the *Triumphs of Temper*, and of other works which shared, along with that, the lavish commendations of the critical in those days. William Hayley was a country

---

[8] As these pages are passing through the press, I observe, in the *Athenæum* for the 14th March 1874, an advertisement inserted by Mr. H. W. Birtwhistle, Halifax. As it gives a more precise account than I had ever seen elsewhere of Blake's work for the *Night Thoughts*, I add it here:— " *Young's Night Thoughts*, with the 537 original coloured drawings, by Blake. 2 vols., 21 inches by 16, red morocco. The letter-press, $8\frac{1}{2}$ by $6\frac{1}{4}$ inches, occupies the centre of each page; and around each page is the drawing, enclosed in a ruled and coloured border. The drawings are clean, perfect, and the colours are bright and fresh as when first put on."

gentleman of some fortune, having a seat at Eartham in Sussex, not far from Bognor: he delighted to style himself "the Hermit of Eartham." He had some good qualities, to which the misdeed of writing unreadable verses, and of getting contemporaries to read them with plaudits, ought not to blind us. He was gifted with amiability, willingness to oblige, the love and the habit of culture according to his lights. Hayley, now aged fifty-six, undertook to write a Life of his friend Cowper, who had died in this same year 1800 (25 April); and Blake was proposed as engraver of the illustrations to the work. He willingly closed with the offer; partly (as he himself has recorded) because in London Fuseli, the bookseller Johnson, and others, made "great objections to my doing anything but the mere drudgery of business, and intimations that, if I do not confine myself to this, I shall not live." For the purpose now in question, it was arranged that Blake should dwell at Felpham, a sea-side village adjacent to Eartham. This latter place had now been let by Hayley, who was himself also living at Felpham in a turreted "marine cottage" of his own construction. Blake took another and very ordinary cottage, still standing, at a rent of £20 a year: his only sister, as well as his wife, lived with him there, though in general, it would seem, she was supported by her other brother James. Blake was at first exceedingly delighted with Felpham, its inhabitants, his personal position and prospects, his cottage, its splendid sea-view and general surroundings. A letter which he addressed to Flaxman on the 21st of September 1800 has often been printed; but, as it is the most readily available among the very few letters which remain to us from the same hand, it must once again reappear in our pages.

"DEAR SCULPTOR OF ETERNITY,

"We are safe arrived at our cottage, which is more beautiful than I thought it, and more convenient. It is a perfect model for cottages, and I think for palaces of magnificence — only enlarging, not altering, its proportions, and adding ornaments and not principles. Nothing can be more grand than its simplicity and usefulness. Simple without intricacy, it seems to be the spontaneous expression of humanity, congenial to the wants of man. No other-formed house can ever please me so well; nor shall I ever be persuaded, I believe, that it can be improved either in beauty or use.

"Mr. Hayley received us with his usual brotherly affection. I have begun to work. Felpham is a sweet place for study, because it is more spiritual than London. Heaven opens here on all sides her golden gates; her windows are not obstructed by vapours; voices of celestial inhabitants are more distinctly heard, and their forms more distinctly seen; and my cottage is also a shadow of their houses. My wife and sister are both well, courting Neptune for an embrace.

"Our journey was very pleasant, and, though we had a great deal of luggage, no grumbling. All was cheerfulness and good-humour on the road; and yet we could not arrive at our cottage before half-past eleven at night, owing to the necessary shifting of our luggage from one chaise to another—for we had seven different chaises, and as many different drivers. We set out between six and seven in the morning of Thursday, with sixteen heavy boxes and portfolios full of prints.

"And now begins a new life, because another covering of earth is shaken off. I am more famed in heaven for my works than I could well conceive. In my brain are studies and chambers filled with books and pictures of old, which I wrote and painted in ages of eternity before my mortal life; and these works are the delight and study of archangels. Why then should I be anxious about the riches or fame of mortality? The Lord our Father will do for us and with us according to His divine will, for our good.

"You, O dear Flaxman, are a sublime archangel —my friend and companion from eternity. In the divine bosom is our dwelling-place. I look back into the regions of reminiscence, and behold our ancient days before this earth appeared in its vegetated mortality to my mortal vegetated eyes. I see our houses of eternity, which can never be separated, though our mortal vehicles should stand at the remotest corners of heaven from each other.

"Farewell, my best friend. Remember me and my wife in love and friendship to our dear Mrs. Flaxman, whom we ardently desire to entertain beneath our thatched roof of rusted gold. And believe me for ever to remain your grateful and affectionate

"WILLIAM BLAKE.

"Felpham, September 21st 1800, Sunday morning."

In a different letter we find Blake saying: "One thing of real consequence I have accomplished by coming into the country, which is to me consolation enough; namely, I have re-collected all my scattered thoughts on art, and resumed my primitive and original ways of execution in both painting and engraving, which, in the confusion of London, I had very much lost and obliterated from my mind."

At the end of 1801 Hayley began some *Ballads on Anecdotes relating to Animals*, which Blake illustrated: the proceeds of sale, if any there were, went to the artist by the author's good-will. Most of his working hours, always most industriously filled up, were spent in the literary squire's house. The illustrations for the projected *Life of Cowper* were engraved in due course; and in 1803 some designs which Maria Flaxman, the sculptor's sister, had produced in illustration of the *Triumphs of Temper*: these remained unpublished until 1807. Miniature-painting also now occupied Blake to some small extent: he produced a portrait, in this style, of the Rev. John Johnson, Cowper's cousin, and others of some of the neighbouring gentry, to whom Hayley introduced him. Generally, he accepted whatever commissions came in his way, apposite to his powers or otherwise: one however, offered to him through Hayley's introduction, he declined—that of painting a set of hand-screens for a lady. He learned something of Greek during his connection with the Hermit: and it may here be observed that the extreme meagreness of his early schooling was supplemented afterwards by some smattering of Latin, and by studying French sufficiently to read that language, and also, at the age of sixty, as much Italian as was needed for skimming Dante.

It must not be supposed, however, that all went smooth with Blake at Felpham. Among the few of his extant letters are ten addressed to his attached friend Mr. Butts; some of these show how sorely, after a while, the fiery idealist chafed under Hayley's patronage—his " genteel ignorance and polite disapprobation," his "affected contempt" and "affected loftiness." He demurred to Blake's style of working, both in design and in poetry; and, shortly before the date of the painter's letter of 6 July 1803, there had evidently been a "scene" between the two ill-assorted *collaborateurs*. Blake, in his own view at least, had had the better of this. He had been set at liberty by his spiritual friends, after a long period of probation, "to remonstrate against former conduct, and to demand justice and truth; which (he adds) I have done in so effectual a manner that my antagonist is silenced completely, and I have compelled what should have been of freedom— my just right as an artist and as a man." In any connection of this sort, between men so radically and irremediably unlike, a time is pretty sure to come when each considers himself rather scurvily used by the other: each sees so clearly the justice and urgency of his own cause, and is by the very constitution of his mind so unable to discern any plausibility in the pleas put forward by the opposite party. We cannot therefore be in the least surprised that Blake became incensed against Hayley: but in justice to the latter we shall do well to remember that the painter's earlier letters had spoken of him in very different terms; for instance (10 May 1801, after an experience of nearly a year and a half)—" Mr. Hayley acts like a prince; I am at complete ease."

While Blake was irritated against Hayley, there occurred a strange matter-of-fact interruption to the course of so imaginative and esoteric a life. This again gave Hayley an opportunity of proving the substantial kindliness of his feeling; nor was Blake slow to acknowledge as much, and to withdraw, in a subsequent letter to Mr. Butts, the harshness of his animadversions upon the Hermit of Eartham. In truth, after making every allowance for Blake, we may not irrationally conclude that the good-humour of the Hermit also had at times been rather strained by the author of *Jerusalem*— a man who affirmed himself to be "under the direction of messengers from heaven, daily and nightly." If Hayley always managed to keep his temper, those "*Triumphs*" which his goose-quill had celebrated in exalted verse had now been further signalized by his own deportment.—Blake himself shall relate for us the vexatious and anomalous incident which befell him in the August of 1803.

"I am at present in a bustle to defend myself against a very unwarrantable warrant from a Justice of Peace in Chichester, which was taken out against me by a private in Captain Leathes' troop of 1st or Royal Dragoons, for an assault and seditious words. The wretched man has terribly perjured himself, as has his comrade; for, as to sedition, not one word relating to the King or Government was spoken by either him or me. His enmity arises from my having turned him out of my garden, into which he was invited as an assistant by a gardener at work therein, without my knowledge that he was so invited. I desired him, as politely as possible, to go out of

the garden: he made me an impertinent answer.
I insisted on his leaving the garden: he refused.
I still persisted in desiring his departure. He
then threatened to knock out my eyes, with many
abominable imprecations, and with some contempt
for my person: it affronted my foolish pride. I
therefore took him by the elbows, and pushed him
before me till I had got him out. There I intended
to have left him; but he, turning about, put himself into a posture of defiance, threatening and
swearing at me. I, perhaps foolishly and perhaps
not, stepped out at the gate, and, putting aside
his blows, took him again by the elbows, and,
keeping his back to me, pushed him forward down
the road about fifty yards—he all the while endeavouring to turn round and strike me, and
raging and cursing, which drew out several
neighbours. At length, when I had got him to
where he was quartered, which was very quickly
done, we were met at the gate by the master of
the house, the Fox Inn, who is the proprietor of
my cottage, and his wife and daughter, and the
man's comrade, and several other people. My
landlord compelled the soldiers to go indoors,
after many abusive threats against me and my
wife from the two soldiers; but not one word of
threat on account of sedition was uttered at that
time. This method of revenge was planned between them after they had got together into the
stable. I have for witnesses [five persons, present
at the time, who will disprove the allegation as to
use of any seditious words]. I have been forced
to find bail. Mr. Hayley was kind enough to
come forward, and Mr. Seagrave, printer at Chichester: Mr. H. in £100, and Mr. S. in £50. . .

I have heard that my accuser is a disgraced sergeant: his name is John Scholfield."

Blake's trial came on at the Chichester Quarter Sessions on the 11th of January 1804. He was charged with "having uttered seditious and treasonable expressions, such as 'Damn the King, damn all his subjects, damn his soldiers, they are all slaves: when Bonaparte comes, it will be cut-throat for cut-throat, and the weakest must go to the wall: I will help him,' &c., &c." Hayley, though suffering from a severe accident in riding, attended and spoke up for the defendant's character; and a vigorous cross-examination damaged the principal witness for the prosecution. The result was an acquittal, which was received with the applause of the auditory. Blake, mindful of the republican and anti-warlike sentiments entertained by himself, and of the many instances in which he had made these prominent, as in the case of Paine, was wont to aver that the soldier must have been sent by the Government or some person in authority to entrap him. This the reader may not be disposed to believe; but it is certainly rather curious that the soldier, if his encounter with Blake was wholly fortuitous and unplanned, should have hit upon that very sort of accusation against him, and have untruthfully charged him with using that very sort of language, which his antecedents rendered *primâ jacie* probable.

The patronage of Hayley, the sojourn at Felpham, were now played out: they had become irksome to a genius and a character in which compromise found no place, and early in 1804 Blake returned to London. "The visions were angry with me at Felpham," was a phrase of his in after years; and the letters which he had addressed from that village to Mr. Butts leave no doubt that considerations of that kind were very prominent at the time in determining his resolve. It had turned out that at Felpham "voices of celestial inhabitants were *not* more distinctly heard, nor their forms more distinctly seen," than in London, spite of the conviction expressed in Blake's letter to Flaxman already quoted. He took lodgings on the first floor of No. 17 South Molton Street, Oxford Street; and soon issued thence the astounding scriptures which he had been elaborating at Felpham, named respectively *Jerusalem, the Emanation of the Giant Albion,* and *Milton, a Poem in Two Books.* These works were not milk for babes, nor stirabout for Hayleys. In the preface to the *Jerusalem,* Blake speaks of that composition as having been "dictated" to him; and other expressions of his prove that he regarded it rather as a revelation of which he was the scribe than as the product of his own inventing and fashioning brain. Blake considered it "the grandest poem that this world contains;" adding, "I may praise it, since I dare not pretend to be any other than the secretary—the authors are in eternity." In an earlier letter (25th April 1803) he had said: "I have written this poem from immediate dictation, twelve or sometimes twenty or thirty lines at a time, without premeditation, and even against my will."

The *Jerusalem* and the *Milton* are the last of the "Prophetic Books," properly to be so called, that ever saw the light, though not the last that

Blake wrote. So curt a performance as the *Ghost of Abel* (issued in 1822), being besides devoid of pictorial design to accompany its words, cannot be taken into account; moreover, it appears to have been composed and engraved as far back as 1788. Others—scores of MSS., a larger mass than the writings of Shakspeare and Milton united—were produced, but no publisher could be obtained for them. "Well," Blake would say after some futile application, "it is published elsewhere, and beautifully bound!" According to himself, he had done six or seven epics as long as Homer, and twenty tragedies as long as *Macbeth*—an assertion not perhaps to be accepted literally. One of his writings is referred to by Mr. Crabb Robinson under the term "a Vision of Genesis, as understood by a Christian Visionary."

It was not destined that Blake should go on writing, as author or as amanuensis, such works as the *Jerusalem* and the *Milton*, in entire solitude of aspiration, of mind, and of habit of work. In the year 1805 he got connected with a speculator who was to play fast and loose with his material interests, and (had he not been protected by unshaken firmness) with his self-respect as well. Mr. Robert Hartley Cromek, a native of Yorkshire, had given over the practice of engraving for the position of a print-jobber and book-maker, and was now about to make his first venture as a publisher. He started schemes of work, enlisted co-operation, vamped up volumes, and pocketed proceeds. Keen as he was, he could be taken in: Allan Cunningham palmed off upon him some of his own spirited ballads as genuine relics of popular song. Commonly, however, the function of Mr. Cromek was not that of being taken in by others, but rather the converse, and the unworldly-minded Blake was doomed to experience his sharp practice, and to resent it bitterly enough, but not the less helplessly. In 1804 and 1805 Blake had produced a series of designs appropriate to that arid yet in some sense forcible poem, Blair's *Grave*, which in those days enjoyed a reputation not easy for us now to conceive. He had himself intended to engrave and publish these very fine designs; but Cromek, having made his acquaintance, and finding him in extremely narrow circumstances (living, as the Yorkshireman afterwards averred, on half-a-guinea a week for himself and his wife), bought the whole series of twelve for the petty sum of £21. Small, miserably small, as this amount obviously is, it was not much out of character with the prices (one guinea to one guinea and a half) which Blake usually received for drawings or water-colours. So far, therefore, the bargain was an endurable one; but only on the express understanding that the engraving also should be Blake's proper handiwork, and paid for, of course, at an ordinary rate. That there *was* such an express though unwritten understanding does not admit of any real doubt: the prospectus issued by Cromek showed as much, and Blake did in fact engrave one or two of the designs in the first instance. But Cromek did not think Blake's style of engraving so likely to attract the public, and to "pay," as that of some other artists. He therefore, in gross breach of faith and to the destruction of Blake's well-grounded expectations of remunerative employment, transferred the engraving-work to another man, and truly a very competent one, Lewis

Schiavonetti, a pupil of Bartolozzi. Neither as a question of generosity nor even of simple honesty can the slightest excuse be suggested for this high-handed proceeding: the utmost that can be said on Cromek's side is that, as Schiavonetti's engravings were likely to prove more popular than Blake's, the credit arising from the joint work would redound partly to the designer, and would thus to some extent indemnify him for the loss of the profit of engraving, and give him a better chance of fair prices for future designs. Nor was this the only grievance that Cromek inflicted upon Blake with regard to the Blair work. An offensively insolent letter which he addressed to the painter in May 1807, refusing to pay the moderate sum of £4. 4s., at which the latter had priced a design for the Dedication of the work (accepted by Queen Charlotte), may be read in Mr. Gilchrist's book, reprinted from the *Gentleman's Magazine*. In that letter, we may observe, Cromek has the grace to admit that the twelve designs for the *Grave* were properly worth at least £63; but this is indeed graceless grace, considering that he only paid £21, cozened Blake out of his right of engraving the works, and finally refused so poor a boon as this supplementary £4. 4s. The book was published in the autumn of 1808, 589 subscribers having been obtained at £2. 12s. 6d. each: Cromek's profits included likewise the money accruing from proof and extra copies. The well-known portrait of Blake by Phillips was engraved as a frontispiece to the volume, which may too truthfully be termed the only work of his which ever found a public during his lifetime. At all periods of his career he had some admirers, and in his later years a few much younger men might almost be regarded as his proselytes or reverential disciples: in the present instance he once—and once only —secured some moderate instalment of general reputation.

Mr. Cromek's misdemeanours against Blake did not terminate with the affair of the Blair designs. In a second transaction he acted still more foully, if we are to believe Blake's account of the matter; and I cannot see why we should not credit it, although the evidence may be somewhat more indistinct. While Schiavonetti was progressing with his engraving work, Cromek called one day on Blake, and saw a pencil drawing which the latter had made of Chaucer's *Canterbury Pilgrims* on their road; and he gave Blake a commission to execute the design—so at least the painter considered. But Cromek, who had in reality wished, and wished in vain, to obtain a finished drawing of the subject from Blake, to be again engraved by some one else, now threw the artist over altogether. Such a bidding from Cromek was indeed not likely to be entertained; for Blake's friends had already circulated, or about this time did put forward, a prospectus with a view to the engraving of this very work by Blake himself, by subscription. Cromek went off to Stothard, and suggested the same subject to him; an oil-picture to cost £63, and to be engraved. Stothard consented, proceeded with his task, and did not withhold the work, during its progress, from Blake's own inspection; a circumstance which may fortunately be construed as indicating that he was not aware of the fraud upon his friend's right of inventive priority, to which he had become a party. Flaxman believed that Stothard was not a wilful misdoer in this matter: and that may not improbably have been one principal motive for the outbursts against Flaxman himself which one finds written by Blake in epigrammatic verse and otherwise. He, when he learned the precise state of the facts, blazed forth in indignation. His wrath was rightfully directed against Cromek; rightfully perhaps to some extent—at any rate naturally—against Stothard, his old and familiar acquaintance. This was the great cause, though not strictly the only incidental occasion, of his breach of friendship with Stothard—who also, on his part, assumed the tone of an aggrieved man, suffering under unjust and unhandsome imputations. The breach was never closed. Several years afterwards Blake—generous and placable at heart, though he had openly spoken his mind against his antagonist to all sorts of people—met him at a gathering of artists, and held out his hand for reconciliation; Stothard refused it. He also called to see Stothard when the latter was ill, but admittance was not vouchsafed him.

The sequel of Cromek's commission to Stothard for the *Canterbury Pilgrimage* is well known. The picture—natural, if debility were the natural thing for such a subject, and agreeable if one chooses to condone the emasculation of Chaucer—was completed, and publicly exhibited, in May 1807, to many thousands of visitors; and, after a considerable interval (Cromek having died meanwhile), the engraving made its appearance, and became immensely popular. As regards Blake also this thorny affair had its sequel. Fired by seeing, at the end of the Blair's *Grave*, a prospectus announcing Stothard's *Canterbury Pilgrimage*, Blake completed his picture (of the class that he termed "fresco") of the same subject, and resolved to exhibit it, along with other pictures and water-colours. The exhibition was opened in May 1809, on the first floor of No. 28 Broad Street, the natal home of Blake, and still the shop of his brother the hosier. He drew up a *Descriptive Catalogue* of the works. This is one of the most singular and entertaining examples of his prose writing, and includes an admirable tribute to the greatness of Chaucer as the classifier and pourtrayer of human character, for his own age and for all ages: in truth, it cannot be said that one knows Blake thoroughly until after perusing the *Descriptive Catalogue*. The admission-fee to the exhibition, including the catalogue, was half-a-crown: the visitors were next to none. Blake then issued a prospectus for engraving his picture of *The Canterbury Pilgrims*, of which Mr. Butts became the possessor, the price to subscribers being £4. 4*s*. The subscribers proved scanty; but the engraving, begun in the autumn of 1809, was brought out in October 1810, considerably preceding the print from his rival Stothard. The two productions are no less unlike than the two men. Blake's is as unattractive as Stothard's is facile, as hard and strong as Stothard's is limp; one face in Blake's design means as much on the part of the artist, and takes as much scrutiny and turning-over of thought on the part of the spectator, as all the pretty fantoccini and their sprightly little horses in Stothard's work, from first to last. Be this said without any undervaluing of the numerous and excellent gifts of this charming designer—gifts which make many of his works precious indeed, and confer no despicable value upon this very picture of the *Canterbury Pilgrimage.*

Always unsuccessful with the public and with patrons, Blake became still more so after this tussle with Cromek and Stothard. He suffered in mind and temper, not to speak of purse; people steered clear of him, and with increasing emphasis pronounced him mad. Towards 1813, however, he was introduced to a new, and (as it proved) a most true and valuable, friend; and gradually, through the latter, to that circle of attached and often enthusiastic acquaintances with whom he was chiefly conversant in his declining years, and who, had he needed any such aid, would have powerfully contributed to keep him in heart and hope. The friend here referred to is Mr. John Linnell the landscape-painter, who still lives among us, and continues to sustain (as nobly as any of our masters, after allowing for Turner as the one without parallel) the great name of our school in this branch of art. It was Mr. George Cumberland, of Bristol, who brought Blake and Linnell together. The latter (we are speaking of full sixty years ago) was then a struggling young man, turning his hand to many sorts of artistic work—principally to portrait-painting. He engraved several of his productions of this class; and Blake was associated with him in some of these prints, which the elder artist would begin, and the junior finish. Through Mr. Linnell, the water-colour painters, John Varley, Richter, and Holmes, became known to Blake:

the latter two had some influence upon him in deepening the scale of colour in his water-colour works. It was with Varley, however, that Blake had the most intercourse. This gentleman, Blake's junior by twenty years, besides being a landscape-painter of uncommon merit, was an adept in astrology: he even received fees for calculating nativities, and some very singular instances are related of the fulfilment of his prognostications. Naturally such a man must have been greatly attracted towards Blake, with his faculty of imaginative vision, and Blake towards him. The Visionary Heads drawn by Blake, of which much has been said by all his few biographers, were executed at Varley's house, and in his presence: Mr. Linnell possesses thirty-six of them, including that unique subject "The Ghost of a Flea." As it is important to understand the mood of mind in which Blake produced these works, and as the condensation of details could hardly be carried beyond what has been done by Mr. Gilchrist, I will here avail myself of that author's words :—

" Varley it was who encouraged Blake to take authentic sketches of certain among his most frequent spiritual visitants. The visionary faculty was so much under control that at the wish of a friend he could summon before his abstracted gaze any of the familiar forms and faces he was asked for. This was during the favourable and befitting hours of night, from nine or ten in the evening until one or two, or perhaps three or four, o'clock in the morning; Varley sitting by, ' sometimes slumbering and sometimes waking.' Varley would say ' Draw me Moses,' or David; or would call for a likeness of Julius Cæsar, or Cassibellaunus, or Edward the Third, or some other great historical personage. Blake would answer 'There he is!' And, paper and pencil being at hand, he would begin drawing with the utmost alacrity and composure, looking up from time to time as though he had a real sitter before him; ingenuous Varley meanwhile straining wistful eyes into vacancy, and seeing nothing, though he tried hard, and at first expected his faith and patience to be rewarded by a genuine apparition. A 'vision' had a very different signification with Blake to that it had in literal Varley's mind. Sometimes Blake had to wait for the vision's appearance; sometimes it would come at call. At others, in the midst of his portrait, he would suddenly leave off, and, in his ordinary quiet tones, and with the same matter-of-fact air another might say 'It rains,' would remark,—' I can't go on—it is gone: I must wait till it returns'; or 'It has moved, the mouth is gone'; or 'He frowns—he is displeased with my portrait of him.' . . . In sober daylight, criticisms were hazarded by the profane on the character or drawing of these or any of his visions. 'Oh it's all right,' Blake would calmly reply. 'It *must* be right: I saw it so.' It did not signify what you said: nothing could put him out; so assured was he that he, or rather his imagination, was right, and that what the latter revealed was implicitly to be relied on,—and this without any appearance of conceit or intrusiveness on his part."

Among the personages whose portraits Blake drew in this mode were the Builder of the Pyramids, Edward the Third as he exists in the spiritual world, a man who instructed Blake in painting, in his dreams, David, Uriah, Bathsheba, Solomon, Mahomet, " Joseph and Mary, and the room they were seen in," Old Parr at the age of forty, &c.

In 1821 Blake removed to the house in which it was fated that his life should close—No. 3 Fountain Court, Strand, close now to Simpson's dining-rooms. Here he occupied the first floor; appropriating one of his two apartments as a reception-room, while the other was his living-room for all purposes—working, studying, cooking, dining, sleeping. It has been made a subject of controversy whether Blake's *ménage* was or was not, under these circumstances, a " squalid " one. To some eyes it did appear so: but one of his then youthful and most sincerely attached friends, Mr. Samuel Palmer, so deservedly admired now as a painter and etcher of landscapes full of nature and of poetry, is very emphatic in repudiating the epithet. "It gives," he says, "a notion altogether false of the man, his house, and his habits. Whatever was in Blake's house, there was no squalor. Himself, his wife, and his rooms, were clean and orderly; everything was in its place." We may readily accept this as a candid and true statement of the matter, viewed by a young man free from the habit or the love of luxury, and construing everything that regarded Blake in the light of the love and enthusiasm which so exalted a seer of spiritual things rightly commanded from a youthful aspirant and disciple. It is the truth, if not the *whole* truth—of which some other aspects were visible to eyes of a different kind.

Blake executed in 1820-21 the only woodcuts

that he ever worked upon, seventeen subjects designed by himself in illustration of the *Pastorals* of Phillips—rough and brilliant, 'prentice work and master's work at once. Towards 1822 he produced his first set of twenty-two water-colour paintings from the *Book of Job:* these were about the last works of his which his old friend Mr. Butts purchased. Soon afterwards that gentleman replaced the series in the artist's hands, so as to serve as an incentive to any other person who might be minded to give him a commission, Blake's monetary position being at this time very low. Mr. Linnell, by a written agreement dated 25th March 1823, engaged him to paint a duplicate set of the designs, and to engrave them. He was to receive £100 for the designs and copyright, and a like sum out of any proceeds. No proceeds, however, were forthcoming from the engravings, the sale of which barely covered the expenses: Mr. Linnell, viewing the equity of the case in a handsome spirit, presented Blake with an extra £50. The engravings from *Job* are executed entirely with the graver,—there is no etching. In this respect the artist was partly influenced by a more particular study, to which Mr. Linnell had lately invited him, of Italian engravings of the date of Marcantonio and Bonosoni, to the latter of whom Blake paid especial heed. The volume of *Job* prints was issued in March 1826, a year later than the date marked on the plates: the price of an ordinary copy was £10. 10s. While this work was still going on, towards the close of 1824, Linnell turned Blake's attention to Dante's *Divina Commedia* as another subject for illustration; and the energetic old man set to, learned in a few weeks Italian enough for his immediate purpose, produced nearly a hundred water-colours (one of the largest series he ever executed), and engraved seven of them to boot. The prints came out at the very close of his career—the year 1827, in which he died. For this work also a sum of £150 had been paid by Mr. Linnell by the time of his friend's decease; and paid on such easy and accommodating conditions that the final months of Blake's life must (it is a satisfaction to reflect) have been passed without wearing anxiety as to money-matters—though indeed he was not wont, under any circumstances, to allow such considerations much space in his mind. According to this arrangement, he received two or three pounds a week as he wanted money, without any sort of pressure as to the prompt production of designs or engravings to correspond with the successive payments; and, with the economical habits of himself and his wife, this was amply as much as he found occasion for. Another of the works which occupied him towards this time was his large tempera-picture (large for Blake, for none of his works was really of very considerable size) representing the Last Judgment, and containing, it is said, some thousand figures. This is at any rate the third instance in which he had treated the same overwhelming theme : the work seems to have remained unsold at his death, and its present whereabouts is uncertain.

We have now reached the latest stages in the life of the exalted visionary, and have little more to record save physical suffering and decay. About the first indication that we find of Blake's failing health occurs in a letter addressed to Mr. Linnell on 10th November 1825, in which he says : " I cannot get well, and am now in bed, but seem as if I should be better to-morrow." Elsewhere we read of "his ankles frightfully swelled, his chest disordered." He continued subject to frequent and painful attacks of cold and dysentery, very generally recurring after any visit paid to Linnell at Hampstead. Such visits, mostly on Sundays, had now become frequent, and were a source of great pleasure, not only to the seniors, but also to the growing family of small Linnells, to whom the aged idealist condescended with paternal fondness. But the Hampstead air was inimical to him: one of his letters (1st February 1826) represents that, even in his youth, he could not go to Hampstead, Highgate, or other northern suburbs of London, without exposing himself to derangements of this kind. Then we hear of "another desperate shivering-fit" (18th May 1826), and "a deathly feel all over the limbs," relieved by going to bed, and consequent perspiration. Another attack came on on the 1st of July 1827, upon his returning home from Hampstead; this was the final one, or at any rate he never rallied from it to much purpose. His physical powers waned without great pain at the last, or any loss of mental capacity. He was frequently bolstered up in bed to go on with the Dante designs: a pencil (one pencil at a time for so great an artist as Blake!) was among his latest purchases. The very last works of his that have been distinctly specified are a coloured example of *The Ancient of Days* and a sketch of his wife. *The Ancient of Days* "when he set a compass upon the face of the earth," one of the figures engraved in the Prophecy of *Europe*, was a favourite design with Blake. Mr. Tatham had offered three guineas and a half for this particular impression, coloured; and, for so comparatively large a price, Blake bestowed his heartiest labour upon the finishing of the tints. "After he had frequently touched upon it," says Mr. Tatham, "and had frequently held it at a distance, he threw it from him, and with an air of exulting triumph exclaimed, 'There! that will do,—I cannot mend it.'" No sooner had he done this than, addressing his devoted wife, he said: "Stay! keep as you are. You have ever been an angel to me: I will draw you." He accordingly made a drawing, described by Mr. Tatham as "a frenzied sketch, of some power,—highly interesting, but not like."

This may have been some few days prior to the 12th of August 1827, which brought Blake's earthly life to a close. On that day (as related by Mr. J. T. Smith) "he composed and uttered songs to his Maker, so sweetly to the ear of his Catharine that, when she stood to hear him, he, looking upon her most affectionately, said—'My beloved, they are not mine! no, they are *not* mine!' He told her they would not be parted; he should always be about her to take care of her." Another friend relates:—"He said he was going to that country he had all his life wished to see, and expressed himself happy, hoping for salvation through Jesus Christ. Just before he died, his countenance became fair, his eyes brightened, and he burst out into singing of the things he saw in heaven." Then his breath began to fail: and he died towards six in the evening, so calmly that the precise moment of his expiring could hardly be fixed. In a manuscript account, drawn up by Mr. Tatham, it is stated that the cause of death was ascertained to be a mixing of the gall with the blood.

Blake was buried in the Bunhill Fields Cemetery; this had been his own wish, as his father and other members of the family lay there already. The grave—an unpurchased common grave—is unmarked by any memorial, and cannot now be traced. He incurred during his life, and at his death he left, no debts; numerous unsold specimens of his designs, engravings, and engraved books, remained. The sale of these, to friendly or admiring purchasers here and there, helped to sustain in moderate comfort the declining days of good Mrs. Blake,[1] who survived her husband about four years—his spirit, as she felt and said, being still with her: she died in October 1831. At first she had been residing in Mr. Linnell's house in Cirencester Place, partly in fulfilment of an old but then abandoned project, according to which both she and Blake would have lived there rent-free in charge of the premises, while Linnell and his family dwelt chiefly at Hampstead. Leaving Cirencester Place, she had afterwards stayed in Mr. Tatham's chambers, under a somewhat similar arrange-

---

[1] Mrs. Blake, so attractive at the time when the painter first saw and loved her, appears to have lost her good looks rather early than otherwise. It is said that an acquaintance who met her again after a lapse of seven years " never saw a woman so much altered." The date to which this anecdote appertains is not defined: the mention of " seven years" inclines me to suppose that it may belong to the year 1794 or 1795, and that the "acquaintance" may have been one of the Flaxman family,—as Flaxman returned in 1794 from a seven years' sojourn in Italy.

ment; and finally had taken lodgings of her own, No. 17 Upper Charlotte Street, Fitzroy Square, where her life terminated. Blake's sister, who had been domesticated with him in the old days at Felpham, survived some years longer; but no particulars regarding her latest period of life remain, save the report that she was extremely poor.

Mrs. Blake had bequeathed to one of her most constant friends the remaining stock of her husband's works, and Mr. Gilchrist informs us—"They have since been widely dispersed, some destroyed." Note-books, poems, designs, in lavish quantity, annihilated: a gag (as it were) thrust into the piteous mouth of Blake's corpse. The fact is—so I have been informed—that Swedenborgians, Irvingites, or other extreme sectaries, beset the then youthful custodian of these priceless relics, and persuaded him to make a holocaust of them, as being heretical, and dangerous to those poor dear "unprotected females" Religion and Morals. The horrescent pietists allowed that the works were "inspired;" but alas! the inspiration had come from the Devil. The words inscribed by Blake upon that very early engraving of his, but with a wholly different intention, recur to our memory—" Such were the Christians in all ages."

3.—BLAKE'S VISIONS, PERSON, CHARACTER, AND INTELLECT.

Before proceeding to other points bearing upon Blake's character, we may as well say here something about his visions—a matter which we have as yet left almost entirely aside, highly important as it is to the understanding of our subject.

It has been stated that he saw his first vision at Peckham Rye, near Dulwich Hill, when he was some ten years of age, or less. He then beheld a tree filled with angels, their wings of star-like brilliancy amid the boughs. But this cannot have been his *first* vision, if we are to rely upon a quaint observation made by Mrs. Blake (in or about 1826) to Mr. Crabb Robinson. She said, addressing her husband: "You know, dear, the first time you saw God was when you were four years old; and he put his head to the window, and set you a-screaming." Clearly, after the quadrennial Blake had seen the present Deity at a window, there remained for him little to experience or explore in the way of visionary revealings. On another occasion, when still a child, he saw angelic figures walking among the haymakers. The next instance is a curious one: it is not properly a vision, but a prevision or intuition, and no doubt one might easily lay more stress on the slight incident than it is worth. The engraver to whom Blake's father first thought of apprenticing him was not Basire, but Ryland, a man of great distinction at the time, engraver to the king, and familiar with many persons of the first eminence. Young Blake, however, disliked the idea of becoming Ryland's apprentice. After leaving his house, he said:—" Father, I do not like the man's face,—it looks as if he will live to be hanged." And, twelve years afterwards, so it proved, the ill-starred Ryland *was* hanged, having committed a forgery on the East India Company. In Westminster Abbey, when drawing there as Basire's apprentice, Blake had a vision of Christ and the Apostles. At a later date he had a habit of speaking which startled many. He would say "I am Socrates," or any one else whose name and personality might be in question —Moses, Isaiah, or other great character. This is sufficiently intelligible if one chooses to remember Blake's point of view, even without supposing that he was a direct adherent of the doctrine of metempsychosis. To him, mind being the eternal substance, and body only the transitory accident, it was open enough to say that his own mind, in so far as it possessed a real apprehension of Socrates, was identical with Socrates—was in truth Socrates; for Socrates himself had been merely a mind housed for a short while in a rather different body. To Mr. Crabb Robinson, who first met Blake in December 1825, he said: "I was Socrates or a sort of brother: I must have had conversations with him. So I had with Jesus Christ: I have an obscure recollection of having been with both of them." Blake, in fact, had a face somewhat, in his old age, resembling that of Socrates, and this at times was made a subject of remark; but he was certainly better-looking than that far from well-favoured philosopher. When living in Hercules Buildings, he had a vision, not clearly defined to us, which hovered over his head at the top of the staircase, and inspired him with the grand figure of *The Ancient of Days*, already referred to: it made a more powerful impression on his mind than any preceding vision. On the same staircase he saw a ghost: the only one that he ever did see, for such apparitions, he would sometimes say, did not often visit imaginative men. It was "a horrible grim figure, scaly, speckled, very awful, stalking down-stairs," and so frightened our painter that he ran out of the house. At Felpham he held converse with many spirits of a less repellent kind—Moses and the Prophets, Homer, Dante, Milton: he described them as "all majestic shadows, grey but luminous, and superior to the common height of men." Milton appears to have been a frequent visitant in later years as well. On one occasion, "I tried," said Blake, "to convince him he was wrong, but I could not succeed. His tastes are Pagan: his house is Palladian, not Gothic." At another time he affirmed: "I have seen him as a youth, and as an old man with long flowing beard. He came lately as an old man. He came to ask a favour of me; said he had committed an error in *Paradise Lost*, which he wanted me to correct in a poem or picture. But I declined; I said I had my own duties to perform." The error in question was "that carnal pleasures arose from the Fall: the Fall" (added Blake) "could not produce any pleasure." With Voltaire also Blake averred that he had had "much intercourse," and that the French philosopher had been commissioned by God to bring into discredit the natural sense of the Bible, of which, however, Blake accepted and championed the spiritual sense. At Felpham, again, in his garden, he saw "a fairy's funeral," of which Allan Cunningham gives a little account as if in Blake's own spoken words, but how far strictly authentic one may feel some doubt. It was "a procession of creatures of the size and colour of green and grey grasshoppers, bearing a body

laid out on a rose-leaf, which they buried with
songs, and then disappeared." In this statement there may have been at least as much of
fanciful invention as of mere acquiescence in
popular superstition. A more decisively superstitious tone of mind appears in Blake's assertion
that some foul spell of Stothard's had caused the
almost total effacing of the original pencil drawing
of the *Canterbury Pilgrims*, which Blake (after he
had shown it to Cromek, with the unpleasant sequel
already related) had hung up over a door in his
sitting-room, leaving it there, exposed to air and
dust, for about a year. There is another story
of an account given by Blake of a meadow in
which he saw a fold of lambs, which turned out
to be sculptured, not living, animals. In itself,
the statement has no importance, and little apparent meaning of any kind: it is, however, of
some interest in connection with the reply which
Blake gave to a lady who asked him *where* he had
descried this sight. "Here, madam," he replied,
touching his forehead: an answer which serves
to caution us against supposing that he either
accepted as literal facts for himself, or wished to
convey literally to others, some of the visionary
or supersensuous incidents of which he made frequent mention. Here is another of them, more
than commonly amusing in point of expression, as
narrated by Blake to Mr. Crabb Robinson. "You
never saw the spiritual sun? I have. I saw him
on Primrose Hill. He said: 'Do you take me for
the Greek Apollo? No! *That*' (pointing to the
sky) 'that is the Greek Apollo: he is Satan!'"

That Blake believed in the *truth* of his visions
is abundantly evident: whether he also believed

in their actual objective *reality* is a different question. I should, however, be minded to answer it in the affirmative, in many instances; but it should always be recollected that the terms applicable to bodily realities, according to which we speak of them as present *de facto* and having a physical subsistence, are not properly or fully relevant to mental or spiritual realities. A few of Blake's own words (from the *Descriptive Catalogue*) may be very fittingly introduced here. "The Prophets describe what they saw in vision as real and existing men, whom they saw with their imaginative and immortal organs; the Apostles the same. The clearer the organ, the more distinct the object. A spirit and a vision are not, as the modern philosophy supposes, a cloudy vapour or a nothing; they are organized and minutely articulated beyond all that the mortal and perishing nature can produce. He who does not imagine in stronger and better lineaments, and in stronger and better light, than his perishing mortal eye can see, does not imagine at all. The painter of this work asserts that all his imaginations appear to him infinitely more perfect and more minutely organized than anything seen by his mortal eye. Spirits are organized men." Blake had a mental intuition, inspiration, or revelation,—call it what we will; it was as real to his spiritual eye as a material object could be to his bodily eye: and no doubt his bodily eye, the eye of a designer and painter with a great gift of invention and composition, was far more than normally ready at following the dictate of the spiritual eye, and seeing, with an almost instantaneously creative and fashioning act, the visual semblance of the visionary essence. Blake thus, in a certain not solely metaphorical sense, veritably *saw* the vision; and, with his imperious, emphatic, and uncompromising mode of speech, he would naturally speak of it as real, without any of those saving clauses, or qualifying concessions to his hearer, which another man would have introduced. But in fact I have understated it in saying that the mental intuition " was *as* real to his spiritual eye as a material object could be to his bodily eye." It was much *more* real. To Blake in very deed, as to how many others in theory or in professed belief, the spiritual was the reality, and the physical was the phantasm—a fleeting and unsubstantial illusion, connate and coetaneous with the bodily five senses. *These* were, for Blake, the untrue reporters about ambiguous simulacra; while the mind was a true criterion and recorder of truths, and the self-evidence of their verity. That he had held converse with Milton—his mind with Milton's mind, his perceptive faculty with Milton's perceptibility—this was a mental truth, therefore, in the full sense of the word, a *truth*. On the other hand, that he held converse with Mr. Crabb Robinson concerning Milton, that his vocal organs uttered sounds of which Mr. Robinson's auditory sense took cognizance, and that his bodily eyes saw the external frame of Mr. Robinson,—that was but a sensory exercise or impression, an evanescent accident, phænomenal not essential.

This is, I think, the intrinsic truth about Blake's visions, although it is difficult to express the exact degree in which, according to his personal impressions and convictions at least, the appearances presented themselves to him spontaneously and unbidden, apart from any self-conscious exercise of imagination or formative power. In such a case, the more active the man himself is, and the more prolific his imagination has been in producing the visions, so likewise the more passive does he become : .the visions are invested, out of his own vital force, with a vitality proper to themselves, and dominate their originator. They had been his objects: he is now their subject. Blake conceived a vision : in conceiving it, he saw it: inasmuch as he saw it, he believed in it: and, believing in it, he spoke of it in terms which affirmed—and necessarily so, according to his intellectual creed—its real existence. Had he been a different man, all these stages of the affair would also have been different; but, such as he was, he expressed himself simply and truthfully. It might be noted moreover that his general mode of life, and especially the abstemious habits to which poverty as well as inclination conduced, were peculiarly likely to foster the visionary tendency, and to convert cogitations into perceptions.

In person Blake was below the middle height, his stature being hardly five feet and a half. He was of robust though rather slender make, and fearless spirit: one instance of which we have already seen in the very summary treatment which he applied to the soldier who had entered his garden, and who, in revenge, accused him of seditious speech. Another instance was an onslaught of uttermost energy and instantaneous success which he committed on some rascal who was battering his wife in the St. Giles district. His dress was simple, and one may well suppose that it was mostly rather shabby than otherwise, though there was nothing in it to attract particular notice out of doors : Mr. Palmer, referring to the year 1823 or 1824, speaks of " Blake in his plain black suit, and rather broad-brimmed but not quakerish hat; " he continued wearing knee-breeches to the last. The same friend says :— " His eye was the finest I ever saw ; brilliant but not roving, clear and intent yet susceptible: it flashed with genius, or melted in tenderness. It could also be terrible ; cunning and falsehood quailed under it. Nor was the mouth less expressive,—the lips flexible, and quivering with feeling." He was short-sighted, and his eyes were prominent, as usual in such cases ; but he wore glasses only occasionally. The head was massive, the brow full and rounded ; it might have been deemed to surge and heave with what was within. The nose has been termed " insignificant as to size ; " but I cannot say that this appears to me to be shown either by the portrait which Phillips painted, or by the sketch done by Blake himself which may be seen in Mr. Gilchrist's book. In the latter likeness especially the nose is of ample size, as are all the other features proportionately—the mouth being the least full. Mr. Robinson has spoken of " the sweetness of his countenance, and gentility of his manner," which, as he says, "added an indescribable grace to his conversation." Wholly destitute as he was of " dignified reserve," he has been called " the politest of men,"—equally courteous to people of every age and rank; and, with all his intensity of spirit and heat of temperament, there was on ordinary occasions " great meekness and retirement of manner, such as belong to the true gentleman, and commanded respect." Blake has himself referred to this in a letter written shortly before he quitted Felpham, and has noticed it as working to his detriment there: "It is certain that a too passive manner, inconsistent with my active physiognomy, had done me great mischief."

The character of Blake is sufficiently displayed in the events of his life, and a few additional observations will be enough. He was eminently single-minded, energetic, impulsive, vehement, without reticence and without indirectness. Every one might know what he thought, what he meant, what he wanted, and what he purposed. He was also incessantly and indefatigably laborious, patiently toiling on, never taking a holiday, turning only from one occupation to another as a relief. Often he would write away at a poem in brief intervals, almost without discontinuing his spell of engraving; but occasionally, it would seem, he pursued his own individual work, in poetry or in designing, to the neglect of other and more paying work which may have been on hand, his ordinary task as an engraver of all sorts of miscellaneous subject-matter. In such cases, his wife, finding it vain to remonstrate from day to day, would at last, when all the house-money was gone, set before him an empty plate: he would take the hint, turn to at some drudgery, and resume the hard earning of his pittance. Earlier verbal reference to waning resources had perhaps only elicited the response, "Oh damn the money! It's always the money!" "He was an early riser," says Mr. Gilchrist, "and worked steadily on through health and sickness. Once a young artist called, and complained of being very ill,—What was he

PREFATORY MEMOIR.

to do? 'Oh!' said Blake, 'I never stop for anything: I work on, whether ill or not.' He never took walks for mere walking's sake, or for pleasure, and could not sympathize with those who did." Another writer, Mr. J. T. Smith, states: "Often in the middle of the night, he would, after thinking deeply upon a particular subject, leap from his bed, and write for two hours or more." His habits were extremely temperate. Money he despised, and fame—the applause of contemporaries or of posterity—he was ready to do without: at the same time, he was by no means indifferent to the claims which he possessed on public regard, and he felt both irritated and indignant at the coldness and apathy with which his works were received, and was always ready to express these grievances as bluntly as he felt them acutely. It may be inferred that—true in this as in other matters to the impressionable artistic temperament—he was too liable to take umbrage and conceive dislikes. This tendency would doubtless have been fostered by his wife, of whom it has been said that " some of the characteristics of an originally uneducated mind had clung to her, despite the late culture received from her husband; an exaggerated suspiciousness, for instance, and even jealousy, of his friends." Thus Blake, open-minded and frank with friend and acquaintance, was also subject to fits of estrangement, which found a splenetic utterance orally and in writing. Nor yet was this waywardness or touchiness the only thing that made him not easy to be approached by most men, or to be kept up with even by the few who approached: by his very birthright, he belonged to the race of the solitary and uncompanioned.

"Blake," it has been well said,[1] "had a difficult and repulsive [repellent] phase in his character. It seems a pity that men so amiable and tender, so attractive to one's desire for fellowship, should prove on close contact to have a side of their nature so adamantine and full of self-assertion and resistance that they are driven at last to dwell in the small circle of friends who have the forbearance to excuse their peculiarities, and the wit to interpret their moods and minds.

> ' Nor is it possible to thought
> A greater than itself to know.'

In this sphinx-like and musical couplet, Blake himself hits the true basis of the reason why men whose genius is at once so sweet, so strong, and so unusual, are largely overlooked during life, and are difficult of exposition when the fluctuations and caprices of life no longer interfere to prevent a fair estimate of their powers and performances." Here and there, however, some stranger capable of appreciating Blake happened to encounter him: the German painter Götzenberger should be especially named. He has left it on record: "I saw in England many men of talent, but only three men of genius,—Coleridge, Flaxman, and Blake; and of these Blake was the greatest."

Let us add (or rather repeat, for we have before had occasion to state the fact, and exem-

---

[1] In an article, *Life of William Blake*, published in the *London Quarterly Review* for January 1869, by way of reviewing Mr. Gilchrist's book. This article, the best of all those I have seen having the same object, was written by Mr. James Smetham,—who, being himself a painter and designer, has more than common qualifications for appreciating Blake, and bringing the reader *en rapport* with him.

plify it by an instance) that, notwithstanding his jealous suspicions and summary aggressiveness, Blake was neither rancorous nor unforgiving. "He seemed incapable of envy" (says Mr. Crabb Robinson), "as he was of discontent." His heart was truly a soft one; and his liberality, considering his extremely restricted means, was more than laudable. On one occasion he lent £40 (almost all the money that he then possessed, and presumably far more than he could mostly command for any purpose whatever) to an acquaintance who was in difficulty. At another time his attention was caught by a young man, evidently in delicate health, who frequently passed his house. He invited the youth indoors; found him to be a student of art; and, seconded by Mrs. Blake, ministered to his wants for some while together with unwearying kindness.

His unworldliness, extreme as it was, did not degenerate into ineptitude: he apprehended the requirements of practical life, was prepared to meet them in a resolute and diligent spirit from day to day, and could on occasion display a full share of sagacity. He was of lofty and independent spirit, not caring to refute any odd stories that were current regarding his conduct or demeanour, neither parading nor concealing his poverty, and seldom accepting any sort of aid for which he could not and did not supply a full equivalent. His conversation was nervous and brilliant, his knowledge various and extensive. This is Mr. Palmer's testimony, and we may probably accept it in the sense in which it is meant; though in the way of accurate scholarship, of precise acquisition of the details of knowledge,

Blake, like many other men of great intellect, had little to vaunt. The same observant and sympathetic friend tells us that, notwithstanding the wild, yet never meaningless, attacks which Blake has written on certain artists (such as Titian, Correggio, Rubens, Reynolds), "in conversation he was anything but sectarian or exclusive, finding sources of delight throughout the whole range of art, while, as a critic, he was judicious and discriminating." In conversing, it should be understood that some of his extremest and fiercest utterances were due to a spirit of opposition rather than anything else: people provoked him by obtuseness or antagonism, and he would make them stare by the opinions he expressed or the affirmations he made. His voice was low and musical. He was gentle and affectionate, loving to be with little children, and to talk about them. Republican and liberty-loving as he was, he had little faith in common demagogues, and entertained a certain curious liking for ecclesiastical governments, thinking less ill of priestcraft than of "soldiercraft and lawyercraft." That he was on the whole and in the best sense happy is, considering all his trials and crosses, one of the very highest evidences in his praise. "If asked," writes Mr. Palmer, "whether I ever knew among the intellectual a happy man, Blake would be the only one who would immediately occur to me." Visionary and ideal aspiration of the intensest kind; the imaginative life wholly predominating over the corporeal and mundane life, and almost swallowing it up; and a child-like simplicity of personal character, free from self-interest, and ignorant or careless of any policy of self-control, though habitually guided and regulated by noble emotions and a resolute loyalty to duty—these are the main lines which we trace throughout the entire career of Blake, in his life and death, in his writings and his art. This it is which makes him so peculiarly loveable and admirable as a man, and invests his works, especially his poems, with so delightful a charm. We feel that he is truly of "the kingdom of heaven": above the firmament, his soul holds converse with archangels; on the earth, he is as the little child whom Jesus " set in the midst of them."

It must be allowed that in many instances Blake spoke of himself with measureless and rather provoking self-applause. This is in truth one conspicuous outcome of that very simplicity of character of which I have just spoken: egotism it is, but not worldly self-seeking. Something also is probably due to the fact that he considered himself to be continually working under direct inspiration or supernatural command; and much assuredly, to his canons of art, according to which the conception or invention of a work was the one thing of supreme importance, and the power of execution indivisibly annexed to the power of invention. If only the idea was strikingly and movingly expressed, that was the execution of the work, adequately carried out, and finally right. Here are a few examples of the style in which Blake was capable of writing about himself. "It has been said to the artist—'Take the Apollo for the model of your Beautiful Man,[1]

---

[1] Our extract is from Blake's *Descriptive Catalogue*, and relates especially to the painting entitled—*The Ancient*

and the Hercules for your Strong Man, and the Dancing Faun for your Ugly Man. Now he comes to his trial. He knows that what he does is not inferior to the grandest antiques. Superior it cannot be, for human power cannot go beyond either what he does or what they have done. It is the gift of God, it is inspiration and vision." "I have now given two years to the intense study of those parts of the art which relate to light-and-shade and colour; and am convinced that either my understanding is incapable of comprehending the beauty of colouring, or the pictures which I painted for you[1] are equal in every part of the art, and superior in one, to anything that has been done since the age of Raphael . . . . I also know and understand, and can assuredly affirm, that the works I have done for you are equal to the Caracci or Raphael (and I am now some years older than Raphael was when he died). I say they are equal to Caracci[2] or Raphael; or else I am blind, stupid, ignorant, and incapable, in two

---

Britons. In the last Battle of King Arthur only three Britons escaped. These were the Strongest Man, the Beautifullest Man, and the Ugliest Man. These three marched through the field unsubdued as Gods, and the sun of Britain set, but shall arise again with tenfold splendour when Arthur shall awake from sleep, and resume his dominion over earth and ocean.

[1] Mr. Butts. This extract comes from a private letter addressed to that gentleman in 1802.

[2] Of course many of us at the present day will think that Blake's works are *more* than equal (in various regards, including some of the highest) to those of the Caracci; whom, indeed, Blake himself did not greatly reverence, though he here couples their name with Raphael's. This was probably an *argumentum ad hominem.*

years' study, to understand those things which a boarding-school miss can comprehend in a fortnight. Be assured, my dear friend, that there is not one touch in those drawings and pictures but what came from my hand and my heart in unison; that I am proud of being their author, and grateful to you my employer . . . . I do not pretend to be perfect: yet, if my works have faults, Caracci's, Correggio's, and Raphael's have faults also." "In the art of painting these impostors sedulously propagate an opinion that great inventors cannot execute . . . . I do not believe that this absurd opinion ever was set on foot till, in my outset into life, it was artfully published, both in whispers and in print, by certain persons whose robberies from me made it necessary to them that I should be hid in a corner . . . . I, in my own defence, challenge a competition with the finest engravings, and defy the most critical judge to make the comparison honestly; asserting in my own defence that this print[1] is the finest that has been done, or is likely to be done, in England, where drawing, the foundation, is condemned, and absurd nonsense about dots and lozenges and clean strokes made to occupy the attention, to the neglect of all real art." "Mr. Blake's powers of invention very early engaged the attention of many persons of eminence and fortune; by whose means he has been regularly enabled to bring before the public works (he is not afraid to say) of equal magnitude and consequence with the productions of any age or country."

---

[1] Blake's print of the *Canterbury Pilgrims.*

Having thus spoken of Blake's person and his character, we must next say a little of the distinctive qualities of his mind. All these were in fact entirely homogeneous, and he would himself have been among the first to scout any wiredrawn distinctions between the several constituents which make up the man—scion and heir of immortality, passing quickly through this terrene life as through a garment. The essence of Blake's faculty, the power by which he achieved his work, was intuition : this holds good of his artistic productions, and still more so of his poems. Intuition reigns supreme in them ; and even the reader has to apprehend them intuitively, or else to leave them aside altogether. They do not invite, nor bear, analysis : they were conceived each as a whole. Or rather one might say that each of them embodies a perception, a vivid perception, of Blake's mind, which he realized to himself in rapid and luminous words. The perception and the words are highly congruous one with another : but it does not always happen that the words indicate to the reader exactly the same thing which they represented to Blake, or with the same force and aptitude : they are to be seized or missed—not expounded and dissected. In many instances, no doubt,— so far as his lyrical poems are concerned—Blake both thought and wrote with the extreme of simplicity. Like an infant, he acquiesces in the appearances of things, and expresses them with a directness of sympathy which cannot be surpassed. Yet here too, and far more so in other instances of a different order of subject-matter, his intuition catches at the *meaning* of the things through their appearances; and the potency of his words is rather in flashing out the meaning than in any process of description.

Along with this faculty of intuition, Blake had a boundless capacity of faith: he could believe in anything, and required no confirmatory evidence, whether of his own senses, or of argumentative reasoning, or of other people's concurrence. Doubt was his loathing:—

> "If the sun and moon should doubt,
> They'd immediately go out."

Of a truth, doubt was not in him: he either believed or repudiated, accepted or rejected. As Mr. Swinburne has said, with his usual exquisite tact of diction corresponding to a clear intellectual perception: "His outcries on various matters of art or morals were in effect the mere expression, not of reasonable dissent, but of violent belief." His mind saw demonstrations, and leaped to conclusions; and the unity of his nature was such that what was apparent to him on one side, or from one point of view, was received as irrefutable from all points of view. This but amounts to another instance of his sense of spiritual insight: to him the information afforded by his mind, his imagination or perception, was true and final information, not subject to the illusions and ambiguities of the five senses and of physical things: it was "a portion of the eternal" admitting of no refutation. A great many things which other people believed or asserted, whether on religious or other subjects, were to Blake nugatory or fallacious: but there was nothing of the sceptic in him. His faith found boundless space for exercise, and pierced the utmost depths of it unflinchingly.

As to his religious belief, it should be understood that Blake was a christian in a certain way, and a truly fervent christian: but it was a way of his own, exceedingly different from that of any of the churches. For the last forty years of his life he never entered a place of worship. That he kept up a practice of private prayer—at any rate, on particular emergencies—appears from the following anecdote. Mr. Richmond (the now well-known portrait-painter, then one of the young men who revered Blake in his advanced age), "finding his invention flag during a whole fortnight, went to Blake, as was his wont, for some advice or comfort. He found him sitting at tea with his wife. He related his distress, how he felt deserted by the power of invention. To his astonishment, Blake turned to his wife suddenly, and said: 'It is just so with us (is it not?) for weeks together, when the visions forsake us. What do we do then, Kate?' 'We kneel down and pray, Mr. Blake.'" He was (as Mr. Swinburne has well pointed out) a heretic, not an infidel. He would zealously and vigorously confute the freethinkers, such as Paine and Godwin, whom he met at the table of the bookseller Mr. Johnson; and would constantly, in later years, uphold revelation and christianity, and argue in a very incensed tone against materialism. But, if his companion were a christian of any ordinary type, he would regard Blake himself as the freethinker and unbeliever, cut off by impassable lines of demarcation from the communion of the faithful. Clearly, Blake's beliefs were not vague to himself, but most express and positive: yet they appear to have been to a certain extent shifting, or at least subject to great variety of relative weight and of application. Moreover (I again recur to Mr. Swinburne) "it must be remembered that Blake uses the current terms of religion, now as types of his own peculiar faith, now in the sense of ordinary preachers; impugning therefore at one time what at another he will seem to vindicate." Thus the task of setting forth Blake's beliefs becomes arduous, and sometimes hardly to be managed. He believed—with a great profundity and ardour of faith—in God; but he believed also that men are gods, or that collective man is God. He believed in Christ; but exactly what he believed him to be is a separate question. Jesus Christ (he said, conversing with Mr. Robinson) "is the only God; and so am I, and so are you." This, from a certain point of view, is fairly intelligible; other remarks which Blake made on the same occasion, if less important, are also more obscure. "He had just before" (as Mr. Robinson relates) "been speaking of the 'errors' of Jesus Christ: Jesus Christ should not have allowed himself to be crucified, and should not have attacked the government. On my enquiring how this view could be reconciled with the sanctity and divine qualities of Jesus, Blake said 'He was not then become the Father.'" "All nations," he averred, "had originally one language and one religion; this was the religion of Jesus, the everlasting gospel." But what did this gospel amount to? "I know of no other christianity and no other gospel than the liberty both of body and mind to exercise the divine arts of imagination." These two passages come respectively from the *Descriptive Catalogue* and the *Jerusalem*: widely sundered though they are, they have a real interdependence. Again, he would say " Christianity is Art," and " Art is Christianity."

These oracles about "imagination" and "art," as identified with "christianity," seem to be rather wild; yet there is a certain pregnancy about Blake's words in general which renders it unbefitting that we should pass over the present *dicta* without making some small attempt to understand them. Nevertheless, it is certain that, as Blake did not reach his conclusions by any cautious steps of induction or deduction, so we, in using those methods, shall not succeed in precisely solving his problems. But to put the point argumentatively: the prominent idea in Blake's mind may, for instance, have been that Christ rejected "the world," and that his doctrine made light of "the natural man." By a rapid transition from the acceptation which these and other like phrases have received in theology, and in the order of moral ideas, to the construction which might be put upon them in a cosmical sense, Blake may have chosen to think that Christ rejected the visible physical world, and made light of the physical constitution of man— the very things that Blake himself was so perpetually resisting, whenever their claims came into collision with those of supersensual existence and imaginative verity. And in this sense it may have been true to his own intellect—and even not entirely untrue or fantastic to other intellects as well—that christianity champions "the divine arts of imagination," which by Blake were summed up in the single emphatic word

"Art." The reader, if disposed to do so, must follow out for himself these and other lines of thought which converge, or may be supposed to converge, towards our poet's laconic and startling axiom.

In immortality Blake seems to have believed implicitly, and (in some main essentials) without much deviation from other people's credence. When he heard of Flaxman's death (7 December 1826), he observed, "I cannot think of death as more than the going out of one room into another." In one of his writings he says: "The world of imagination is the world of eternity. It is the divine bosom into which we shall all go after the death of the vegetated body. This world of imagination is infinite and eternal; whereas the world of generation, or vegetation, is finite and temporal. There exist in that eternal world the permanent realities of everything which we see reflected in this vegetable glass of nature." It may well be doubted, however, whether Blake adhered to the established belief in future rewards and punishments according to the tenour of life which men have led on this earth; and he steadily resisted the acceptance of the common "moral virtues" as the standard of human excellence. What he attended to was difference of character, excellence or meanness of faculty; not what is regarded as the right or the wrong in conduct. Endless capacity for forgiving, and measureless exercise of that capacity, this was his acme—almost his sum-total—of teachable moral or religious obligation, continually repeated, whether in the form of direct precept or otherwise.

> "Mutual forgiveness of each vice,
> Such are the Gates of Paradise."

He once maintained that the Roman-Catholic Church is the only one which teaches the forgiveness of sins: this, and not this alone, may have prompted the liking which he certainly entertained for that communion. As to the "moral virtues," he was not afraid of declaring that they "do not exist: they are allegories and dissimulations." Here is another of his curious utterances bearing on that general subject: it occurs in a conversation held with Mr. Robinson in 1825. "There is no use in education: I hold it to be wrong. It is the great sin: it is eating of the tree of the knowledge of good and evil. This was the fault of Plato: he knew of nothing but the virtues and vices, and good and evil. There is nothing in all that. Everything is good in God's eyes." At another interview a short while afterwards, Blake, as Mr. Robinson notes, "would allow of no other education than what lies in the cultivation of the fine arts and the imagination."

Blake had in all probability read in his youth some of the mystical or cabalistic writers—Paracelsus, Jacob Böhme, Cornelius Agrippa; and there is a good deal in his speculations, in substance and tone, and sometimes in detail, which can be traced back to authors of this class. Not that he borrowed intentionally, or was at all in the way of following out anybody's system as such: but some of these ideas commended themselves to his mind, and, transfused through that, found expression along with others for which he was probably indebted to no precursor. Swedenborg also he had read, and he respected him, but with measure. "Any man of mechanical talents" (he writes in the *Marriage of Heaven and Hell*) "may, from the writings of Paracelsus or Jacob Böhme, produce ten-thousand volumes of equal value with Swedenborg's; and, from those of Dante or Shakspeare, an infinite number."[1] Several of his leading doctrines closely resemble those which were promulgated by Marcion, the celebrated heretic of the second century : Blake might without great impropriety be numbered among those long-extinct sectaries the Marcionites. Marcion held that there was an irreconcileable opposition between the Creator of the world and the Christian God, and their respective systems, the Law and the Gospel. He believed in two, or perhaps three, original principles. One he named the Good; another, the visible God, the Creator; the third was the Devil, or perhaps Matter, the source of evil. Theodoret says that even four such principles were recognized; the one which we have placed third being in this arrangement divided into (3) Matter, and (4) the Devil, the ruler of Matter. Marcion could not discern in Nature, nor yet in the Old Testament, that love which is manifested in the Gospel. He regarded the Creator, the God of the Old Testament, as "*malorum factorem*," or author of suffering. Jesus

---

[1] It would be interesting (at any rate to the few readers of Blake's mystical writings) if some thoroughly competent writer, supplementing the masterly performance of Mr. Swinburne, would trace out the relation between the speculations of Blake and those of other mystics. I believe that M. Jules Andrieu, now among us in London, one of the most deserving of honour among the survivors of the much-maligned Parisian Commune, possesses, in almost unequalled degree, the knowledge requisite for such an undertaking— not manageable at all save by a few.

was not the Messiah promised by this God to
the Jews, but was the son of the unseen and un-
named God, and had appeared on earth as a man,
possibly only phantasmal, to deliver souls, and
overthrow the dominion of the Creator. He de-
livered from hades, not the saints (such as Abel
and David), but the opponents of the Creator
(such as Cain, Esau, Dathan, Abiram, Korah,
&c.). Marcion condemned marriage, as being
subsidiary to the propagation of new slaves of
the Creator; he denied the resurrection of the
body; fasted on the sabbath, as an act of protest
against the repose of the Creator on that day;
and rejected the whole of the Old Testament, and
much of the New, especially those passages where
Christ speaks of the Creator as his father. The
student of Blake's writings will find in them some
things strictly conformable to these doctrines
of Marcion, and other points nearly enough related to the same order of ideas.

To illustrate the extreme divergence of Blake's
way of speaking of certain points in christian
theology from what is customary with the orthodox, I give the following brief extract from *The
Marriage of Heaven and Hell.* It may be read as
supplementary to the axiom "Art is Christianity."
"Then Ezekiel said: 'The philosophy of the East
taught the first principles of human perception.
Some nations hold one principle for the origin,
and some another. We of Israel taught that the
Poetic Genius (as you now call it) was the First
Principle, and all the others merely derivative;
which was the cause of our despising the priests
and philosophers of other countries, and prophe-
sying that all gods would at last be proved to

originate in ours, and to be the tributaries of the Poetic Genius. It was this that our great poet King David desired so fervently, and invoked so pathetically, saying—By this he conquers enemies, and governs kingdoms. And we so loved our God that we cursed in his name all the deities of surrounding nations, and asserted that they had rebelled. From these opinions, the vulgar came to think that all nations would at last be subject to the Jews. This,' said he, 'like all firm persuasions, is come to pass; for all nations believe the Jews' code, and worship the Jews' God, and what greater subjection can be?' I heard this" (Blake subjoins) "with some wonder, and must confess my own conviction."

One of the matters most observable, and at times most puzzling, in Blake, is the contempt with which he treats the body and all its acts, as contrasted with the spirit and its functions,—and, on the other hand, the unflagging zeal with which he upholds the acting-out of natural human desires, and repels and denounces all the coercive devices of the formalist, and even the regulative distinctions between right and wrong propounded by the moralist. Yet there is a clue to these seeming contradictions. Blake believed in man as a divine emanation, an eternally subsisting revelation of deity. Man was essentially a spirit; but, in this mundane transit, invested with a body, and communicating with the infinite through the medium of the five senses. Man, the free divine spirit, was at liberty to do, and right in doing, whatsoever his spiritual essence dictated—he was a law to himself, and none other law existed; and, in the mundane condition, the body, as organ and vehicle of the spirit, was rightly employed in putting into effect the spiritual desires and aspirations, which, in this physical world, became necessarily conversant in many respects with physical things. Where Blake contemned the body was in its severance from or substitution for the spirit. To trust the five senses, to believe in their intimations as final, or as corrective of the intuitions of the spirit, this was his abhorrence. The spirit had other and superior knowledge than any which the five senses could minister; but the service of the senses, as service and not guidance to the spirit, as executors and not dictators of the free-will, was wholly legitimate and commendable in this transitionary and hebetated state of life, since no better might be. "Act out all your spiritual desires, whether the spirit or the body be the appointed medium of action." "Be not careful of the things of the body, rather hold them in small account, and let not the body overrule the spirit." These are two separate precepts (given here not in Blake's own language, but by way of condensing many scattered items of his teaching): separate, but not in the least degree incompatible when one considers them singly and relatively. Blake preached forth both, and both with great emphasis, liable sometimes to mislead his auditor.

Despising sense whenever its evidence or its claims are made to conflict with those of spirit, Blake constantly fell foul of Newton and Locke, authors of "a philosophy of the five senses"; men who could not be contented with perception and conviction, but must investigate, forsooth, and ponderate, and verify, and find out. Hence too, in part, his still greater and more rabid animosity against Lord Bacon. "The great Bacon, as he is called (I call him the little Bacon), says that everything must be done by experiment." That was one great offence; another was the tone of diplomacy and statecraft (things peculiarly odious to Blake) apparent in the politician's *Essays* and other writings. "Bacon, Locke, and Newton," said Blake to Mr. Robinson, "are the three great teachers of atheism, or Satan's doctrine." Nor did the authors of classical antiquity, taken in a body, fare better at the hands of our mystic; their delight in war, and no doubt their worship of the powers of Nature, being damnatory charges against them. "The stolen and perverted writings" (thus runs a passage from the preface to the poem *Milton*) "of Homer and Ovid, of Plato and Cicero, which all men ought to contemn, are set up by artifice against the sublime of the Bible. But, when the new age is at leisure to pronounce, all will be set right, and those grand works of the more ancient and more consciously and professedly inspired men will hold their proper rank, and the Daughters of Memory [the Muses] shall become the Daughters of Inspiration. Shakspeare and Milton were both curbed by the general malady and infection from the silly Greek and Latin slaves of the sword.... We do not want either Greek or Roman models, if we are but just and true to our own imaginations—those worlds of eternity in which we shall live for ever, in Jesus our Lord."

Blake may be termed a pantheist, as well as mystic. In the essence and elements of the human soul, its aboriginal powers and passions, he recognized no evil: at least, this appears to have been his enduring doctrine when he defined and formulated it, for no doubt he, like other audacious and impulsive thinkers, said many things from time to time which could not be made to square exactly with the ideas which he laid down with decisive solemnity *ex cathedrâ*. "Without contraries is no progression. Attraction and repulsion, reason and energy, love and hate, are necessary to human existence. From these contraries spring what the religious call good and evil. Good is the passive that obeys reason: evil is the active springing from energy. Good is Heaven; evil is Hell." This extract comes from *The Marriage of Heaven and Hell*, which title we thus perceive to imply intrinsically "the union of reason with energy;" and we need hardly explain that Blake was not the sort of man to consider that reason was the only thing grand and noble, to the exclusion of energy. When he calls the one "good," and the other "evil," we are to understand both these terms in a plastic and fluent sense, by no means the same as would be given to them in a tract of the Society for Promoting Christian Knowledge. The strenuous exertion of human faculty, of whatever kind, was not hateful to Blake, although he may have identified it, in a certain deep and enlarged sense, with "evil." What he did intensely and thoroughly hate, with an active detestation difficult of comprehension to most people, was the formality of moral and religious precisians; the dividing and ticketing of the human-divine being, constituted of soul and body; the labelling of one portion of him, or one direction of his spiritual energies, as right, and another as wrong; the elaboration of rules, and exact, rigid, self-applausive adherence to them; the whole stock-in-trade of the professed moralist, and *apparatus criticus* of the pharisee. The character in which he abhors and renounces Satan is that of " the Accuser of Sins." The monarch of hell might be the antagonist of many things accounted sacred, and might exercise wild volcanic forces in many inconvenient directions, and yet incur small blame from Blake: but it is a different matter when the same personage accuses others of sins. He has no business to consider that such and such things are sins, or to run up bills of indictment against people who are fulfilling their own destinies, or putting their own free-will into act, or suiting their own tastes. *There* lies the fatal flaw in Satan. "Every religion that preaches vengeance for sin is the religion of the enemy and avenger, and not of the forgiver of sin; and their God is Satan named by the divine name."

We have now gone through the incidents in the life of Blake, and have taken some general view of his person, his character, and, however imperfect, of his mind and line of thought. We have found him to be spiritual-minded, mystic and visionary, lofty, energetic, hard-working, superior to circumstance. We shall next recur to a question which we asked almost at the threshold of our investigation—Was he mad?

The first thing to be observed upon this query is that it cannot be answered, to the enquirer's personal satisfaction, unless he has first familiarized himself with Blake's actual work in fine art and in letters, more especially with the so-called Prophetic Books. If he has done this, he is certain to have formed some opinion on the question, or at any rate to tend towards one opinion or the other; and he will not be easily moved therefrom by the conclusion of other enquirers. For my own part—with the deepest reverence for Blake, the keenest enjoyment of a great deal of his work, and an inclination to accept the rest of it as in some way or other justifiable to the author's intellect, and responsive to, and representative of, his large conceptions and deep meanings—I must nevertheless avow that I think there was something in his mind not exactly sane.[1] I apprehend that there are in the Prophetic Books many passages which show the author to have been possessed by ideas which he could not regulate or control—indeed, he himself proclaimed as much when he asserted that he wrote under immediate dictation, and without the exercise of any option of his own; and, what is far more symptomatic in the same direction, I think he every now and then "boiled over" (if the expression may be allowed) into words which have no definable relevancy to anything that deserves to be called a thought or idea. I cannot pretend to furnish—what has baffled many persons incomparably more qualified than myself for such a task—a fair definition of the term "Madness;" but, when I find a man pouring

---

[1] Mr. Smetham expresses himself very much to the same effect. "We cannot but, on the whole, lean to the opinion that somewhere in the wonderful compound of flesh and spirit—somewhere in those recesses where the one runs into the other—he was 'slightly touched.'"

forth conceptions and images for which he professes himself not responsible, and which are in themselves in the highest degree remote, nebulous, and intangible, and putting some of these moreover into words wherein congruent sequence, and significance of expression or of analogy, are not to be traced, then I cannot resist a strong presumption that that man was in some true sense of the word mad.

To call Blake simply a madman would be ridiculous and despicable; even to call him (as some have done) an inspired madman would be most incomplete and misleading. But it may, I think, be allowable to say that he was a sublime genius, often perfectly sane, often visionary and *exalté* without precisely losing his hold upon sanity, and sometimes exhibiting an insane taint. To me this appears to be the true statement of the matter; nor do I think it derogates from a respectful and grateful acceptance of Blake's work. We have his product before us, and are constrained to form some estimate of it. There are portions of it which not one of us can possibly hoodwink himself into receiving as the right sort of thing—we *must* condemn them as faulty and even heinous, according to any true standard of art. If we eliminate them as coming from the mad chink of Blake's mind, we leave undamnified the far larger proportion of his work to which the same censure does not apply. But if, on the other hand, through timorous respect and consideration for his genius, we flinch from this conclusion, we are then compelled to say that Blake, in full possession of his rationality, could write much that was fatuous and nonsensical—"balderdash," to use a plain word—as well as much that was noble and admirable; and this leaves an uneasy sense of insecurity in his reader, and casts a slur over the whole body of the author's work. For he must be a "queer fellow" (to use one of Blake's own phrases) who, being sane, can write the sort of thing which, had it proceeded from a madman, we should recognize as altogether in character. At the present day, the word "enthusiast" bears only a secondary and diffused meaning, and is mostly a term of commendation; but in our older writers it designates a person of morbid spiritual and religious self-consciousness, a fanatic partly insane. In both senses the word applies rightly to Blake. In his accustomed moods he is an enthusiast in the modern sense; a glorious enthusiast at whose feet we can sit in veneration, and hear divine strains from his lips, and see his hand prolific in magical creations. But there are moments not unfrequent when he becomes an enthusiast in the older sense, and then we are permitted to close our ears and eyes; under penalty, if we open them, of being forced to pronounce the words a thick-coming and contorted jargon, and the pencilled forms an indiscriminate shadow-dance.

The imputation of madness seems to have beset Blake from his earliest years: it is not simply a deduction arrived at by those who have conned his completed work with amazement. "One day," writes Mr. Gilchrist with reference to the artist's childhood, "a traveller was telling bright wonders of some foreign city. 'Do you call *that* splendid?' broke in young Blake. '*I* should call a city splendid in which the houses were of gold, the pavement of silver, the gates ornamented with precious stones.' At which outburst hearers were already disposed to shake the head, and pronounce the speaker crazed." Wordsworth, after reading the *Songs of Innocence and Experience,* spoke of them as the productions of "great but undoubtedly insane genius." Dr. Malkin, the Head Master of Bury St. Edmund's Grammar School, writing[1] in vindication of the claims of Blake as a man of uncommon genius, remarks : " The sceptic and the rational believer, uniting their forces against the visionary, pursue and scare a warm and brilliant imagination with the hue-and-cry of 'madness' ... By them, in short, has he been stigmatized as an engraver who might do tolerably well if he was not mad." Blake himself (in his manuscript *Public Address,* intended to accompany the engraving of the *Canterbury Pilgrims*) writes : " Ye English engravers must come down from your high flights. ... It is very true what you have said for these thirty-two years : I am mad, or else you are so. Both of us cannot be in our right senses. Posterity will judge by our works." Again (in the manuscript *Vision of the Last Judgment*) : " The painter hopes that his friends, Anytus, Melitus, and Lycon, will perceive that they are not now in ancient Greece ; and, though they can use the poison of calumny, the English public will be convinced that such a picture as this could never be painted by a madman or by one in

---

[1] In that very curious book entitled *A Father's Memoirs of his Child, by Benjamin Heath Malkin,* 1806. This is an account of an astonishingly precocious little Malkin, who died in his seventh year: the frontispiece to the volume is designed partly by Blake.

a state of outrageous manners; as these bad men both print and publish by all the means in their power." Flaxman is perhaps glanced at under the name of Anytus, or Melitus, or Lycon. The reader will see, in two of the rhymed epigrams in our volume each of them addressed to Flaxman, the phrases "You call me mad," and "Thou call'st me madman." In the *Examiner* newspaper for 17 September 1809 appeared an abusive article upon Blake's Exhibition, speaking of him as "an unfortunate lunatic whose personal inoffensiveness secures him from confinement": this sounds like the mere low-minded insolence of a literary fish-fag, yet it probably means what it purports. As I have already observed, Mr. Gilchrist (and here Mr. Swinburne is at one with him) repudiates the idea that Blake was, in any admissible sense of the word, "mad." He quotes the opinions to the contrary expressed by Mr. Linnell, Mr. Palmer, Mr. Butts, Mr. Cornelius Varley, and others who were acquainted with Blake; and goes so far as to say that the term "mad" is "one which none who knew the visionary man personally, at any period of his life, thought of applying to him." But here Mr. Gilchrist wrote with less than his usual accuracy. The opinion entertained at times by Flaxman—or at any rate supposed by Blake to be entertained by the distinguished sculptor and old friend—has just been quoted: Mr. Crabb Robinson also considered Blake insane—as indeed Mr. Gilchrist himself acknowledges elsewhere.

It has likewise been said that Blake, however strange in some of his writings or designs, always behaved rationally in the affairs of practical life.

This, making some slight allowance, appears to be true. There are people who might object that he was unduly and unaccountably indifferent to money-making and worldly position; but I for one would not admit that as derogating in any way from his sanity of mind—rather as testifying to the greatness, if also in this epoch the uncommonness, of his character. If it is true that he seriously proposed to his wife to introduce into the household a second sharer of his bed and board, this must be counted a not strictly rational proceeding, even if we leave aside the question of morals; but we are always to remember that he did not carry any such proposal into effect, nor can we be certain that he ever so much as suggested it.

Again, it might be averred that he somewhat exceeded the bounds of healthy reason, as well as of good feeling, in the imputations which he would now and again cast on his friends and acquaintances. There is in especial one epigram of his concerning Hayley never yet put into print: it exists in the MS. book belonging to Mr. Dante G. Rossetti of which mention will again be made in our volume, and which Mr. Gilchrist drew upon. Blake evidently had no idea of ever printing it, or showing it about: he wrote the lines merely as a vent to feelings of pettishness and exasperation.

"*On Hayley's Friendship.*
When Hayley[1] finds out what you cannot do,

---

[1] In the original MS. this name, and also the name in the heading of the epigram, stands written simply "H—y." There is no manner of doubt that Hayley is intended.

> That is the very thing he'll set you to.[1]
> If you break not your neck, 'tis not his fault :
> But pecks of poison are not pecks of salt.
> And, when he could not act upon my wife,
> Hired a villain to bereave my life."

The last couplet conveys two distinct and most grave charges against poor Hayley; charges to which one can hardly suppose Blake himself to have lent any real credence. He seems rather to have been writing in a spirit of wilful and wanton perversity: the more monstrous and obviously untenable the accusation, the more pat it comes under a pen guided by mere testiness. It is exactly the spirit of a "naughty little boy." The phrase "when he could not act upon my wife" has a somewhat indeterminate, though manifestly virulent, meaning: the other statement, that Hayley "hired a villain to bereave my life," can only (it would seem) relate to the affair of the soldier Scholfield, who accused Blake of using seditious words, and thereby subjected him to trial on a criminal (not in reality a capital) charge. Now the fact is that Hayley, so far from hiring this villain to bereave Blake's life, had (as we have already seen) come forward immediately as his bail, and afterwards as a witness on his behalf. Blake, if he believed that Hayley had plotted against his life, can hardly have been quite sane: and, if he disbelieved it and yet wrote it, our conclusion as to his state of mind at that particular moment need only differ in detail. I may here point out that the line,

---

[1] This probably refers to the well-intentioned efforts of Hayley to procure work for Blake in the way of miniature-painting, and other such minor industries of art.

"Hired a villain to bereave my life,"

is repeated in this epigram from the poem *Fair Eleanor* in the *Poetical Sketches*: the other line also,

"And when he could not act upon my wife,"

seems to have some affinity to the course of the story in *Fair Eleanor*—more affinity at any rate to that effort of the Macphersonian romancing faculty in verse than to aught that we can suppose to have taken place in real life between Mr. Hayley and Mrs. Blake.

4.—BLAKE'S FINE ART.

Blake's splendid, terrible, and daring imagination was embodied with equal force in the art of design, and in that of poetry. "Execution," he has said, "is the chariot of genius"; and never did that charioteer reveal himself in more unmistakable guise than in the handiwork of Blake. To see one of his finer tempera or water-colour pictures, or of his partly colour-printed partly hand-coloured engraved designs, or of his designs engraved by himself on the ordinary system, is a new experience—one that you cannot prepare for nor forestall. The mysterious meaning of the work, its austere intensity of presentment, the rush (as it were) of spiritual and vital force into all its forms, animating them with strange fires of life and frenzies of endeavour, the rapture of effort and of repose, the stress and the hush, give these works a different character from aught else. In fact, they have not so much the semblance of inventions (highly inventive though they manifestly are in the ordinary æsthetic sense of the word) as of visions—or, to recur to terms that we have already employed, of revelations or intuitions. There is severity, and there is beauty, each in a high degree: but what impresses the spectator most (consciously, or in many cases unconsciously) is the strength of receptivity or response in the designer—the energy with which he has clutched at the vision, the closeness of rendering with which he has succeeded in imparting it to others. It is like Iris in Homer, who receives a message from the God, and then recites it at length in the same identical words. Blake too has received the message, and he repeats it to us: and there is a tone in it which, although we never heard the original words, we perceive of a surety to be caught from the commissioning god, supernal or tartarean. For Blake by no means confines himself to the crests of Olympus, but is versed in the murk of Hades, and the recesses of the innermost and nethermost pit.

If the ideas and the style of Blake were original, his processes of execution were original also. The way in which he engraved his principal books, from the *Songs of Innocence* to the *Jerusalem* and the *Milton*, was, I believe, adopted from no predecessor; whether we regard the actual method of engraving employed, supplemented as it was by the colouring of the prints, or the intimate intermixture of engraved writing and designs, in which, as one may truly say, the art is made to permeate the poetry, insomuch that the union of the two becomes something different from what either of them would be alone, or both in mere mechanical juxtaposition. Blake himself, in a prospectus which he issued in 1793, spoke of his having "invented a method of printing both letter-press and engraving in a style more ornamental, uniform, and grand, than any before discovered." Another peculiarity, almost or quite original, is the independence which the designs, spite of this very close union, preserve for themselves, as distinct from the poetry: the connection of the two, in point of subject-matter, being often indistinct and dubious, and sometimes apparently null. Thus the designs (in many instances, but of course not in all) do not constitute illustrations of the text, but accompaniments to it, or supplementary suggestions and reinforcements. Terror is heaped on terror, or loveliness wedded to loveliness: each enters the mind by a separate avenue, of eye or ear, and impresses besides a different image upon it, but not a discordant one. It may be added that, if the writing is frequently unintelligible or nearly so, the allied design is the same: we feel its potent and arcane influence, but cannot dismember this into articulated meanings.

We have referred to three species of Blake's artistic work: his temperas or water-colours, his coloured engravings, and his uncoloured engravings. As to details affecting these productions, a good deal might have to be said by way of criticism, were we now concerned with that: powerful but often audacious and exaggerated drawing, strained or impossible attitudes, conventional and sometimes vapid faces, accessories reduced to the barest rudiments, and generally a disposition to leave off as soon as the conception is conveyed in form and colour, whether or not the work has been carried on up to the recognized standard of executive completeness. The water-colours, and along with them the tempera-pictures in their degree, are generally pale and washy in colour, slight in handling; and, throughout the whole range of Blake's art, there is a great deal of what we term "old-fashioned"—primitively jejune and stiff, not without puerility. The colour-worked engravings have greater strength and depth than the water colours, and are in numerous instances most forcible, not only in the idea of the thing to be done, but in the practical doing of it. The uncoloured engravings—of which the chief examples are the Young's *Night-Thoughts*, the *Job*, the Dante, and (engraved by an alien hand) the *Grave*—include many of Blake's sublimest inventions and noblest treatments,—the *Job* in especial, which is in some points of view his masterpiece. Yet in the *Night-Thoughts* we find a certain hardness and crudity of execution; and in the *Job* the characteristic mannerisms of form and of action appear in very ample measure, while the precision of handiwork makes these blemishes perhaps less condonable than in the more rapidly touched and freely handled designs which were engraved with a view to colouring. All minor points of this kind, however, may be left almost unnoticed, in such an account of Blake as ours: they merely need to be glanced at, not enlarged upon. Next after his majestic imagination, fertile in awfulness and portent, yet often also sunny and lambent like an of April sky, full freshness and of promise,—and after his potent wielding of the human form, as expressive of energy, aspiration, ardour, and all of the divine or dæmonic in man—next after these great qualities we should perhaps place the treatment of light, and especially of flame, as Blake's highest distinction in art; although, indeed, his mastery over colour likewise, in certain vivid combinations of simplicity and of intensity, is very marked and admirable.

It may be as well to give here, from Blake's MS. book previously spoken of, three memoranda showing his peculiar and ingenious processes of engraving:

"*To engrave on pewter*.[1] Let there be first a drawing made correctly with black-lead pencil: let nothing be to seek. Then rub it off on the plate, covered with white wax; or perhaps pass it through press. This will produce certain and determined forms on the plate, and time will not be wasted in seeking them afterwards. *To wood-cut on pewter*.[2] Lay a ground on the plate, and smoke it as for etching. Then trace your outline, and, beginning with the spots of light on each object, with an oval-pointed needle scrape off the ground, as a direction for your graver. Then proceed to graving, with the ground on the plate; being as careful as possible not to hurt the ground, because it, being black, will show perfectly what is wanted. *To wood-cut on copper*. Lay a ground as for etching. Trace, &c., and,

---

[1] Pewter had been used by other engravers before Blake—for instance, by Albert Dürer.

[2] The engraved designs by Blake to *Little Tom the Sailor* (a ballad written by Hayley) are examples of this process. The rather incongruous name which Blake bestowed upon it is of course to be understood as meaning "engraving on pewter *in relief*." Some methods of engraving on metal in relief had been known and practised from of old.

instead of etching the blacks, etch the whites, and bite it in."

Blake's so-called frescoes, which are properly rather tempera-pictures than anything else, were painted in water-colour on a ground of glue and whiting laid on canvas, linen, or panel. Those on canvas or linen have in many instances cracked, and been ruined by damp. White was laid on, and mixed with the colours, which were tempered with carpenter's glue. Blake was pleased, at a later date in his life, to find that this process, of his own re-invention, was mentioned in the mediæval treatise of Cennino Cennini. His colour-printed designs were sometimes executed in oil and water-colour combined. In such cases he would first draw his design on millboard, strong and thick, and paint it in oil-colour, of such kind and in such a state of fusion as to blur readily when printed off on paper. He then finished up with water-colour the roughly stamped and "accidental-looking" impression on the paper. For a second impression, he repainted his outline on the millboard, thus slightly varying the several prints.

The earliest known painting by Blake, a water-colour afterwards varnished, was *The Penance of Jane Shore in St. Paul's Church*: this was done towards 1778, and some other historic-romantic subjects soon afterwards. *War unchained by an Angel—Fire, Pestilence, and Famine, following*—dated in 1784, is the first of his ideal inventions, or rather the first to which a definite date can be affixed. The earliest tempera-picture, 1785, is *The Bard* (from Gray), which was re-exhibited in the collection at Burlington House in 1873—a resplendent and wonderful piece of colour, in which

PREFATORY MEMOIR.

gilt is freely used, and a very bold realization in form of Gray's poetic framework. In the same year were produced the first of his scriptural treatments—the three water-colour subjects from the history of Joseph which were to be seen in the International Exhibition of 1862. A few others of his works, most remarkable for power or for subject-matter, may here be particularized. It would be beyond our scope to describe or criticize them: the mere titles, in some instances, speak for themselves, and testify to the imaginative force of the designer. 1795, *The Lazar House*, from Milton, called also *The House of Death*, colour-printed. *Elohim creating Adam*, similar, truly a stupendous thing. *Newton*, similar. Towards 1801, *Heads of the Poets* (eighteen), executed in tempera for Hayley's library at Felpham: Homer, Euripides, Lucan, Dante, Chaucer, Spenser, Tasso, Shakspeare, Sidney, Camoens, Milton, Dryden, Otway, Pope, Young,[1] Cowper, Voltaire, Hayley. 1803, *The Sacrifice of Jephtha's Daughter*, water-colour. Towards 1805, *Fire*, similar. 1808, *The Last Judgment*, tempera, painted for the Countess of Egremont, and described by Blake in some detail, in a letter addressed to Mr. Ozias Humphrey, the miniature-painter. Nine designs from *Paradise Lost*, water-colour. Towards 1809, *The Spiritual Form of Nelson guiding Leviathan, in whose wreathings are enfolded the nations of the earth*, tempera. *The Spiritual Form of Pitt guiding Behemoth*,

---

[1] I have recently been informed that the two heads here named (as in the catalogue drawn up by me, and printed in Mr. Gilchrist's vol. 2) Euripides and Young are more probably Demosthenes (who was not however a poet) and Blair.

similar. *The Ancient Britons: In the last battle of King Arthur only three Britons escaped,—these were the Strongest Man, the Beautifullest Man, and the Ugliest Man*, tempera.[1] 1811, *The Judgment of Paris*, colour-printed. 1822, *The Wise and Foolish Virgins*, water-colour. *The Compassion of Pharaoh's Daughter* (Finding of Moses), similar. *Moses erecting the Brazen Serpent*, similar. *Job confessing his presumption to God*, similar, (a different design from any of those in the engraved *Job* series: of these, two separate sets of water-colours exist, one belonging to Mr. Linnell, and the other to Lord Houghton). *Bathsheba at the Bath, seen by David*, tempera. *The Plague stayed at the Threshing-floor of Araunah the Jebusite*, similar. *The Entombment of Christ*, water-colour. *The Sealing of the Stone of Christ's Sepulchre, and setting of the Watch*, similar. *The Angel rolling the stone from the Sepulchre*, similar. *Christ appearing to the Apostles after the Resurrection*, tempera. *Satan exulting over Eve*, similar. "*Thou wast perfect till iniquity was found in thee*," (a figure of Lucifer), water-colour. *An Allegory of the Spiritual Condition of Man*, (tempera, one of Blake's largest works, some 5½ feet by 4 in dimensions: not unlike a Last Judgment in general conception.) *The Characters in Spenser's Faery Queen*, water-colour. *The River of Life*, similar. "*Pity, like a naked newborn*

---

[1] I *believe* there is a tempera-picture of this subject, concerning which Blake wrote some of the most striking and interesting pages of his *Descriptive Catalogue*. I have not however seen any such picture, but only a water-colour in the ordinary mode of execution.

babe," &c. (quotation from *Macbeth*), colour-printed. *Hecate*, similar. *The Accusers of Theft, Adultery, and Murder*, similar.

It is not an easy thing to express in words that degree of natural truth, charm, and observation, which is to be found in Blake's work, combined as it is with a haughty disregard of the simple visual facts of Nature, whenever he chose, and he often did choose, to neglect these. It was truly a *sovereign* disregard: he would be the king over Nature—the Ahasuerus to repudiate her as Vashti, or to reach out the sceptre towards her as Esther. Clearly, he was born, like every other great artist, with the seeing eye—with the power to discern appearances rapidly, vividly, and intensely, and to reproduce them at once if in demand, or to store them up for future application, direct or indirect. Many things that he saw he loved, and he painted them masterfully or tenderly. "May God," he once said in his old age to a very lovely little girl, "make this world to you, my child, as beautiful as it has been to me:" and doubtless he was thinking then of the material visible world, as well as of the general tenour of life-long experience. But his ideal or abstract faculty acted with far greater strength than his simple power of perception and realization: he gazed *athwart* Nature, and drew, to be contemplated by the mind and partly by the eye, what he saw at the end of the perspective. The artist is a sub-creator: such most preëminently was Blake. After marvelling, with awe and worship, at the ocean, or the sunlit zenith, or the star-paved midnight sky, or the wonders of the spirit-informed human frame, we have all felt that a drop of water, a blade of grass, a grain or two of sand, a golden hair from a woman's head, are equally incommensurable evidences of the creative energy: the soul bows down before them with the same unfathomed sense of the unknown and the unknowable. Blake furnishes us, in his degree, with a like experience: along with shapes of vast imaginative appeal, he gives us here and there a little touch of natural beauty and truth—a low horizon, a winding path, a sprig of leafage—purely and clearly felt by himself, and thoroughly enjoyable. The working of his ideal perception upon such materials is mainly in the way of simplifying and condensing: it may transmute but not falsify. He conveys to us their remote suggestions, and their intimate presence. Often he is wilfully oblivious of objects of this class: but, when disposed to use them, he shows that they are not alien from his mind, or from his eye and hand.

In taking leave of the subject of Blake's work in the designing art, we cannot do better than collect together a few of his observations on the relations of outward nature to the artistic faculty in general, and more particularly to his own:—

"Practice and opportunity very soon teach the language of art. Its spirit and poetry, centred in the imagination alone, never can be taught: and these make the artist."—"Natural objects always did and do weaken, deaden, and obliterate, imagination in me."—"The man who asserts that there is no such thing as softness in art, and that everything is definite and determinate, has not been told this by practice, but by inspiration and vision; because vision is determinate and perfect, and he copies *that* without fatigue. Everything *seen* is definite and determinate. Softness is produced by comparative strength and weakness, alone in the marking of the forms. I say these principles would never be found out by the study of Nature, without con- or in-nate science."—"No one can ever design till he has learned the language of art by making many finished copies both of Nature and Art, and of whatever comes in his way, from earliest childhood. The difference between a bad artist and a good is that the bad artist *seems* to copy a great deal, and the good one *does* copy a great deal.... Servile copying is the great merit of copying .... Invention depends altogether upon execution or organization. As that is right or wrong, so is the invention perfect or imperfect. Michael Angelo's art depends on Michael Angelo's execution altogether."—"To learn the language of art, *Copy for ever* is my rule. But models are difficult—enslave one—efface from one's mind a conception or reminiscence which was better."— "Men think that they can copy Nature as correctly as I copy imagination. This they will find impossible: and all the copies, or pretended copies, of Nature, from Rembrandt to Reynolds, prove that Nature becomes to its victim nothing but blots and blurs. Why are copies of Nature incorrect, while copies of imagination are correct? This is manifest to all. The English artist may be assured that he is doing an injury and injustice to his country while he studies and imitates the effects of Nature. England will never rival Italy while we servilely copy what the wise Italians, Raphael and Michael Angelo, scorned, nay abhorred, as Vasari tells us. What kind of intellects must he have who sees only the colours of things, and not the forms of things? No man of sense can think that an imitation of the objects of Nature is the art of painting, or that such imitation (which any one may easily perform) is worthy of notice—much less that such an art should be the glory and pride of a nation . . . . If the art is no more than this, it is no better than any other manual labour."—" Next time I have the happiness to see you,[1] I am determined to paint another portrait of you from life, in my best manner, for memory will not do in such minute operations; for I have now discovered that, without nature before the painter's eye, he can never produce anything in the walks of natural painting. Historical designing is one thing, and portrait-painting another, and they are as distinct as any two arts can be. Happy would that man be who could unite them! . . . If you have not nature before you for every touch, you cannot paint portrait; and, if you have nature before you at all, you cannot paint history . . . . Nature and Fancy are two things, and can never be joined; neither ought any one to attempt it, for it is idolatry, and destroys the soul."—" I assert for myself that I do not behold the outward creation, and that to me it is hindrance and not action. 'What!' it will be questioned, 'when the sun rises, do you not see a disc of fire, somewhat like a guinea?' 'Oh no, no! I see an innumerable company of the heavenly host, crying 'Holy, holy, holy, is the Lord God al-

---

[1] Mr. Butts. This passage is extracted from a letter addressed to that gentleman in September, 1801.

mighty!' I question not my corporeal eye, any more than I would question a window, concerning a sight. I look through it, and not with it."

To these remarks on Nature and Imagination I will add a few of those which Blake has left us regarding other artists. As in almost all that came from the same hand, there is a great deal *in* them. But the reader who wishes to profit by them, and not to be simply misled or exasperated, must understand and apply them—must not extract from them, as for his personal guidance, a meaning as crude and unmodified as the phrase in which it is couched. Blake, alike in perception and in intellect, scorned the curb: he did not mince matters to his hearer or reader—still less when he was writing (as in some of these utterances) mere private memoranda. The frequently recurring abuse of Titian, as a bad colourist and what not, is rather surprising to the reader not yet fully broken into Blake's *dicta*, and must always remain worthy of rejection. One fact to be remembered is that very probably Blake had never yet seen a genuine (or at any rate never a first-class) Titian. Those were not the days of National Galleries, of Exhibitions of Old Masters at British Institution or Burlington House, and of fairly accessible private collections of the like class.

"This man [Sir Joshua Reynolds] was here to depress art: this is the opinion of William Blake.... While Sir Joshua was rolling in riches, Barry was poor and unemployed, except by his own energy; Mortimer was called a madman; and only portrait-painting was applauded and rewarded by the rich and great. Reynolds and Gainsborough blotted and blurred one against the other, and

divided all the English world between them. Fuseli, indignant, almost hid himself: I am hid."—
"Poetry, as it exists now on earth, in the various remains of ancient authors; music, as it exists in old tunes or melodies; painting and sculpture, as they exist in the remains of antiquity, and in the works of more modern genius; each is Inspiration, and cannot be surpassed: it is perfect and eternal. Milton, Shakspeare, Michael Angelo, Raphael; the finest specimens of ancient sculpture and painting and architecture, Gothic, Grecian, Hindoo, and Egyptian,—are the extent of the human mind. The human mind cannot go beyond the gift of God the Holy Ghost. To suppose that Art can go beyond the finest specimens of Art that are now in the world is not knowing what Art is: it is being blind to the gifts of the Spirit."
—" This picture [one of Blake's own, *Satan calling up his Legions*] was likewise painted at intervals, for experiment on colours without any oily vehicle. . . . These pictures, among numerous others painted for experiment, were the result of temptations and perturbations, labouring to destroy imaginative power by means of that infernal machine called *Chiaroscuro*, in the hands of Venetian and Flemish Demons. . . . The spirit of Titian was particularly active in raising doubts concerning the possibility of executing without a model, and, when once he had raised the doubt, it became easy for him to snatch away the vision time after time;[1] for, when the artist took his

---

[1] The reader who gives a little attention to these words will readily perceive that there is nothing trivial or absurd about them,—only a different way of putting the facts. The

pencil to execute his ideas, his power of imagination weakened so much, and darkened, that memory of Nature, and of pictures of the various schools, possessed his mind, instead of appropriate execution resulting from the inventions.... Rubens is a most outrageous demon, and, by infusing the remembrance of his pictures and style of execution, hinders all power of individual thought; so that the man who is possessed by this demon loses all admiration of any other artist but Rubens, and those who were his imitators and journeymen. He causes to the Florentine and Roman artist fear to execute ; and, though the original conception was all fire and animation, he loads it with hellish brownness, and blocks up all its gates of light except one,[1] and that one he closes with iron bars,—till the victim is obliged to give up the Florentine and Roman practice, and adopt the Venetian and Flemish. Correggio is a soft and effeminate and consequently a most cruel demon, whose whole delight is to cause endless labour to whoever suffers him to enter his mind... He infuses a love of soft and even tints without boundaries, and of endless reflected lights, that confuse one another, and hinder all correct drawing from appearing to be correct; for, if one of Raphael's or Michael Angelo's figures was to be

---

influence on Blake of Titian's pictures (or, as he prefers to phrase it, "the spirit of Titian") was such that Blake felt uneasy as to his own power of executing a painting without models; and, being thus discouraged, he failed in attempting, without models, to realize his conception. All that follows is equally open to a rational interpretation.

[1] This sounds more applicable to Rembrandt than to Rubens.

traced, and Correggio's reflections and refractions to be added to it, there would soon be an end of proportion and strength, and it would be weak and pappy and lumbering and thick-headed, like his own works: but then it would have softness and evenness by a twelvemonth's labour, where a month would with judgment have finished it better and higher."—" While the works of Pope and Dryden are looked upon as the same art as those of Shakspeare and Milton, while the works of Strange and Woollett are looked upon as the same art with those of Raphael[1] and Albert Durer, there can be no art in a nation but such as is subservient to the interest of the monopolizing trader. Englishmen! rouse yourselves from the fatal slumber into which booksellers and trading dealers have thrown you, under the artfully propagated pretence that a translation or a copy of any kind can be as honourable to a nation as an original, belying the English character in that well-known saying, 'Englishmen improve what others invent.' This even Hogarth's works prove a detestable falsehood. No man can improve an original invention; nor can an original invention exist without execution organized, delineated, and articulated, either by God or man. . . . The unorganized blots and blurs of Rubens and Titian are not art; nor can their method ever express ideas or imaginations, any more than Pope's metaphysical jargon of rhyming. . . . I do not condemn Rubens, Rembrandt, or Titian, because they did not understand drawing, but because

---

[1] Blake evidently considered (along with some other connoisseurs) that Raphael had himself at times engraved designs of his own.

they did not understand colouring: how long shall I be forced to beat this into men's ears? I do not condemn Strange or Woollett because they did not understand drawing, but because they did not understand engraving. I do not condemn Pope or Dryden because they did not understand imagination, but because they did not understand verse. Their colouring, graving, and verse, can never be applied to art: that is not either colouring, graving, or verse, which is unappropriate to the subject. He who makes a design must know the effect and colouring proper to be put to that design; and will never take that of Rubens, Rembrandt, or Titian, to turn that which is soul and life into a mill or machine."

5.—Blake's Writings.

The character of Blake's poetry bears, it need hardly be said, a considerable affinity to that of his work in the art of design; he himself, it is said, thought the former the finer of the two. There is, however, no little difference between them, when their main elements are considered proportionally. In both, Blake almost totally ignores actual life and its evolution, and the passions and interactions of men as elicited by the wear and tear of real society. True, individual instances might be cited where he has in view some topic of the day, or some incident of life, simple or harrowing, such as social or dramatic writers might take cognizance of. But these also he treats with a primitiveness or singularity which, if it does not remove the subjects from our sympathy—and a few cases of very highly sympathetic treatment are to be found—does at least leave them within the region of the ideal, or sometimes of the intangible. As a rule, Blake does not deal at all with the complicated practical interests of life, or the influence of these upon character; but he possesses the large range of primordial emotion, from the utter innocence and happy unconscious instinct of infancy, up to the fervours of the prophet, inspired to announce, to judge, and to reprobate.

This range of feeling and of faculty is, as we have just said, expressed equally in the designs and in the poetry of Blake, but not in the same proportions. In the designs, the energetic, the splendid, the majestic, the grand, the portentous, the terrific, play the larger part, and constitute the finer portion of the work; while the softer emotions, and the perception of what is gentle in its loveliness, are both less prominent in quantity, and realized with less mastery and sureness. In the poems these conditions are reversed. We find Blake expressing frequently and with the most limpid and final perfection—in some of its essential aspects, unsurpassed or indeed unequalled—the innocent and simple impulses of human nature; the laughter and prattle of a baby, the vivid transforming freshness of youthful love, the depth and self-devotion of parental affection, the trust in the Father whom the eye hath not seen. Very noble utterance is also given from time to time to some subject of discipline or of awe to the human soul, or even of terror: but generally it is not with these topics that Blake deals in his lyrical poems. He reserves them for his Prophetic Books, written in a style which, though poetical and rhapsodic, does not bring the works within the pale of verse, and barely allows them to obtain access to the human understanding. It is in these scriptures, rather than in the poems properly so called, that we have to seek for the written counterpart of that supernatural stress and that sense of the appalling—now profound in its quietude, now almost bacchant in its orgies—which tell upon us so potently in his designs; and certainly the written form of all this is by no means equal to the plastic one. Leaving these Prophetic Books for the present, we may say of the other rhythmic poems that the spiritual intuition of which we have already spoken as Blake's most central faculty, and a lyric outflow the purest and most spontaneous, fashioning the composition in its general mould, and drifting aright each word and cadence, are the most observable and precious qualities. This statement as to the wording and cadences must of course be understood with due limitation; for Blake, exquisitely true to the mark as he can come in such matters, is often also palpably faulty—transgressing even the obvious laws of grammar and of metre. Power of thought is likewise largely present in several cases; not of analytic or reasoning thought, for which Blake had as little turn in his poems as liking in his *dicta*, but broad and strong intellectual perception, telling in aid of that still higher and primary faculty of intuition.

Blake had more natural mastery over the oracular sublime than over the heroic sublime, and incomparably greater practice in the former. When he attempted the latter, he generally lost himself in an Ossianic tumidity and mistiness; he would himself have accepted as praise any criticism assimilating him with Ossian, as he openly professed to admire and believe in the volume ushered into the world by Macpherson. The Ossianic tendency is to be traced, for instance, in the poem *Fair Eleanor*, one of the *Poetical Sketches*, and most especially in a long unpublished demi-poem named *Tiriel*. *Gwin, King of Norway*, also in the *Poetical Sketches*, is a more than commonly favourable specimen of the same Ossianic afflatus, blended with that of our old ballads. In the *Fair Eleanor*, another superadded influence, derived from the *Castle of Otranto* or the like thrilling romance, can also be surmised.

I have already made mention of the sequence of Blake's lyrical writings, printed during his lifetime: the *Poetical Sketches*, *Songs of Innocence*, *Songs of Experience*. The *Book of Thel* (which, although not strictly lyrical nor rhymed, I have thought fairly admissible into the present collection) came out in the same year as the first series of the *Songs*. The other poems—among which the *Broken Love* may be cited for its excellence, and *The Everlasting Gospel* for its importance in scale and purport—are mostly of uncertain date; probably the great majority of them were written later than the *Songs of Experience*, but I have no reason for regarding any of them as the product of the closing years of Blake's life. He was thirty-seven years of age at the date (1794) of the publication of the *Experience*: and, allowing for some exception here or there, I infer that all his extant lyrical work was executed before he had lapsed into the fifties. The *Poetical Sketches* are simply astonishing; whether we regard the fact that they were written between Blake's twelfth and twentieth years, or reflect that they thus preceded even the first publications of Cowper and of Burns, not to speak of other and later authors in whose work the modern spirit and tone of poetry are more distinctly perceptible. Blake, in truth, when in his teens, was a wholly unique poet; far ahead of his contemporaries, and of his predecessors of three or four generations, equally in what he himself could do, and in his sympathy for olden sources of inspiration. In his fragmentary drama of *Edward the Third* we recognize one who has loved and studied Shakspeare to good purpose: and several of the short lyrics in the *Poetical Sketches* have the same sort of pungent perfume—indefinable but not evanescent—that belongs to the choicest Elizabethan songs; the like play of emotion,—or play of colour, as it might be termed; the like ripeness and roundness, poetic, and intolerant of translation into prose. At the time when Blake wrote these songs, and for a long while before, no one was doing anything of at all the same kind. Not but that, even in Blake, lines and words occur here and there betraying the *fadeur* of the eighteenth century.[1]

It cannot be said that he ever surpassed in absolute lyrical gift, nor yet indeed in literary finish, the most excellent things in his earliest volume. The *Songs of Innocence*, however, are,

---

[1] Take for instance the line (from a peculiarly lovely and very early poem in the *Poetical Sketches*),
 " And Phœbus fired my vocal rage; "
or this from the couplets *To Mrs. Butts* (1800),
 " Receive this tribute from a harp sincere."

taken in their totality, fully up to the same mark; and they have the additional value conferred by unity of scheme, and relation of parts. Some of the little poems included in this series are the most perfect expression ever given (so far as I know) to babe-life—to what a man can remember of himself as an infant, or can enter into as existing in other infants, or can love as of the essence of infancy. Blake was a believer (with more or less exactness of dogma) in the preëxistence of the human soul. These poems are very like the utterance of a babe, sentient at once of its present infantine and of its past matured existence; feeling the life and thinking the thoughts of infancy, yet feeling and thinking all this through the medium of a higher consciousness, a fullness of spiritual stature which once was, and again shall be. The comparative merit of the *Songs of Innocence* and the later-written *Songs of Experience* has been debated by competent critics, with diverse conclusions. To me it seems that the finest compositions in the *Experience* are fully as admirable as the finest in the *Innocence;* the unsuccessful items, however, being more numerous, and the faulty elements throughout producing a more damaging effect. The tone of thought, necessarily more varied, is also, in a sense, more elevated, but not so constantly well sustained or at unity with itself.

The *Songs of Experience* here and there, and also the *Book of Thel* (not to speak of examples even in the earlier poems) show us something of the obscure side of Blake's poetry; his arbitrary use of words and symbols, and a certain way he had of *hurrying* his conceptions into shape. Clearly, no poet had conceptions more immediate: Blake, by an inchoate method of execution, where things are said with as much abruptness as vividness, and are indicated or approximated rather than exhibited, and so left to explain themselves or not as the case may turn out, succeeds in conveying to his reader a good deal of this same immediate impression felt by himself. It cannot be so sudden and striking to the reader as it was to the writer; but the very obscurity serves to make it rapid. The reader, while he feels that explanation is needed (and explanation can only be a lengthy process, and so far conflicts with the immediateness of impression) has a sense also of something hastily presented to him, and as hastily withdrawn. He snatches a meaning, or else must miss it; for, before he has time to think it out, another image has replaced the former one. In some of the remaining poems the obscurity increases; and a certain proportion of them is really not intelligible, save by an effort of conjecture: I may cite *The Crystal Cabinet*, *The Mental Traveller*, and *William Bond*. The two former, however, with all their difficulty, are exceedingly fine; and some others of our volume, especially *Broken Love* and *Auguries of Innocence*, rank among Blake's noblest performances. *The Everlasting Gospel*, again, is in parts enough to baulk the interpreting faculty of the most ingenious, were it required to substitute a precise explanation for the *furor* of the poet, itself combined out of the passion of worship and the passion of contradiction. This extraordinary poem, and the great majority of those which follow it in our volume, were not published during Blake's life. *The Everlasting Gospel*, in fact, had never till now been published anywhere in full; the others, with comparatively few exceptions, appeared for the first time in Mr. Gilchrist's book. Along with *The Everlasting Gospel*, some other brief compositions are now for the first time reproduced in a printed shape from the MS. book by Blake belonging to Mr. Dante G. Rossetti. These waifs and strays include a few of the *Epigrams and Satirical Pieces on Art and Artists;* some of which, as also of the *Couplets and Fragments*, are more grotesque than vivacious, and a few not far removed from pointless absurdity. Every now and then, however, Blake shows a real epigrammatic faculty: he hits a stinging and ringing stroke, the sound of which is easily remembered by whoever heard it, and the sensation of it assuredly never forgotten by the person to whom it was administered.

Of some of Blake's early poems, it has been observed by a very discerning critic,[1]—and the same remark might be applied to his poetical works generally—" They have the grandeur of lofty simplicity, not of laboured pomp; a grandeur like that which invests our imaginations of the patriarchs. By a well, beneath a palm-tree, stands one who wears but a linen turban and a

---

[1] The gentleman who, under the signature of "B. V." wrote some articles in the *National Reformer* in 1866, reviewing Mr. Gilchrist's book. This is the same writer who has produced in 1874, also in the *National Reformer*, an extremely remarkable poem, of philosophical meaning and symbolic or visionary form, named *The City of Dreadful Night*. It was preceded, three or four years ago, by another poem, fully as noticeable but practically unknown, entitled *Weddah and Om el Bonain*, an oriental story of passion and adverse fate.

simple flowing robe, and who but watches browsing sheep, and camels drinking: yet no modern monarch, however gorgeously arrayed and brilliantly surrounded, can compare with him in majesty." And again: "Every man living in seclusion, and developing an intense interior life, comes to give quite a peculiar significance to certain words and phrases and emblems. Metaphors which to the common bookwrights and journalists are mere handy counters, symbols almost as abstract and unrelated to the things they represent as are the x and y and z used in solving an algebraic problem, are, for *him*, burdened with rich and various freights of spiritual experience. They are ships in which he has sailed over uncharted seas to unmapped shores; with which he has struggled through wild tempests, and been tranced in divine calms; in which he has returned with treasures from all the zones: and he loves them as the sailor loves his ship. His writings may thus appear, to any one reading them for the first time, very obscure, and often very ludicrous: the strange reader sees a battered old hull, where the writer sees a marvellous circumnavigation."

The latter of these two extracts applies more particularly to the *Prophetic Books*, to which we must now devote some little attention. Among writers concerning Blake, the only one who has ever conned these works without being bewildered and stunned, and hounded into desperation and denunciation, is Mr. Swinburne: he has made a real study of the books, in the spirit at once of an admirer and an investigator—an enthusiastic admirer of what is great in Blake, and an undaunted investigator of what is profound, or intelligible, or difficult, or frantic, in the books. He has probed each of them singly, and all of them collectively, feeling that what Blake regarded as a sublime religious revelation is probably as well deserving of attention as some of the other less neglected manifestations of the combined faculties of faith and of poetic rapture. One of his observations may be extracted here, as needing to be borne in mind on the very threshold of any such disquisition. "There are two points in the work of Blake which first claim notice and explanation; his mysticism, and his mythology. This latter is in fact hardly more, in its relation to the former, than the clothes to the body, or the body to the soul. To make either comprehensible, it is requisite above all things to get sight of the man in whom they became incarnate and active as forces or as opinions." I shall not attempt here to do over again in a hurry and inadequately what Mr. Swinburne has done deliberately, and with excellent judgment and insight; but would in the main refer the reader to that gentleman's book, supplemented by only a few remarks in extension of what I have already said with respect to Blake's ideas and his writings.

Ample evidence exists to satisfy us that Blake had real conceptions in the metaphysical or supersensual regions of thought—conceptions which might have been termed speculations in other people, but in him rather intuitions; and that the Prophetic Books embody these in some sort of way cannot be disputed. He did not want them to be exactly understood, in the analytical, unravelling sense. "Allegory addressed to the intellectual powers" (he has written *à propos* of the *Jerusalem*), "while it is altogether hidden from the corporeal understanding, is my definition of the most sublime poetry." The Prophetic Books have indeed sublimity and power in large measure; invention both of mythology and of imagery; and much which, if it does not take hold of the imagination of the reader, does at least appeal to it. Yet, after everything that ought to be allowed in favour of the Prophetic Books has been conceded, I must confess my opinion that they are, taken as a whole, neither readable nor even entirely sane performances. They are dark and chaotic to the extremest degree; ponderous and turbid; battling and baffling, like the arms of a windmill when the wind blows shiftingly from all quarters; full of action as inconceivable as the personages, and personages as insoluble as their acts; replete with uncouth and arbitrary nomenclature,—hieroglyphics sometimes seemingly void of demotic equivalents. Urizen, Fuzon, Los and Enitharmon[1] (Time and Space), Theotormon, Ahania, Har and Heva, Orc, Rintrah, Palamabron; and, for places, Golgonooza, Bowlahoola (Art and Law), &c.—such are the names with which Blake condemns us to become familiar before we can so much as begin to follow out his revelations and his myths. Various passages are truly formless, according to any admissible standard of poetic or

---

[1] Mr. Oliver Madox-Brown has pointed out to me that *Los* must be an anagram of *Sol* (quite an appropriate name for the Time spirit). Following this clue, one can turn *Enitharmon* into *An^erithmon*, numberless, limitless. *Orc* may possibly be made out of *Cor*.

rhapsodic form: a much greater number yield no stable or tangible sense,—they hurtle in your ears, and are gone. Notwithstanding all this, the greatness of the man—the directness and force of his mind, and sometimes its vigorous grasp as well—are abundantly evident in the Prophetic Books. A reader susceptible to poetic influences cannot make light of them; nor can one who has perused Mr. Swinburne's essay affect to consider that they lack meaning—positive and important, though not definite and developed, meaning. If an intellectual man were relegated to entire solitude for some months or years, with nothing to read except Blake's Prophetic Books, he would naturally study and ponder them; piece together their myths, trace their connection, reason out their system. If at the end of the process he considered these works altogether right and fine, or even absolutely free from a tinge of something other than sanity, he would have arrived at a conclusion different from mine: but I have no hesitation in thinking that he would relish the books vastly more at the close than at the commencement of his studies, and that his admiration for them would be all the stronger in proportion to the elevation and amplitude of his own mind. He would be quite capable of ranging them among the most inspired, as certainly among the most uncommon, productions of the human intellect.

We have already run over the names of the Prophetic Books; but will here add a few words, chiefly to point out the main bearings of them in relation to some of the special dominant ideas which pre-occupied Blake.

The poem of *Tiriel*, now for the first time

published,[1] is not precisely a "Prophetic Book"; rather a mystic legendary story, of a primæval or Titanic kind—a piece of "Cyclopean architecture" in verse; corresponding, in the narrative class, to what the other Prophetic Books represent in the visionary or mythic-doctrinal class. Blake evidently at one time attached some considerable degree of importance to *Tiriel*, as he illustrated it with a series of designs in Indian ink, twelve in number.[2] It has a certain (as one might term it) Indo-Ossianic grandeur. The story,

---

[1] This poem exists in Blake's handwriting, and the MS. was, until recently, the property of Mrs. Gilchrist. It was read by me prior to the publication of Mr. Gilchrist's *Life of Blake* in 1863. While the present edition of Blake's Poems was in preparation, I had not an opportunity of re-examining the composition, so as to provide for including it in the contents of this volume; finally, however, it has been forthcoming, and I am clearly of opinion it ought not to be omitted. *Tiriel* appears printed at the *end* of our collection: its correct place, according to order of date, would, I conceive, have been just before or just after *Thel*. Blake's MS. of *Tiriel* is neatly executed, and is evidently not the rough first draft: the handwriting appears to me to belong to no late period in his life. This character of handwriting prevails up to near the close of the poem. With the words (in section 8) "I am Tiriel, King of the West," a new and less precise kind of handwriting begins; clearly indicating, I think, that Blake, after an interval of some years, took up the poem and finished it, perhaps in much more summary fashion than he had at first intended.

[2] These are entered in my catalogue of Blake's designs in Gilchrist's vol. 2, "Uncoloured Works, No. 156." They are certainly, as Mr. Swinburne has pointed out, meant to illustrate *Tiriel*, although this fact is only dubiously suggested in my catalogue. Mr. Swinburne (pp. 199, 200, of his book) gives a brief exposition of the probable purport of *Tiriel*, not, in essentials, much unlike what I find to say about it in the text.

merely as a narration, is clear enough, but the *raison d'être* of the agents and incidents is anything but perspicuous. A brief account of the personages will perhaps assist us to as much understanding of the poem as can be needed by way of introduction. Har and Heva (named also in *The Song of Los*) are here encountered. They are shown as lapsed, through extreme old age, into a second childhood, and tended by their nurse Mnetha: they symbolize, I apprehend, some such aboriginal pair of universal parents as Adam and Eve. They are the parents or progenitors of Tiriel, "King of the West," who, at the end of the poem, reproaches Har for his misgovernment of his children. Tiriel represents, perhaps, tyrannic coercion of thought and character, more especially what we call "hypocrisy." He has misruled his own children, by repression and terrorism, as much as Har had spoiled his by trusting all to uncultured animal instinct. Tiriel's sons are denounced and cursed by him as rebels, and finally his curse slays the great majority of them. He is, throughout the course of the poem, a blind and despairing outcast, hating and hated. He has a strong and mighty brother, Ijim, and an oppressed and desolate brother, Zazel; both of them now at last despising him. After a Babel of anathemas, denunciations, and eyeless gropings, Tiriel also expires, and the poem closes.

Of the published, or rather engraved and purchasable, Prophetic Books, the earliest is *The Book of Thel* (1789), shorter and more idyllic than others, quasi-rhythmical, and not difficult to follow in its general scope and particular evolution, though there are various details likely to give the reader pause: it is reproduced in our volume. *The Marriage of Heaven and Hell* (1790) is a magnificent work, and may be counted the very greatest monument of Blake's genius as a writer. It is in the highest degree startling, and demands careful thinking on the reader's part: if this is accorded, it can be understood and laid to heart. The chief subject-matter is the nature of good and evil (with reference to which a short passage has been extracted at our p. lxxxvi.), and their reciprocal necessity. Though permeated with poetic fire and energy, the work is undisguisedly in prose. *The Visions of the Daughters of Albion* (1793) proclaims the vigorous and "emancipated" views which Blake entertained on questions of sexual relation. This book, and those which remain to be mentioned, are not exactly prose, nor yet exactly poetry, so far as the form of the composition is concerned. They are written in a rhapsodical turmoil of thought and of imagery, which finds its most fitting expression in measures not meted out, rolling and semi-rhythmical, often moreover printed with gratuitous and troublesome disregard of metrical sequence, doing less than justice to the sound of the words. They surge on, overlapping the sense and the reader's faculty of analytical attention, flecked here and there with resonances and recurrences. This way of writing conformed in some degree to the Ossian type, but of course with much more volume of sound, corresponding to its exaltation, if also its shadowiness and sometimes its inflation, of motive. Blake himself, in some prefatory words to the *Jerusalem*, has characterized the form of it as follows:—

"When this verse was first dictated to me, I considered a monotonous cadence (like that used by Milton and Shakspeare, and all writers of English blank verse, derived from the modern bondage of rhyming) to be a necessary and indispensable part of the verse. But I soon found that, in the mouth of a true orator, such monotony was not only awkward, but as much a bondage as rhyme itself. I therefore have produced a variety in every line, both in cadence and number of syllables. Every word and every letter is studied, and put into its place. The terrific numbers are reserved for the terrific parts, the mild and gentle for the mild and gentle parts, and the prosaic for inferior parts : all are necessary to each other."

America, Europe, Africa, and *Asia* (the *Song of Los*)—produced from 1793 to 1795—are entitled "Prophecies;" not so much that they profess to foreshadow future events as that they present a stupendous panorama contemplated by a mystic in vision. *The Book of Urizen,* followed by *The Book of Ahania* (1794-95), derives more particularly from the theological side of Blake's mind —his conceptions regarding the Creator, as distinct from the Supreme Benevolence; Urizen himself being by far the greatest dramatic imagination which Blake has attained to or bequeathed to us, and in a certain way really potent and taking despotic possession of the mind. He represents the "jealous God" of the Old Testament, as reinterpreted by the seer into a different range of religious ideas. *Jerusalem, the Emanation of the Giant Albion* (1804), differs considerably from the earlier Prophetic Books, both in subject and in manner, although referable to the same general fount of inspiration. It is no doubt adverted to in the following very impressive passage from the *Descriptive Catalogue*, and the battered and panting commentator cannot hope to put the matter much more clearly. "The Strong Man represents the human sublime; the Beautiful Man represents the human pathetic, which was, in the wars of Eden, divided into male and female; the Ugly Man represents the human reason. They were originally one man, who was fourfold: he was self-divided, and his real humanity slain on the stems of generation, and the form of the fourth was like the Son of God. How he became divided is a subject of great sublimity and pathos. The artist has written it under inspiration, and will, if God please, publish it: it is voluminous, and contains the ancient history of Britain, and the world of Satan and of Adam. The Giant Albion was Patriarch of the Atlantic: he is the Atlas of the Greeks,—one of those the Greeks called Titans." And elsewhere: "Albion our ancestor, Patriarch of the Atlantic Continent, whose history preceded that of the Hebrews, and in whose sleep, or chaos, creation began. . . . Imagination is surrounded by the Daughters of Inspiration, who, in the aggregate, are called Jerusalem." A few words of further characterization may be borrowed from Mr. Swinburne. "The enormous *Jerusalem* is simply a fervent apocalyptic discourse on the old subjects,—love without law and against law; virtue that stagnates into poisonous dead matter by moral isolation; sin that must exist for the sake of being forgiven, forgiveness that must always keep up with sin,—must even maintain sin, that it may have something to keep up with and to live for. Without forgiveness of sins, the one thing necessary, we lapse each man into separate self-righteousness, and a cruel worship of natural morality and religious law. For Nature (oddly enough, as it seems at first sight) is assumed by this mystical code to be the cruellest and narrowest of absolute moralists. Only by worship of imaginative impulse, the grace of the Lamb of God, which admits infinite indulgence in sin, and infinite forgiveness of sin—only by some such faith as this shall the world be renewed and redeemed." But Mr. Swinburne cautions the possible (I will not say the probable) reader against so much as essaying to understand some parts of the plan of the *Jerusalem*. "Neither let any attempt to plant a human foot upon the soil of the newly-divided shires and counties, partitioned though they be into the mystic likeness of the twelve tribes of Israel. Nor let any questioner of arithmetical mind apply his skill in numbers to the finding of flaws or products in the twelves, twenty-fours, and twenty-sevens, which make up the sum of their male and female Emanations." The poem named *Milton* (1804) reveals various *arcana* on the like moral and other subjects; among them (to quote again from Mr. Swinburne) "the incarnation, and descent into earth and hell, of Milton—who represents here the redemption by inspiration, working in pain and difficulty before the expiration of the six thousand years" (*i.e.*, the period of mundane existence, according to Mosaic chronology). The only remaining and very brief Prophetic Book, *The Ghost of Abel* (published in 1822), takes a dramatic form, once more enforcing the doctrine of the forgiveness of sins. The inscription which precedes it may be given here,—both as a compendious example of the union of quaintness, profundity, and mysticism, which the Prophetic Books exhibit, and as reminding us of the long lapse of time during which the great-souled Blake wrote on, and found next to no listeners—from a date preceding the first volume of Cowper to a date only two years before the death of Byron.

" To Lord Byron in the Wilderness.—What dost thou here,
    Elijah?
Can a poet doubt the visions of Jehovah?
Nature has no outline, but Imagination has:
Nature has no time, but Imagination has:
Nature has no supernatural, and dissolves: Imagination is
    Eternity."

6.—EDITORIAL DETAILS.

The Prophetic Books, at which we have now given a hasty and half-shuddering glance, are excluded from the present edition of Blake's poems; exception being made in favour of *Tiriel*, and of *The Book of Thel*, as already mentioned. Our collection professes to give only the lyrical poems, and two or three others naturally associated with them; whereas the Prophetic Books are not exactly poems at all in point of form, and are certainly not lyrical poems. It would nevertheless be highly desirable that these books, now practically inaccessible, should be republished one day in ordinary book-shape; Blake will be but imperfectly known even to his enthusiasts until this is done. The series should include *The French Revolution,* and should be completed by the addition of two works, one of which has never yet got beyond the MS. stage of existence:—1. *Vala, or the Death and Judgment of the Ancient Man, a Dream of Nine Nights,* which Mr. Linnell possesses, but which perhaps no human being ever read: 2. *Outhoun,* which appears to have really existed as an engraved and illustrated book, but which remains as yet totally untraceable.

With the exception of this very extraordinary—and in candour it must be added very unreadable—series of works, our edition presents the whole body of Blake's poetry.[1] It includes the *Poetical Sketches;* the *Songs of Innocence* and of *Experience; Thel; Tiriel;* the verses thinly scattered among other books written by Blake, or in his correspondence; the miscellaneous poems that were first published in Mr. Gilchrist's book, and afterwards (by Mr. Pickering) partly reproduced, following an edition of the *Innocence and Experience,*—the majority of these miscellaneous compositions coming from the MS. book that belongs to Mr. D. G. Rossetti, and the remainder from another MS.; and finally various poems, also from Mr. Rossetti's MS. book, that had as yet not been published at all, or at any rate not in full. Of the chief of these, *The Everlasting Gospel,* all but a few lines appear—but not as a continuous unbroken composition—in Mr. Swinburne's book:

---

[1] Or, in literal strictness, the whole body of it except three compositions, omitted here on grounds of copyright. These are (1) a sort of grotesque ballad named **Long John Brown and Little Mary Bell,** in all respects an unregrettable item; and (2 and 3) two slight songs, **By a Shepherd,** and **By an Old Shepherd.**

others had been omitted from Mr. Gilchrist's, as not being of sufficient value or substance to figure in that selection of Blake's best things. In the present complete edition, however, it seems only reasonable to include them, as they are, in my judgment, good enough or curious enough for preservation. There are still some others in the same MS. book which, for one reason or another, are not inserted here,—mostly because they are loose, scrappy, unfinished jottings, not to be numbered, even by lax indulgence, among the works that can represent Blake to the present and future generations of readers. One of these, entitled *The Marriage Ring*, has been printed by Mr. Swinburne: to me it appears a performance of too much tenuity and caprice for reproduction here. The same gentleman has given a second previously unpublished scrap, from a different source, beginning

"A fairy leapt upon my knee:"

this also I omit, for a like reason. Another specimen of the compositions that I miss out from the text is the epigram on Hayley quoted on p. xciii. of this memoir. As a poem, it is not worthy of preservation; but it has its use in the way of elucidating Blake's mental peculiarities.

In reproducing the *Poetical Sketches* in the present volume, I have followed the reprint which was published by Mr. Pickering in 1868, under the editorship of Mr. R. H. Shepherd. I thus forego certain emendations which were introduced by my brother into that earlier reprint which appears in Mr. Gilchrist's book, vol. 2, of some selected poems from the same series. These emendations were indeed great improvements, and they rectify various annoying and inexcusable laxities in point of metre or syntax, or here and there of expression. It is therefore with considerable reluctance that I abandon them, and do Blake the disservice of again presenting him without their aid. My brother felt that he could introduce them (as observed in his prefatory note) " without once in the slightest degree affecting the originality of the text ": nor do I intend to express here any opinion to the contrary effect. There is, however, I conceive, a certain degree of difference between the treatment which may be legitimately applied to extracted poems reprinted for the first time, and serving partly to illustrate and adorn a biographical record, and the same poems when they form a portion of an edition of the author's works, simply as such. At any rate, as the compositions in question have been already reproduced at a date intermediate between that of my brother's editing and of the present volume, and were then printed in their original shape (which term includes their occasional original shapelessness), I have not felt justified in recurring to another form of the same poems, which, if better, as it assuredly is, is also less absolutely exact.

Let me but hope that Blake's spirit, if conscious of what is here being done for the maintenance of his name and fame, would not resent this damaging adherence to authenticity. Blake at times (as we may remember), when limning his visionary sitters, had to exclaim, " He frowns—he is displeased with my portrait of him." He in his turn might now perchance frown and be

PREFATORY MEMOIR.   cxxxiii

displeased at finding that the present re-issue of the *Poetical Sketches* furnishes a "portrait" of himself—a reflex of his "spiritual form"—less advantageous than another which is already current among readers and admirers of his work. But I am fain to hope the reverse; with which trust, and the preceding faint elucidations, I commit to public regard this first collected edition of Blake's Lyrical Poems.

W. M. ROSSETTI.

PREFACE TO THE REVISED EDITION.

A FEW paragraphs will suffice here by way of preface; other details, relevant to Shelley's poems and to the present republication of them, being supplied in the Memoir, and in the notes at the close of the volumes.

The fact that the previous editions of Shelley were the reverse of scrupulously correct has frequently been remarked upon; as, for instance, thus by a poet who is also a keen critic, Mr. Allingham :—" Hardly any great poet, certainly no modern one, has been so inaccurately printed as Shelley. Helps to the very necessary revision are in existence, and ought quickly to be used."* And thus by Mr. Swinburne, when the present revised edition was already in an advanced stage :—" It is seldom that the work of a scholiast is so soon wanted as in Shelley's case it has been. The first collected edition of his works had many gaps and errors patent and palpable to any serious reader. His text is already matter for debate and comment, as though he were a classic newly unearthed." †

If we enquire *why* Shelley has suffered so much in the printed form of his poems, we shall find that the responsibility rests upon three defendants—Shelley himself, Casualty, and Mrs. Shelley.

Shelley was essentially careless as a writer. Spite of his classical education and tastes, and his cultivated perceptions of

---

* *Nightingale Valley*, p. 282 (1860).   † *Fortnightly Review*, May 1869.

many kinds, he was at all times capable of committing, and incapable of avoiding, slips of grammar and syntax—slips which may indeed be called small, but which are not the less gross—and other oversights, such as rhymes left unsupplied, or nullified by writing the wrong word. In another sense, however, he was *not* a careless writer. Though no poetry bears a more visible stamp of inspiration, his MSS. show that this inspiration did not subside at once into its true and final verbal medium. The false starts, cancellings, blottings, and re-writings, which his first drafts exhibit, are a surprising and bewildering phenomenon. At length one comes upon the right reading—

"Pinnacled dim in the intense inane."

Casualty also played a considerable part in the mischances of Shelley's printed works. Thus *Queen Mab* was only privately printed, and then piratically published; the *Revolt of Islam* is a slightly modified re-issue of a withdrawn book; *Epipsychidion*, *Hellas*, and the volumes containing *Rosalind and Helen* and *Prometheus Unbound*, were printed in England while the poet lived in Italy, and without his having any proofs to revise; *Œdipus Tyrannus* was printed under similar circumstances, and immediately suppressed; *The Cenci* and *Adonais* had the minor misfortune of being first printed in alien Italy, though under the author's own eye; *Julian and Maddalo*, the *Witch of Atlas*, and a number of shorter poems, were posthumous publications; the *Triumph of Life* remains a stately fragment amid many minor *debris*.

Mrs. Shelley brought deep affection and unmeasured enthusiasm to the task of editing her husband's works. But ill health and the pain of reminiscence curtailed her editorial labours: besides which, to judge from the result, you would say that Mrs. Shelley was not one of the persons to whom the gift of consistent accuracy has been imparted; for even this too is a gift in its way, not wholly to be improvised for the occasion.

In preparing the present edition for the press, I have been enabled to collate the collected edition supervised by Mrs. Shelley (in its three current forms of publication) with the original printed texts of all the poems, save only the semi-private first *Epipsychidion*. I have also, through the liberality of Mr. Garnett, received various snatches of verse, mostly fragmentary, hitherto not printed in any form; and have had the privilege of deciphering for myself a MS. book of Shelley, belonging to his son, and containing very considerable additions to the unfinished tragedy of *Charles the First*. Of the principal poems (or the great majority of them) the MSS., I understand, are not now known to exist.

I have innovated to some extent upon Mrs. Shelley's distribution of the poems; thinking it more reasonable that works of substantial length, such as *Rosalind and Helen*, *Julian and Maddalo*, and *Epipsychidion*, should appear among the longer poems, instead of among the miscellaneous poems of their respective years. On the other hand, I have placed among fragments a good number of pieces which really are fragmentary, but which had hitherto been intermixed with the complete compositions. I have also, in all subdivisions, carried out more minutely the record of dates, and (save as concerns the translations) the sorting of the poems according to that criterion. A glance at the table of contents will show the reader what these subdivisions are,— Principal Poems, Miscellaneous Poems, Fragments, Translations, and Appendix, as well as the dates of the several works. These are the dates of *composition*, not necessarily of first publication.

The Appendix is a feature new to any edition of Shelley. It contains a number of his juvenile writings extracted from divers sources, some variations of the printed text of the poems, and other odds and ends. Anything that I have found of an earlier date than 1813, when *Queen Mab* was printed, I treat as a juvenile poem. I must here avow and premise, for the use of all gainsayers, that I regard the main body of these juvenile poems as being not only poorish sort of stuff, but absolute and heinous rubbish; the "clotted nonsense" of a boy in whom even an acute literary prophet would have failed to divine, as in any wise conceivable, the author of *Alastor* at twenty-three years of age, of *Prometheus Unbound* at twenty-seven, and of a most glorious and in some respects unexampled body of poetry accruing up to that dark day of July when the inexorable waves of the Mediterranean closed over a brain and a life still below the rounded manhood of thirty. "Why, then," it may pertinently be asked, "give ampler publicity to all this vile stuff, capable only of derogating from that typical Shelley created for the homage of continents and of centuries?" I answer: Because it interests me as being Shelley's, and ought in my opinion to interest everybody to whom the later developments of that astonishing mind are dear. To find that Pope, whose manhood produced the *Satires*, had in boyhood the capacity which goes to the *Ode on Solitude*, is interesting,—and that apart from the merit which these juvenile verses possess;—to find that Shelley, whose manhood produced *The Cenci* and the *Witch of Atlas*, had in boyhood the incapacity which babbles in the poems of *St Irvyne*, is also and indeed equally interesting. At twenty-three, Shelley as author of *Alastor* is an unusually mature youthful poet; even at twenty, as author of *Queen Mab*, his powers have attained an exceptional ascendant in a certain direction: but at seventeen or eighteen his poetic product is rant and resonance, twaddle and tinsel. Surely this is a fact which may be subjected to some more appropriate treatment than mere hiding out of sight. Such at least is my own sentiment on the subject; and, knowing myself to be not wanting in enthusiasm and reverence for Shelley, I feel justified in acting according to it. I might indeed have felt some hesitation in dragging out into the light of scorn immature writings totally unpublished as yet; but, as a matter of fact, few such have been at my disposal. Six juvenile productions, hitherto unprinted, do, however, appear in the Appendix. Another (written probably in 1811) is in the possession of Mr. Frederick Locker, who obligingly communicated it to me; and this is a very curious scrap, not wanting in *verve* and piquancy, but too unpleasant, in its tone regarding family matters, to see the light of publication. Substantially, therefore, I have simply reproduced, in connexion with Shelley's standard works, those earlier failures which already exist elsewhere in print.

Besides this Appendix, a certain number of pieces, either wholly unprinted till now, or else not printed among the works of Shelley, distinguish the present edition from all predeces-

PREFACE TO THE REVISED EDITION. xv

sors.* No omission from any writing whatever, I need hardly say, has been made on any ground of assumed "propriety," moral or religious. As Shelley did not write, so neither do I revise, for babes and sucklings.

The question how a re-editor should treat the works of a great poet, when confessedly inaccurate in some respects, is of the highest importance. I shall not debate the various sides of the question, for there will be plenty of people to show that the modes of treatment which I have *not* adopted are severally right; I therefore confine myself to saying what I have done, and briefly why. I have considered it my clear duty and prerogative to set absolutely wrong grammar right; as thus—

> "Thou too, O Comet, beautiful and fierce,
> Who *drew'st* [*drew*] the heart of this frail universe;"

and to set absolutely wrong rhyming right; as thus—

> "Beneath whose spires which swayed in the red *flame* [*light*]
> Reclining as they ate, of liberty,
> And hope, and justice, and Laone's name,
> Earth's children did a woof of happy converse frame";

and to set absolutely wrong metre right; as thus—

> "This plan might be tried too. Where's General
> Laoctonos? It is my royal pleasure,"

instead of

---

* The reader may like to see here the exact list of these pieces. They are as follows:—

[Introduced from printed sources] Lines written in the Bay of Lerici; To —— (Thy dewy looks sink in my breast); Scene from Tasso; Orpheus; To his Genius; Fiordispina (a portion); Love, Hope, Desire, and Fear; Prologue to Hellas; Sonnet to Byron; Fragments of an Unfinished Drama (a portion); Lines (We meet not as we parted); Homer's Hymn to Venus; First Canzone of the Convito; Matilda gathering Flowers; Fragments 3, 4, 5, 6, 7, 8, 21, 22, 28, 29, 49, 50, 51, 52, 53, 54, 55, 64, 96. [Hitherto unprinted] Lines (If I walk in autumn's even); Marenghi (the majority); Lines written for Miss Sophia Stacey; Time Long Past; The Boat on the Serchio (a portion); Fragments of an Unfinished Drama (a portion); Charles I. (the majority); Fragments 9, 23, 24, 25, 66, 67, 68, 69, 70, 71, 87, 88, 89, 90; From Virgil, the Tenth Eclogue.

In the Appendix, only two items come from the collected editions—Singing, and the variation from Prometheus Unbound. Eleven items had never been printed—The Solitary; To Mary, who died in this Opinion; Mother and Son; The Mexican Revolution; To Ireland; To —— (O thou); Eyes; a Hate Song; the second version of the Epithalamium; and the omitted lines from the Indian Serenade, and the Recollection. All the residue is from outlying printed sources.

> "This plan might be tried too. Where's General Laoctonos?
> It is my royal pleasure."

Annexed to this is another duty, that of pointing out any and every such change; this is done in my notes. In speaking of "absolutely wrong" grammar, rhyming, and metre, I by no means include a vast number of laxities in these matters—laxities which are a genuine portion of Shelley's poetic intention and performance, and which it would be presumption in me so much as to censure. These are of course left untouched; and along with them not a few things which, though in strictness even absolutely wrong, may also be fairly understood to appear as Shelley meant them to appear, or as he would not have troubled himself to prevent their appearing. I have made it a point to follow the readings of the original editions, unless some strong presumption should arise that these readings are erroneous, and those of subsequent editions correct. Some instances occur in which I have felt quite uncertain which was correct among different readings, and then I have chosen the one I myself prefer. I have also with scrupulous exactness attended to the punctuation of every line; and (a minor yet not wholly unimportant point) have made the marginal setting of type throughout the volumes such as to represent the true interrelations of rhythm and rhyme—a matter left hitherto at sixes and sevens. The interruption of foot-notes in a page of fine poetry is, I conceive, always some sort of annoyance; and even the numbers or other marks in the text calling attention to notes at a later page come under the same disfavour. Convenient they assuredly are to the tiro or the student: as certainly are they tiresome to the expert. On the whole, it has appeared to me best to remove all notes from the foot of the page to the end of the poem or subdivision, and to give no figures or marks of reference. My own notes come in mass at the end of the respective volumes.

As to conjectural emendation—that most dangerous and lethal weapon, but still, I apprehend, a lawful and needful weapon in the hands of a re-editor—I am well aware that I shall have offended some readers, and perhaps disappointed others. Among friends of high critical qualifications whom I have consulted, some have urged me onwards in the path of emendation, and others withheld me. I have tended more towards lagging behind than towards outstripping my own theoretic standard in this regard, acting very generally on the rule that a conjectural emendation should not be tolerated, unless it is either a stopgap expedient against a patent and formidable blunder, or else convincing in a very high degree indeed. Good or bad, many or few, my conjectural emendations are of course all set forth in the notes, and can be cancelled as errata by any reader who may consider them in that light.

The notes do not aim at being excursive, critical, or explanatory, nor to any large extent even illustrative. Such illustration as they supply is chiefly from Shelley's own writings: mainly, the notes profess to be textual, and no more. They specify all modifications of the text * which rest on my own authority, and a fair proportion even of those which depend upon MSS., or the safest editions. I have no fear of having specified too few minute points in these notes—too many, rather.

I have expressed, and must here repeat, my obligations to Mr. Garnett, who, waiving all rights of priority and personal research, has freely imparted to me whatever Shelleyan items he had at command, whether MSS., transcripts, or details of any kind elucidating the text of the poems; including the book containing *Charles I.*, for permission to use which I am indeed primarily indebted, through Mr. Garnett, to the owner, Sir Percy Shelley. It is a gratification to acknowledge also valuable advice or assistance from Captain Trelawny, Mr. Browning, Mr. W. Bell Scott, Mr. Swinburne, Mr. Allingham, Mr. C. B. Cayley, Mr. G. S. D. Murray, my brother, and others. Captain Trelawny's information has been especially valuable both for the poems and for the memoir, and commands my most respectful and grateful thanks.

No man is better qualified than a re-editor of Shelley to affirm that authors, editors, and printers, are all fallible. To flatter myself that the present edition is free from errors of purpose on my part, or from casual oversights, would be the height of folly,

---

* Not including, however, small changes of punctuation which make no marked difference of meaning; nor changes of spelling or printing, such as "wrapped" instead of "wrapt," or "linkèd" instead of "linked." In these respects I have (properly speaking) systematized rather than altered.

and would be my best title to detraction. But I can say that the editorial work has been to me a true labour of love, and has been gone through diligently and deliberately. Indeed, the pleasure of having anything to do with Shelley's poems is to myself so great that I should have been my own tormentor had I stinted or slurred work in any particular.

W. M. ROSSETTI.

PREFACE

BY THE EDITOR.

THE ready and wide acceptance of my annotated Library Edition of the Works of Shelley induces me to believe that there is place for an edition of the text, given accurately from the most authentic sources without annotation of any kind. In the following pages, therefore, I have separated from the extensive notes and appendices of the Library Edition the text as there printed, adopting also the same principles of arrangement. There must be many students of Shelley who have no time or inclination to go into the pros and cons of textual discussion, but who would gladly have under their hands in a portable and readable form the ipsissima verba of the master in what has the best claim to be considered their ultimate developement. To this class of readers, variorum readings even are of no sufficient interest to compensate for repetition and the distraction of coming to a conclusion on the relative merits of the several readings; and for such, it will be enough to have the ultimate work in its entirety and integrity.

The present Edition contains every poem or fragment of verse by Shelley which has ever as far as I am aware been published, and a few dozens of lines not included in any previous edition. All his prefaces, dedications, notes, and mottoes are given, together with all his poetic translations, and an appendix consisting of the whole series of Juvenilia, from the *Verses on a Cat* written when he was some eight years old to the remarkable poem by which he is still perhaps most widely known—*Queen Mab*. This I have given in its original form among the *Juvenilia*; while including in the series of mature works, notwithstanding the considerable repetitions involved, the revision made in 1815 under the title of *The*

Dæmon of the World—which I was enabled to complete from the copy mentioned in Medwin's and Middleton's Lives of Shelley. And there are other instances in which studies and cancelled passages of importance are retained as a portion of the text of Shelley's poetry, albeit including lines and expressions which occur in the finished forms.

To produce in the case of Shelley as near an approximation as may be to the text that the poet intended to issue, is a more than ordinarily difficult task,—not from any lack of materials, for the mass of material extant is astonishing when we consider the vicissitudes to which his works have been subjected. The difficulty is in deciding what shall be the authority for the text in each particular poem. In respect of books seen through the press by himself, there ought to be no difficulty whatever, except as regards isolated words and stops; but unfortunately he did not revise while at press one half of the entire bulk of his poetry, several of the volumes having been printed in England while he was abroad, and read through the press by friends. The proportion of his mature works, from *Alastor* onwards, which had the advantage of his personal revision when in type, would, I think, be liberally estimated at one third; and the largest of the volumes seen through the press by himself is infamously printed. Generally speaking, however, where there is no manuscript extant, the text as printed in Shelley's life-time must be accepted as the nearest obtainable approach to an authority; and even when there is a manuscript extant, it is by no means a final authority as a matter of course. The relative value of a poem as printed in Shelley's life-time and as written out by him must depend not only upon the revision of the press by the author or his substitute, but upon the technical quality of the printer's work, and the amount of care bestowed upon the manuscript. If the printed version is obviously a careless piece of typography, it loses much of its authority even though seen through the press by Shelley himself. This is preëminently the case with *Laon and Cythna*; and the extant manuscript fragments tend to shew that the printer had not one of Shelley's best manuscripts to work from. *Alastor*, on the contrary, seems to me a very creditable piece of printer's work, on the whole; and, if a manuscript of that volume were discovered, I should not expect it to authorize more than two important verbal alterations. The *Rosalind and Helen* volume, again, of which proof sheets were certainly not seen by Shelley, is inferior to the *Alastor* volume as an authority; but probably the manuscript of the eclogue itself would be found very hasty and inconsistent in the matters of detail in which alone the printed text is suspicious to any great extent.

These three instances are merely typical of the kind of consideration applicable to every one of Shelley's volumes; and to reprint his published series just as they stand, without correcting palpable errors, would thus be an inadequate attempt to approach the genuine text. I have therefore not scrupled to remove many small blemishes of three classes, (1) those for which the printer is clearly responsible, (2) those for which Shelley may be responsible, but would certainly have removed if he had observed them, and (3) those for which Shelley's substitute for the time being is probably responsible. No alteration has been made unless I have felt sure the original was not what Shelley meant it to be, or would have wished it to be; and, I may almost add, unless it has been perfectly obvious what change should be made. Conjecture has no part nor lot in the matter.

It is easy enough to go on the assumption that everything in a text is right, and reprint it in fac-simile; and it is not much less easy to go on the opposite assumption that everything a little out of one's ordinary experience is wrong, and alter it forthwith. But the difficulty, with such texts as Shelley's, is to discriminate between unintentional inaccuracies in printing or writing and intentional eccentricities of style, metre, punctuation, and orthography. In my opinion the least correct of all the volumes published by Shelley during his life-time is very far pleasanter to read, and very much nearer the fact of his intention, than any of the posthumous texts published up to the year 1876. The chief reason of this I take to be a want of veneration on the part of his editors,—a failure to perceive that Shelley's eccentricities, even his errors if errors there be, must be far more interesting to intelligent humanity at large than any punctilious correctness not Shelley's. Even if the aggregate genius of the present generation were brought to bear upon the task of systematizing Shelley's style and grammar and so on, we might perhaps not obtain anything comparable to the real Shelley; and I conceive it to be a good service to his memory to restore in every instance what he wrote or meant to write. I have therefore adopted as a principle, that it is better to leave unchanged any doubtful passage, about which there may be several opinions, and which is not, as a matter of certainty, corrupt.

Corrupt as nearly all the posthumous texts of Shelley certainly are, the course of my studies has led me to think that the original editions are not nearly so corrupt as they are generally said to be, or as might be expected, and also that much has been called corrupt which is really nothing but elliptical, or unusual in point of grammar, of construction, of orthography, or of punctuation. Sufficient allowance has not been made for unusual features of Shelley's work which were deliberate, or which he would have seen no reason, as far as we can judge, for altering. To take as an example a single curious instance of seeming inconsistency, I would draw attention to his use of the interjection *O* or *Oh*. Throughout his works *O* and *Oh* are used interchangeably without any apparent rule; and, more than this, they are sometimes followed by a comma, sometimes by no stop at all, sometimes by a note of exclamation. To me it appears most objectionable to interfere with this irregularity. Whatever Shelley's view on this small but important word may have been, I do not presume to think he unerringly carried out that view in writing; but *O* is so constantly used within a line or two of *Oh*, that I cannot think he would have left so many of these divergences of practice had they been wholly unintentional. Of the half-dozen different ways of using the two forms of interjection, no two, if minutely considered, are of precisely the same metric value; and it is hardly fantastic to suppose that a slightly different intonation or stress is indicated by these slightly different interjections, though Shelley may have been wholly unconscious of any intention in the matter, and have simply written in each case what seemed to convey the weight of thought and word his mind was uttering.

The bearing on metric effect of what at first sight may appear to be mere slovenlinesses of grammar, orthography, and punctuation, is not easy to estimate in the case of so subtle a master of music as Shelley: I suspect his punctuation often depended more on euphony than on grammar; and it must always be intrinsically safer to leave the text as it is in these minute particulars than to tamper with it, unless there be a strong presumption that it has become corrupt since it left his hands. At all events, not only has this seemed to me *safer* and more in accordance with editorial obligations; but I have even thought it well worth while to preserve in the present text so much of the minute history of Shelley's mind as is unfolded to us in the peculiarities and inconsistencies of his orthography &c.,—at least when it has seemed likely that the orthography &c. were his, and deliberately adopted. But here again there are difficulties; for occasionally we come upon divergences of practice for which there is double and conflicting authority. In such cases, if I find clear evidence of a certain rule recognized by Shelley, I do not hesitate to apply his rule in correction of the text even where there is some sort of manuscript authority against the change,—because very often the manuscript giving such authority is either hastily dashed off or seemingly immature, and the change such as the poet might reasonably be expected to have made when reading the proof-sheets, or whenever he discovered the departure from his own rule. I have of course often left the punctuation or orthography of the text as I found it, even in cases where I have not been convinced of its being precisely as Shelley left it, but where the matter was of very little importance, *and could not possibly be decided.*

In the first volume of the present edition Shelley's various mature poetic issues are reprinted in chronological order, with the exact titles which he gave them, the dedications, mottoes, &c., and with the original arrangement of contents preserved. This plan seems to me to afford a marked artistic advantage. There is a decided interest in knowing precisely what Shelley thought appropriate as minor poems to append to his larger ones; and although this knowledge might of course be afforded even in a rearranged edition, still the effect must be lost in such an edition. That effect in such an instance as that of the poems issued with *Prometheus Unbound,* is simply magical. Never since the age dominated by the genius of Æschylus was anything of like lyric exaltation produced in dramatic literature; and never, perhaps, since, in our poet's own words, "God first dawned on Chaos," had there been any human soul that "panted forth a flood of rapture so divine" as that incomparable group of lyrics which follow the incomparable fourth act of *Prometheus*,—still sounding in diverse echoing keys and under infinite variations of melody the same intense intellectual passion, the same most holy love of humanity, the same godlike perception of ideal beauty. A "flood of rapture" still more divine remained to crown the work of the master in *Epipsychidion*, and a still more certain grasp on the combined resources of the lyric and dramatic crafts was yet to be shewn in *Hellas*,—the one put forth by itself, the other with a single lyric of astonishing fitness; but the fact remains that the selection and arrangement of lyrics to accompany *Prometheus* was a thing unequalled in perceptiveness; and in that case, at all events, the highest importance is to be attached to the preservation of Shelley's order among these lesser poems,—lesser only than greater things of his own, and greater than anything lyric to be found elsewhere in modern literature. At the same time I have not hesitated to interpolate, between the poems published with *Alastor* and Shelley's next published poem *Mont Blanc*, the recently discovered Second Part of *The Dæmon of the World*—so as to place the two parts of that redaction in sequence and leave the poem to be conveniently apprehended as a whole. To the mass of posthumous poems, translations, and juvenilia, no rigid principle of reproduction could be usefully applied; here an editor has a larger option; but of one thing I am convinced, that all distinctly immature work should form a separate chronology ending with *Queen Mab*. Shelley lived to protest against its being published at all; but, as it has now become an inalienable part of the world's possessions, all we can do out of respect to his memory is to assign to it the position which he assigned,—that of a juvenile work—albeit the book has had a more decided career than perhaps any other poem of striking immaturity in our literature.

It has seemed to me that the best plan for the arrangement of the rest of Shelley's poetry is to follow up the series of mature works published in his life-time, with the principal posthumous poems produced contemporaneously with that series; to place next in order the small posthumous poems of the same period, grouped under separate years, as Mrs. Shelley grouped them; and to keep the translations apart, at the end of the mature works, and arrange them according to the chronology of the original authors.

In carrying out this arrangement I have innovated somewhat in the matter of fragments. The fact that a poem was unfinished did not with Shelley form *per se* an obstacle to its publication; for we have *A Vision of the Sea*, ending abruptly in the middle of a sentence, put forth by him in his life-time, as were also *The Dæmon of the World* and *Superstition*; and the fragment of *Prince Athanase* was also sent for publication. Thus I have been obliged to introduce fragments into the chronological series of reprinted volumes; and it certainly seems to me better to follow the same principle in regard to the posthumous fragments, and group them with the poems of each year. I think they have a stronger interest so grouped than when separated and arranged in an independent chronology. They thus shew more readily what Shelley was doing, as far as we can ascertain, in the way of original poetry, in each year. For these reasons I have imported the *Fragments of an Unfinished Drama, Charles the First*, and *The Triumph of Life* into the series of principal posthumous poems; and for similar reasons I have placed cancelled passages, belonging obviously to given poems, immediately after such, instead of in a separate section.

The *Letter to Maria Gisborne* has been brought into the series of principal or more important posthumous poems, because, though comparatively short, it is among the most perfect and to my mind important of Shelley's smaller compositions, and is in some respects unlike all else.

It ought perhaps to be explained that the poems which are arranged between *Julian and Maddalo* and *The Mask of Anarchy*, namely *Prince Athanase* and a few lyrics, are so placed to carry out an intention expressed by Shelley: he told his publisher that *Prince Athanase* was to accompany *Julian and Maddalo*, and he afterwards sent for the same purpose some poems which he described as all his "saddest verses raked up into one heap." Both the specified works appeared for the first time in *Posthumous Poems*; and the rest here arranged in connexion with those two are chosen from the same volume as answering to the description given above.

The question why there should be any need to do more than simply reprint those poems which were printed in the first instance under Shelley's own supervision, invites further consideration. We have heard enough and too much about Shelley's being "a careless writer,"—enough because such truth as there is in this current assertion has been long ago laid to heart by those who are discerning in such matters, and too much because very few are discerning, and the text that cost the greatest lyric poet of England infinite pains to elaborate has been held fair ground whereon every clumsy or thoughtless emendator (or rather innovator) might do just what suited his fancy.

If, therefore, we admit at all that Shelley was a careless writer, we must guard such admission round about with saving clauses, and clearly understand in what sense the intrinsically damaging word *careless* is used. That he would have done himself no credit before a Chinese board of examiners in pen-craft and orthography and the punctilio of smart composition, may be safely admitted; and those who would fain fit his compositions for presentation before such a board are not qualified by natural proclivity for the labour of editing the works of a great poet. But that he was careless as an artist in any sense in which it behoved such an one to be careful, is amply refuted by the fact for which Mr. Garnett vouches in the following striking paragraph from the *Relics of Shelley*, pages xi and xii:

"They [the pieces in the *Relics*] appear to have been hitherto overlooked, for the reason that must also serve as an excuse for the imperfect manner in which they are even now presented to the public—the extremely confused state of these books [Shelley's manuscript note-books], and the equal difficulty of deciphering and connecting their contents. Being written in great haste, and frequently with pencil, the hand-writing is often indistinct of itself; and rendered far more so by erasures and interlineations *ad infinitum*. Shelley appears to have composed with his pen in his hand, and to have corrected as fast as he wrote; hence a page full of writing frequently yields only two or three available lines, which must be painfully disentangled from a chaos of obliterations. Much that at first sight wears the appearance of novelty, proves on inspection to be merely a variation of something already published; and sometimes the case is reversed, as in the *Prologue to Hellas*, so buried in the MS. of that drama (which has in itself on the average ten lines effaced for one retained), as to be only discoverable or separable upon very close scrutiny." Mr. Garnett adds a note to the effect that, when Shelley wrote for the printer, his handwriting was "singularly neat and beautiful"; and it seems to me that the proportion of lines rejected and lines retained in his rough drafts, taken in connexion with the quality of his "printer's copy," is the best possible proof of due care. As regards the statement that his drafts for the printer were beautifully written, I can confirm that from the evidence of the copy of *Julian and Maddalo* which he sent from Italy to Hunt, to have published: not only is the writing most careful and beautiful; but the punctuation is at once eminently characteristic and peculiar, and generally adequate and accurate from the poet's own point of view. This is still more noteworthy, inasmuch as Shelley wrote the poem out with his own hand twice at least, in ink. One copy is in a book among those in Sir Percy Shelley's possession; the other, on what seem to be the gilt-edged leaves of a pocket-book, is that already referred to, of which a specimen is given in fac-simile in the Library Edition.

That the confused note-books described by Mr. Garnett imply care, not the reverse, must be evident to any one who thinks for a moment: these were Shelley's means of putting his thoughts on record at once as they came burning upon him; and they were never meant for any one's guidance but his own. It was a need inherent in the fiery exaltation of his lyric mood that the result should be set down at once; and, for mere temporary *memoranda*, it mattered not how intricately one poem might be blended with another. He knew how to disentangle and write them fairly, or dictate them to Mrs. Shelley; and, had he lived to have the slightest suspicion how we should venerate every scrap of paper bearing the impress of his hand and pen, he would, we may be sure, have taken ample care to place these note-books beyond our reach.

The subject of Shelley's method of composition, a right understanding of which is the first requisite for any one aspiring to edit his works, would be a very fruitful theme for prolonged discussion. In one of the keenest and at the same time most enthusiastic of recent contributions to Shelley literature this theme is very happily touched upon. I refer to an article in *The Edinburgh Review* for April 1871, written *à propos* of Mr. Rossetti's edition of Shelley,—an article which I am authorized to connect with the name of Professor Thomas S. Baynes of St. Andrew's University, and which I cannot do better than quote.

"It is," says Professor Baynes, "a curious psychological problem how it is that amongst modern poets Shelley should be distinguished by his comparative neglect of minute verbal accuracy; how it comes to pass that the text even of poems which he himself carefully revised should be so extremely imperfect." Negligence, care, imperfection! This is a strange association of words; but in that association Professor Baynes seems to me to go right home to the facts of the case. The problem, he says, is, how it happens that in the poems which Shelley himself revised "there are grammatical laxities and metrical oversights, which are not only stumbling-blocks to readers of ordinary cultivation, but the despair of acute and accomplished verbal critics.

"This uncritical negligence, the want of minute accuracy in the details of his verse, seems to us intimately connected with the whole character of Shelley's mind, and especially with the lyrical sweep and intensity of his poetical genius. He had an intellect of the rarest delicacy and analytical strength, that intuitively perceived the most remote analogies, and discriminated with spontaneous precision the finest shades of sensibility, the subtilest differences of perception and emotion. He possessed a swift soaring and prolific imagination that clothed every thought and feeling with imagery in the moment of its birth, and instinctively read the spiritual meanings of material symbols. His fineness of sense was so exquisite that eye and ear and touch became, as it were, organs and inlets not merely of sensitive apprehension, but of intellectual beauty and ideal truth. Every nerve in his slight but vigorous frame seemed to vibrate in unison with the deeper life of nature in the world around him, and, like the wandering harp, he was swept to music by every breath of material beauty, every gust of poetic emotion. Above all, he had a strength of intellectual passion and a depth of ideal sympathy that in moments of excitement fused all the powers of his mind into a continuous stream of creative energy, and gave the stamp of something like inspiration to all the higher productions of his muse. His very method of composition reflects these characteristics of his mind. He seems to have been urged by a sort of irresistible impulse to write, and displayed a vehement and passionate absorption in the work that recalls the old traditions of poetical frenzy and divine possession. His conceptions crowded so thickly upon him, were embodied in such exquisite verbal forms, and so enriched by illustrations flashed from remote and multiplied centres of association, that while the fever lasted his whole nature was carried impetuously forward on a full tide of mingled music and imagery. From this exuberance of poetical power some of his critics have reproached him with accumulating image upon image without pausing to select, discriminate, or contrast them. And it is no doubt true that there are passages in which metaphors and similes are heaped on each other in almost dazzling profusion. But even in his most opulent and ornate descriptions there is hardly a trace of conscious labour or deliberate effort. In his higher work the brilliant diction and splendid imagery glow with kindled emotion, and are wrought into the very substance of the poem by the sustained vehemence and rapture of his impassioned verse. Many of his most exquisite pieces were in this way produced almost at a sitting—at a single heat, as it were—and some of his longest poems, such as *The Revolt of Islam* and *The Cenci*, were completed in a few months. Once engrossed with a great poetical conception, all his powers were kindled to a pitch of the highest intensity, and amidst the crowding realities of imagination the whole world of sense grew pale and dim, and everything around became for the time unsubstantial as a dream.

"This power of complete and passionate absorption in an ideal world of his own had marked Shelley from his earliest years. The stories told of his boyhood and youth strikingly illustrate this feature of his character. . . Shelley himself, however, gives the most vivid picture of this abstracted mood in the description of the poet by one of the spirits in *Prometheus* :—

> He will watch from dawn to gloom
> The lake-reflected sun illume
> The yellow bees in the ivy-bloom,
> Nor heed nor see, what things they be ;
> But from these create he can
> Forms more real than living man,
> Nurslings of immortality !

Shelley's 'nurslings of immortality' were produced in such seasons of rapt and exulting vision, and they bear in every part authentic and indelible marks of their origin. The verbal obscurities and metrical defects that have given his critics so much trouble are amongst these marks. The thoughts and feelings and images that crowded upon him he was in the habit of committing to paper with the utmost rapidity, and so that the expression was clear and rhythmical enough to be for the moment a kind of musical transcript of what was passing in his own mind, he was satisfied. He could not pause to elaborate the niceties of diction while new and stimulating thoughts, fresh and more brilliant images, were every moment pressing for utterance. If any difficulty as to word or phrase arose, instead of staying to remove it, he left a blank and passed on to embody the fresh visions of ethereal beauty that filled the inward eye before they again faded into the obscurity out of which they had so swiftly arisen. Or he would sometimes give within brackets tentative or alternative expressions, to be afterwards examined and decided on more at leisure. When he returned to revise and complete the unfinished or fragmentary piece, his mind evidently kindled afresh into something like its first ardour, and the work was matured under conditions of poetical excitement similar to those that accompanied its birth. And once fairly finished he busied himself to get the new creation of his brain printed as soon as possible. His eagerness to publish and the reason he gives for it are highly interesting and characteristic. 'If you ask me,' he says, writing to his friend Trelawny, 'why I publish what few ' or none will care to read, it is that the spirits I have raised haunt ' me until they are sent to the devil of a printer. . .' The real reason was, of course, that his mind being full of new conceptions he wanted to be free for fresh creative efforts. In this way, having once published a poem, he considered himself to have done with it, and rarely attempted afterwards anything in the shape of critical revision. Nor in the first printing did he make any important alterations or correct the press with any great care."

In regard to the last sentence but one, it is right to remark that *The Revolt of Islam*, at all events, Shelley was anxious to revise for a second edition, and in fact enquired with some instance of Mr. Ollier whether an opportunity was likely to occur. "I have many corrections," he says (*Shelley Memorials*, page 153), "to make in it, and one part will be wholly remodelled." And again (page 159), "I could materially improve that poem on revision." I have been unable to ascertain that he ever carried out this project, though Medwin mentions having seen a revised copy. The circumstances must be taken for what they are worth in contemplating Shelley's mental attitude towards those works that he had seen safely launched from the press.

In the expression, "Nor in the first printing did he make any important alterations or correct the press with any great care," Professor Baynes does not of course imply any want of due earnestness; but here again I must partially dissent. The unique proof-leaf inserted in Shelley's own copy of *Laon and Cythna* seems to me to indicate modifications important enough; and I think there is at all events a strong probability that great fastidiousness, involving in the event pretty considerable revisions of the proof sheets, are at the root of the strikingly corrupt state of the original edition of *Laon and Cythna*. The *Alastor* volume bears no evidence of careless revision; and *The Cenci* and *Adonais*, printed in Italy under Shelley's own supervision expressly in order to avoid error, though characteristically inconsistent in minute details, shew remarkably few actual errors left undetected by Shelley. What he may have done in the way of modification on the proof-sheets, there are no *data* on which to form a hypothesis. With this note of partial dissent, I return to Professor Baynes's remarks; and they certainly qualify to some extent the expression from which I have dissented: "Not that Shelley was careless as to expression, or at all wanting in critical power. On the contrary, he had the finest instinct for language, which he had early cultivated so as to acquire a wonderful mastery over the more vivid, ideal, and expressive elements of poetical diction. But for this, indeed, with his rapid habit of composition, eagerness to print, and neglect of all after revision, the verbal difficulties of his poems would be far more serious than they are. Again, his prose writings show that he possessed a critical faculty of the rarest delicacy and penetration, a power of philosophical analysis of the keenest edge and finest temper. But the persistent exercise of this faculty upon his own poetry would have required an amount of deliberation and delay, a coolness of temperament, a power of standing aloof from his own work and regarding it in a purely objective point of view wholly foreign to Shelley's nature. In seasons of inspiration he concentrated his whole soul on the work in hand, wrought strenuously to invest his poetical conceptions with 'the light of language,' and present them to the world in the most perfect form, and having done so he deliberately left them to their fate. To have occupied himself afterwards in touching and retouching the finished work would have been in his view a waste of time. Such careful and minute critical revision could in any case only be undertaken in intervals of leisure as a reaction and relief from creative effort. But Shelley was always producing; the completion of one poetical work being almost invariably followed by the commencement of another."

Still, we know that, before his poems went to the press he did not regard it as a waste of time to touch and retouch them; and I must confess I do not think he would ever have regarded as a waste of time the removal of anything that he recognized as a blemish. But our current notions on the subject of artistic blemishes are crude, narrow, and conventional; and I do not believe Shelley would have admitted as blemishes one fiftieth of the small inconsistencies of detail which his editors have been at so much pains to remove. It is perfectly true that, as Professor Baynes says, the longer poems rarely display "perfect evenness of verbal and metrical finish,"—Shelley's ideal of perfection being in fact something much higher than that,—so much so that we might as soon expect perfect evenness of utterance from his own inspirers the West Wind and the Skylark as from Shelley, whose highest technical feat was the production of works of art perfectly artless in aspect, and having the air rather of growth than of elaboration. "His finest passages," continues Professor Baynes, "have a witchery of aërial music, an exquisiteness of ideal beauty, and a white intensity of spiritual passion... But the very qualities of mind and heart out of which these perfections spring carry with them the conditions of relative imperfection in the minor details of his work. The lyrical depth and impetuosity of feeling which carries Shelley on, and gives such freedom and grace to the poetical movement of his kindled thought, is unfavourable to perfect smoothness and accuracy in the mechanical details of his verse. He was often, in fact, too completely absorbed in the glorious substance of his poetry to give any minute attention to subordinate points of form. Thus, although from native fineness of ear his lines are never unrhythmical, the rhyme is often defective, and sometimes the metre as well. And while his thought, even in its most subtle refinements, is always lucid, the expression, from haste or extreme condensation, is sometimes far from being clear." I have freely quoted these remarks because they are admirable in themselves and appropriate to the subject in hand, and also because I think they enforce by implication the principles of editing which I have desired to follow. The lesson that we have to learn is that it was inherent in the very nature of Shelley's mind that certain unevennesses, inconsistencies, and divergences of practice should find place in his work, and that, instead of suspecting corruption where these occur, we should feel satisfied of incorruption, and do all in our power to preserve the fruit of his spirit intact,—not try to make it like the fruit of some other and lesser spirit.

I trust I have shewn that the word *careless* will not do to apply to Shelley's views of the attention to be bestowed on the details of his work. In any case it may be noted that the manuscripts of *Julian and Maddalo* and *The Mask of Anarchy* alone afford ample evidence on this point, and seem to me to shew that he took somewhat elaborate pains to redact and punctuate his poetry. I cannot doubt that, having set himself determinedly to go through the punctuation and minor detail of a fairly written poem about to go to press, he was only prevented from consistently revising it throughout, by getting once more implicated in the ardour of realization,—an ardour differing only in degree from that of composition. A curious instance of minute care presents itself in the manuscript of *The Mask of Anarchy*—written mainly by Mrs.

Shelley, but completed and revised by Shelley. In stanza xxix the second line seems on close examination to have been originally written by Mrs. Shelley thus—

A planet like the morning lay;

which laxity, very likely to have been Shelley's in the ardour of composition, is carefully altered to the line in the text—

A planet, like the morning's, lay;

and that this minute change was actually made with Shelley's hand, it needs no expert to decide beyond a doubt.

Traces of moments when minute care gave out (displaced according to my view by renewed ardour) occur in the manuscripts of both *Julian and Maddalo* and *The Mask*, and for that matter in numerous others which I have consulted; but the general impression left on my mind is that, had Shelley lived to collect and revise his own poetical works, he would probably have produced a text that would have left very little for editors to do.

Concerning Mrs. Shelley's editions there is nothing to be said derogatory to the admiration and gratitude which we all owe her. It is not surprising that, in the proximity of so radiant a source of light, she should have seen no need for studying minutely the details of a series of texts, faulty from several causes, and irregular to some extent owing to changes of method on the part of the author. In her life-time the period had not arrived for the study of characteristic irregularities and changes in minute matters connected with Shelley's works; and she had quite enough to do in searching out new poems and passages of poems from among the mass of confused and undigested manuscripts which he left. On the text itself she probably worked pretty hard: but the measure of original genius with which she was herself endowed, though marking her out for independent admiration, was rather a disqualification than otherwise for the editing of texts. Still, she must, through her intimate acquaintance with the mind and heart of Shelley, have been enabled to preserve and supply much of the spirit of his works that no one else could have seized in a situation similar to that in which she worked; and it is also fair to assume that some of the more important variations between the original and posthumous editions of his poems rest on something more than the intuition of his widow,—that she had, in some instances, manuscript authority for modifying passages in his poetry. That she also modified without such authority, there is no reasonable doubt; so that a re-editor has, necessarily, to use his own judgment, and whatever means are at his command, to discriminate between the authoritative and unauthoritative variations of Mrs. Shelley's editions from the originals. I have carefully collated every page of the originals with the two collected editions of 1839, and sometimes with later editions, and have adopted such verbal variations as seem to be improvements, and as have a decided air of authority; but the changes in orthography and punctuation shewn by the posthumous editions are, no doubt, as a rule unauthoritative, and probably, to a great extent, printing-house changes.

Beside the fact that Mrs. Shelley's editions are the only authority for much of the text of the posthumous works, we must remember that it is impossible to say how much of revision may have been floating in her mind from old experience of her husband's personal utterances,—what he may have noted in copies of his poems belonging to her, or what he may have said to her about general or special imperfections to be amended. And this consideration should make us careful in rejecting important changes made in her editions. I will not say that the two editions of 1839 must hold quite the same position in Shelley literature as Heming and Condell's folio of 1623 holds and will ever hold in Shakespeare literature,—I will not say this, because, for the bulk of Shelley's works, the earlier editions are certainly more authoritative than the later; but I do say that there is an analogy between the editions of 1839 and the folio of 1623,—which analogy will remain as long as the study of English literature lasts.

The remarks made thus far in connexion mainly with the text of such poems as were published during Shelley's life-time of course apply in a great degree to posthumous works also; but, in editing these, change of method necessarily arises from change of materials. The largest mass of posthumous poetry is the volume issued by Mrs. Shelley in 1824 under the title of *Posthumous Poems*; but this has been steadily followed by one instalment after another of more or less precious and wonderful poetry, up to the years immediately past; and even yet the process is not complete, for there are still buried works of Shelley's. The volume of *Posthumous Poems* was followed by *The Mask of Anarchy* in 1832 and *The Shelley Papers* in 1833. The first collected edition of 1839 added somewhat to the known mass of Shelley's verse; and the second collection of that year added far more—among other additions giving the practically unpublished *Œdipus Tyrannus* and the absolutely unpublished *Peter Bell the Third*. Mrs. Shelley made no later additions, as far as I am aware; but the Lives by Medwin and Hogg added a little, and in 1862 there came Mr. Garnett's Relics. In 1870 Mr. W. M. Rossetti gave several pieces not before published; in 1876-7 there were still a few items left to make their first appearance in my Library Edition; and even the present edition has its contribution to the mass. Of some poems the text grew gradually under Mrs. Shelley's disentangling hand, some being incompletely issued in the volume of 1824 and added to afterwards; and in some cases the process of disentanglement has been carried on by later hands. In framing the present text, whatever posthumous work I have taken in the main from any of the several sources other than Mrs. Shelley's editions, I have submitted to a rigid collation with those editions whenever the poems occurred there as well as in the other books drawn upon. Such poems have, as Shelley's own issues have, been collated with both of Mrs. Shelley's editions of 1839. Indeed, in every case where further collation seemed desirable (and many such cases have presented themselves), several later editions also have been consulted; and wherever a manuscript has been available to me, I have collated the text with it word by word and point by point. In regard to any slight variation of this edition from the current texts, whether in orthography, punctuation, capitalling, or other minute particulars, it is to be understood in a general way that I have adopted the reading, either of the manuscript, or of one of Mrs. Shelley's editions. In the case of poems first given by Mr. Garnett and Mr. Rossetti, I have permitted myself some little liberty of variation from the text before me in these small details; and there is good reason for this slight relaxation: Mr. Garnett assures me that the manuscripts from which he has made transcripts have been very deficient in punctuation,—an assurance amply confirmed by my own experience; and as both

Mr. Garnett and Mr. Rossetti, who have given these transcripts to the public, disagree with me as to the utility of preserving Shelley's punctuation, I have not felt called upon to follow the pointing of the *Relics*, or of Mr. Rossetti's edition, as the case may be, but have punctuated the pieces as I should imagine Shelley punctuating them in a more advanced stage than that in which he left them. This has been to treat them as I must have done had the manuscripts been deciphered by myself instead of Mr. Garnett.

For the rest, before settling the text either of the first or of the second volume of this edition, I have carefully weighed every change made or proposed in the two-volume edition which Mr. Rossetti issued in 1870—always provided such change seemed to him important enough for record in a note. Truth to tell, the like has been done in regard to many changes not thus recorded; but it did not seem necessary to collate the text line by line with Mr. Rossetti's as with Mrs. Shelley's; nor have I made any rigorous examination of Mr. Rossetti's unannotated edition (Moxon's *Popular Poets*), or of the three-volume re-edition of 1878, the general tendency of which, so far as it varies from the edition of 1870, is in the direction, not of further emendation, but of reversion towards readings accepted before 1870. Mr. Rossetti adheres however to his view of systematizing the punctuation &c. from an external point of view, whereas it seems to me that, from the close inspection of manuscripts in various stages of advancement, a great deal as to Shelley's ways in small matters is to be learnt. The manuscripts often shew apparently trifling details that should, on my theory, be followed implicitly, as being intentional. Thus, in the careful manuscripts from which *Julian and Maddalo* and *The Mask of Anarchy* are given, it would be, if accidental, a very curious coincidence that the system of turned commas is precisely the same. In each poem, in the earlier part, where the speeches are short, the quotation-marks are repeated at the beginning of every line; but when in *Julian and Maddalo* we come to the monologue of the maniac, a single turned comma before each paragraph is made to suffice: similarly, when we come in *The Mask of Anarchy* to the invocation forming stanzas xxxvii to xci, the turned commas are at the beginning of each stanza only, and not of each line.

It may perhaps be expected that I should indicate more

particularly within what limits I have exercised the editorial prerogative. It has already been stated that in regard to the work issued in Shelley's life-time, conjecture has not been admitted. It remains to say, as regards the posthumous poems, that, wherever I have noticed certain words spelt otherwise than there is reason to believe Shelley spelt them, I have restored what I think his spelling: thus, *inchant*, being the spelling of that word for which I have found authority, that orthography has been adopted whenever *enchant* has been observed in the posthumous poems; and the same remark applies to *inwoven* and *enwoven*. I have also, whenever the word *passed* has come under my notice, substituted *past*,—knowing that such was Shelley's habitual way of spelling the word. But, although these changes are made in the mature posthumous poems, they are not as a matter of course made in such of the *Juvenilia* as Shelley printed himself: there, the original forms are as a rule minutely preserved.

Finding good reason to think that words ending in *ize* were duly spelt by Shelley with a *z*, I have, whenever I have observed an *s* in that termination in the posthumous poems, substituted a *z*. Shelley's text has probably suffered in this respect from the same agency that is operating to the damage of other texts in this matter, to wit the persistent indolence of compositors, who, when "at case," can pick up an *s* with much less trouble than a *z*.

In the matter of quotations in Latin, Greek, and other foreign tongues, I have not sought to bring any scholastic interference to bear on what I have thought was deliberately written by Shelley: obvious printers' errors in these quotations, I have removed; but in other cases I have not thought it worth while to supply or correct accents and so on; for those who know more of the grammar of foreign tongues than Shelley did will not be misled,— those who know less will not be annoyed. In regard to the epigram from the Greek Anthology on the title-page of *Adonais* and the verses from Moschus at the head of the preface to that poem, as well as the quotations from Homer and Plutarch in the Notes to *Queen Mab*, the exact Greek scholar will find much to criticize; but I suspect these extracts give us pretty accurately the measure of Shelley's own exactness at the periods in question.

In the verses from Lucretius quoted at the head of *Queen Mab*, however, a printer's error, *juratque* for *juvatque*, has been corrected; but I have even left the titles of, and extracts from, French works as I found them in the *Queen Mab* Notes, the errors in accents &c. affording evidence as to Shelley's scholarship or accuracy in the year 1813, and having thus an intrinsic value for the student of the poet.

The only matter in which I have consciously departed from what I believe to have been Shelley's practice is that of past tenses and participles in *ed*. In this case accents have been supplied as a help to the reader whenever there was no doubt that the final syllable was meant to be separately sounded. To anyone technically familiar with the rhythmical manner of Shelley, this is almost always decided beyond a doubt by the scansion; but there are some few cases in which a line will scan equally well with the final *ed* mute or sounded. As far as I know Shelley never supplied the accents, so that wherever one occurs it is to be reckoned as a minute deviation from the original text.

For ease and simplicity of reference all poems exceeding in length a sonnet or fourteen lines have been numbered in the margins, unless already divided in the original editions into numbered stanzas, and indeed in some cases of long or irregular stanzas it has been thought useful to give a marginal numeration also; but no new numeration of stanzas has been introduced into Shelley's editions as reprinted in Volume I. Such helps as the insertion in the head-lines of "Canto I" &c., "Act I, Scene I" &c., are invariably given whether Shelley's editions give them or not; and I have sought to make the wording of the head-lines as useful as possible.

As a rule Shelley's own editions have been followed in the matter of indentations (or "indentions" as they are technically called); though of course there as elsewhere there are occasional errors to be corrected in working from his editions. In Volume II, in a general way, the setting of lines is arranged so that the "indentions" have some correspondence with the rhymes; but there are two forms of verse in which this plan has not been followed, —*terza rima* and the Sonnet. In printing the *terza rima* poems in simple groups of three lines, the present edition follows those of Mrs. Shelley, who, I doubt not, followed in this respect the indication of Shelley's manuscripts,—especially as we find the same arrangement in the stanzas of cognate form employed in the *Ode to the West Wind*. In giving the sonnet without "indentions," the invariable practice of Shelley's own printed volumes is followed; and in such of his manuscript sonnets as I have seen there are no intentional "indentions,"—merely the same irregularity of margin that we generally find in his manuscripts. As the writing of these two highly artificial forms of verse has ever been matter of much controversy and strong opinion, it is unlikely that Shelley's own way of writing them was unconsidered: it should therefore be followed.

Of the two fragments of verse which have not appeared in any edition of Shelley except the present, the *Fragment of a Satire on Satire* (Volume II, page 210) is reprinted from Professor Dowden's recent volume *The Correspondence of Robert Southey with Caroline Bowles*. Professor Dowden gave it from a transcript furnished to him by Mr. Garnett. The *Lines to William Godwin* (Volume II, page 162) have not, I believe, been printed before: they were written by Shelley on a letter addressed to him by Godwin, dated "Skinner Street, Apr. 29, 1817," proposing an eligible investment for Shelley which was also to benefit Godwin, and suggesting a subscription for the payment of the Hunts' fine. The lines seem to be a poetic comment on the situation of Godwin—an eagle caught by night, facing and defying tempests. The couplet in *Hellas* (lines 76-7)—

> As an eagle fed with morning
> Scorns the embattled tempests' warning,

will at once recur to readers of this fragment; and it is most remarkable that this figure should have remained so long in Shelley's mind.

H. BUXTON FORMAN.

46 MARLBOROUGH HILL, ST. JOHN'S WOOD,
May 1882.

EDGAR ALLAN POE.

"..... Amabam pulchra inferiora et ibam in profundum, et dicebam amicis meis: Num amamus aliquid nisi pulchrum? Quid est ergo pulchrum? et quid est pulchritudo? Quid est quod nos allicit et conciliat rebus quas amamus? Nisi enim esset in eis decus et species, nullo modo nos ad se moverent. . . . . Et ista consideratio scaturivit in animo meo ex intimo corde meo, et scripsi libros."

S. AUGUSTINI EPISCOP. *Confess.* lib. iv. 20.

WE must all have observed, I am sure, with a great deal of pleasure, how much the literature of our American kinsmen has been spreading amongst us within the last few years. Such men as Washington Irving and Cooper were familiar friends from the first; but they both founded, more or less, on our own classical models. Irving's whole tone of thought and style, for instance, is English; his sentiment is essentially English. But we are now beginning to get acquainted with writers amongst the Americans who are really national—in the sense that American apples are national. Emerson has a distinct smack of the rich and sunny West; just as the honey in Madeira tastes of violets. Lowell's humour in the "Biglow Papers" is as gloriously Yankee as Burns's humour is gloriously Scotch. Is not the genius of Hawthorne a real native product? And from whom but an American could we have expected such a book as we had the other day in the *Whale* of Herman Melville? such a fresh daring book—wild, and yet true—with its quaint spiritual portraits looking ancient and also fresh, as though Puritanism had been *kept fresh* in the salt water over there, and were looking out living upon us once more. These writers one sees, at all events, have our old English virtue of pluck. They think what they please, and say what they think. And while M'Fungus is concocting philosophical histories in the style of the last century with drums on our ears, these other open-hearted men are getting into all our hearts, and making themselves friends by our firesides. An Englishman ought to require no apology from one who introduces an American Poet to him. I have undertaken this office very cheerfully with regard to EDGAR ALLAN POE. I owe his acquaintance, as

I owe much of the happiness of my life, to the society of friends devoted to art and poetry. His music has made several summers brighter for me; and now that his reputation (the man himself died just three years ago) is appealing for recognition to the English "reading public," I feel that I ought to say a few words about him. At all events, this notice may serve as a finger-post to direct the wanderer to a *tumulus* as worthy of honour as any that has been made on the earth lately.

EDGAR ALLAN POE was a native of Virginia; and as Virginia is richer in good families than other American States, we learn that he was of honourable descent. The name is not a common one in England. There was a Dr. Poe, physician to Queen Elizabeth; and there is a highly respectable family of the name in Ireland who bear the same coat-armour as the doctor. The poet's great-grandfather, who married a daughter of Admiral M'Bride, was probably of the same *stock*. *His* son was a quartermaster-general in the American line; and his grandson David, the poet's father—commencing an "eccentricity" which, we shall see, ran in the blood afterwards—married an enchanting actress of uncertain prospects. Having achieved this, David Poe (who was a younger son) took to acting himself; but both he and his wife died young, leaving three children destitute. Edgar (who was born at Baltimore in January 1811) accordingly began the world,—for he was thrown thus early on his " own resources,"— as naked as a cherub.

Mr. Allan, a rich gentleman who had no children of his own, adopted Edgar, brought him to England, where he put him to school at Stoke-Newington. Edgar, who was a " spoilt child "—a beautiful, witty, precocious boy,—remained at school there for some five years. In 1822 he returned to the United States; went to the academy at Richmond; and thence to the University at Charlottesville. Always he signalised himself by early intellect, quickly learning all that came in his way, brilliant, vivacious, passionate, always—but always "eccentric" in proportion; so that, what with intemperance and insubordination, this youth,—

> . . . . . To whom was given
> So much of earth, so much of heaven,
> And such impetuous blood,

—was expelled from the University. Distant rumours, and—what fly faster than even rumours— bills, kept Mr. Allan informed of the youth's progress. Mr. A., who seems to have been a good-natured old gentleman of the school of MICIO in the *Adelphi*, could pardon a great deal; but there are limits to the patience even of a MICIO. Edgar, finding that his bills recoiled on himself as boomerangs do, seems to have tried his satire on the worthy man; and, after writing a sharp letter, went off to the Mediterranean to free the Greeks from the Turkish yoke. We rarely hear of a more heroic project!

I like to think of Poe in the Mediterranean. With his passionate love of the Beautiful,—in " the years of April blood," in a climate which has the perpetual luxury of a bath,—he must have had all his perceptions of the lovely intensified wonderfully. What he did there we have now no means of discovering. He never reached the scene of war, which was doubtless a great loss to the Greeks; but he turned up, whence or how no man knows—in St. Petersburg. The American Minister, it seems, had to relieve the youth from " temporary embarrassment;" and he returned to his native land. He now appears to have thought that it was time for his friends to exert themselves. Mr. Allan was once more kind and forgiving, and Edgar was entered as a cadet at the Military Academy. In the groves of *that* academy he did not remain long, we may be sure; the fact was, he was " cashiered."

It seems to have been about this time that he published, while still a boy, his first volume of poems —those comprised in his later collections as " Poems written in Youth." I agree with all that Lowell says of their wonderful precocity, though I by no means agree with Lowell in his depreciation of Chatterton.

There are, of course, obvious traces of imitation, adoptions of the metres of Scott, imitations of the verse of Byron. But there is the keenest feeling for the Beautiful, which was the predominant feeling of Poe's whole life; there is the loveliest, easiest, joyfulest flow of music throughout. There is, too, what must have been almost instinctive, an exquisite taste—a taste which lay at the very centre of his intellect like a conscience.

We should notice here two phenomena in this volume, both of importance to one who wants to understand Poe as man and poet. There is no trace of any depth of spiritual feeling; no "questioning of destiny;" none of those traces of deep inward emotion which, like the marks of tears, we see on the face of so many a modern muse. On the other hand, though it appears only too certain that his wild passions carried him into most unhappy self-abandonment, his verse is all as pure as wild flowers. This is the way in which the boy Edgar—the rejected of the Military Academy, the rake of Charlottesville, noted for "intemperance" and "other vices"—writes about a girl:—

To Helen.

Helen, thy beauty is to me
  Like those Nicéan barks of yore
That gently, o'er a perfumed sea,
  The weary way-worn wanderer bore
  To his own native shore.

> On desperate seas long wont to roam,
>   Thy hyacinth hair, thy classic face,
> Thy Naiad airs have brought me home
>   To the glory that was Greece,
> And the grandeur that was Rome.
>
> Lo, in yon brilliant window-niche
>   How statue-like I see thee stand,
>   The agate lamp within thy hand!
> Ah, Psyche, from the regions which
>   Are holy-land!

Could anything be more dainty, airy, amber-bright than this is? Its elegance is Horatian. It is *merum nectar*, as Scaliger says of the Ode to Pyrrha. I do not believe what is asserted, that this was written when Poe was fourteen; but it was undoubtedly written in his earliest youth. Now, Poe may have done this and done that. Youths brought up by fine good-natured old Micios, particularly if their "veins run wine," as is believed of some, will do many strange things. There are hundreds of youths as "wild" as Poe; but this one wrote the above poem. *That* is the interesting fact. A fragment of song like this comes out of the inner being of a man, and the capability of producing it is *the* fact of his nature.

These poems had, as was natural, great success He was already known as a youth of "genius," one who had shown a certain power of a mysterious character, one who breathed the breath of that sacred wind which "bloweth where it listeth." But he was still as irregular as ever, having been created to be so, seemingly. He entered as private into a regiment, and again disappeared from his friends. We have a striking account of his next appearance from Mr. Griswold's memoir of him. He turned up once more, "thin, pale, and ghastly," the mark of poverty branded upon him, and began the world now regularly as a "literary man." He soon got employment; he was a scholar, had read a great deal, and was not wanting in people to encourage him. There still remained, however, one step to take. Edgar, while his income was about a hundred a-year, thought it was time to marry. He married accordingly—a most beautiful girl, of course. She was his cousin, Virginia Clemm—" as poor as himself," says Griswold, grimly. A most amiable, lovable, and lovely person, however,—which some people think the most important consideration,—she appears to have been. Whenever the curtain of Poe's private life is pulled aside,—which is not frequently, for his biographers and countrymen tell us more of his misdoings generally than of his home,—for he had a home,—we get a glimpse of her beautiful face—cheerful, affectionate, always—sad, alas, latterly, but still, like Oriana's, "sweet" as well as "pale and meek." How little do we know of the wives of famous men! What idea do we carry away of any of the three

Mrs. Miltons? Of all the goodness of the wife of "brave old Samuel?" Of the tenderness and affection of Mrs. Fielding? To us they are barely names; but we ought to hear more of them.

Poe's life henceforth is the life of a man-of-letters by profession, and, on the whole, it is a melancholy history. No man can complain that there is not in the literary profession as much—indeed, there is more—allowance made for frailties, eccentricities, shortcomings of all kinds, than there is in other departments of active life in our modern social state. When, therefore, we find Edgar Poe quarrelling with so many people with whom he had business relations, continually in miserable embarrassments when he had a pen which could command money, what can we say? A career like that of our old Savages and Boyses,—as his, too often, was,—what can we make of it? We must even admit that his misery was mainly caused by the "dissipation" which we find universally attributed to him. All his aspirations, his fine sensibilities, sought wildly for their gratification through the medium of the senses. The beauty which he loved with his whole soul, he madly endeavoured to grasp in the forms of sheer indulgence Like Marlow's *Faustus*, he used his genius to procure him self-gratification; and always at the end of such a career, it is the devil, as our pious old singers believed, who waits for the hero.

In truth, it was the Beautiful that he loved with his entire nature. In sorrowful forms—sombre or grotesque forms—brilliant and musical, or scientific forms, he sought the Beautiful; and in all these forms his writings have embodied it. In his life, too, he loved the emotions which the Beautiful produces; but we know from the *Phædrus*,—old wisdom yet new,—" that though the beautiful be the dearest and most lovable of all things," yet that " he who hath not been lately initiated in the mysteries, or rather has become depraved, he is not easily excited to the true beauty itself, but only to a certain likeness of it, which goes by its name; and so he does not venerate it, but after the manner of animals striveth after pleasure." And thus Edgar Poe drew a sensual veil across the vision of his soul, and in that blinded way sinned; and sinning, suffered.

Other men have been as reckless as he in their youth, yet have escaped out of it, and risen into clear day. But he did not,—he made strong efforts,—he fell, however, finally.

From the period of his marriage, as I have said, he made literature his profession, and was connected at different periods with leading American journals. Occasionally he produced one of the few poems which compose his collection; "The Raven" in particular excited immense attention. He wrote Tales and Essays, and Reviews of all that was noticeable in

American literature; the latter, in his work the *Literati*, I have read, and admire their sharp cutting vividness of analysis. They show a man of large and various literary attainments (he always passed for one of the best scholars in America), with a spice of that bitterness which sprang from his misanthropy; for poor Edgar, as Griswold dryly and solidly informs us, "considered society as principally composed of villains!" He hated and despised the blockheads who, perhaps from no virtue of their own, were exempt from *his* failings and consequent sufferings; but, unhappily, the blockheads, in their condemnation of Edgar, were but too often in the right. Yet let not such, there or elsewhere, be too harsh on the failings of a fine nature, and the degradation of a noble mind. Who shall explain the mysteries of temperament? Who calculate the force of circumstances? The spiritual part of this man, of which a specimen remains with us, was highly beautiful, and allied to the perennial beauty! Let solid excellence of the epitaph-description remember, that perhaps all its parlour virtues are not worth one hour of Coleridge's remorse.

I have hinted above that it is difficult to get such details of the better part of Edgar's life as would enable me to give some little picture of him. WILLIS has written a fine graceful sketch, both manly and tender, of him, and describes him as "a winning, sad-mannered gentleman." But Willis never visited his home, and cannot be said to have been intimate with him. Yet we hear of the air of simplicity and elegance which pervaded the poet's house—we have a glimpse of it from the pen of Francis Osgood,—we see the poet industrious, playful, with his beautiful and affectionate Virginia with him, and her mother, whose name is never to be mentioned in the history of Poe's life without signal honour. Maria Clemm, his mother-in-law, was truly a mother to him, faithful to him through all the strange fortune which he underwent with true womanly constancy.

His portrait, prefixed to the American edition, is a very interesting—a very characteristic one. A fine thoughtful face you see at once, with lineaments of delicacy, such as belong only to genius or high blood. The forehead is grand and pale, the eyes dark, gleaming with sensibility and the light of soul. A face of passion it is, and in the lower part wants firmness,—a face that would inspire women with sentiment, men with interest and curiosity.

His wife died,—they had had no children. His "Annabel Lee" records his recollection of her with something more than tenderness. I suppose his wayward ways caused her much sorrow; but they loved each other truly. She seems to have been a simple affectionate creature, contented on very easy terms, rich with a heart that could bear much, and, most likely, placed its highest hopes elsewhere. She, at all events, did her duty in all purity and goodness, and is gone where these virtues are better understood than here.

Poe had been lecturing on the "Universe" in 1848, and producing his strange great book *Eureka*, on which I shall not attempt to speak critically. In the autumn of 1849 he had, after a sad fit of insane debauchery, made one vigorous effort to emerge. He joined a Temperance Society,—he led a quiet life,— and his marriage was talked of. But on the evening of the 6th of October, 1849—a Saturday evening— passing through Baltimore on his way to New York, accident threw him among some old acquaintances. He plunged into intoxication; and on the Sunday morning he was carried to an hospital, where he died that same evening, at the age of thirty-eight years. No details have been given of this last scene: let us be thankful that we bear not that pain in our memory!

It remains that I should say something of his genius, and the fruits of it which remain with us. Of his character what is there to say? "Theory" of it, or how to "explain" this and that about such a problem, so as to pronounce what his life meant,— only the presumption of pedants ventures on decisions about these matters now-a-days, There is something about the "mystery of a Person"* which we should be very cautious in explaining, though

* CARLYLE.

there are some who think that from a *post-mortem* examination of the body you can learn the soul of a man. The conditions of a man's life, complex as they are, make the real understanding of his character very difficult. Too often, particularly in artificial ages like ours, a man's whole career has to be run, like a race at a fair, in a sack. Many a man never gets fair play—sometimes is born with a constitution that won't permit it—sometimes is born into circumstances that will not. Let us be charitable. Southey's "Doctor," when he heard of a Toper, was wont to say compassionately, "Bibulous clay, sir—bibulous clay!" I would not put forward this compendious excuse for Poe; but we must allow for infirmity in the man. He was indulged early; he was seduced by example. *Because* he left traces of something high and beautiful in him in spite of this, don't let us make that a reason for being harsher on him than on the frail mortals of his race. One pious scribbler told us—very soon after his death—(have they not in America, as here, a rule at all cemeteries that "no dogs are admitted?") that

His faults were many, his virtues few!

But I learn from those who knew him—men like my friend BUCHANAN READ, himself a fine, graceful, tender poet—that his friends loved him, and that those who understood him pardoned his infirmities. Much more should they be pardoned now to one.

> Whose part in all the pomp that fills
> The circuit of the summer hills,
> Is—that his grave is green.   BRYANT.

It has been remarked of him that he united singularly the qualities of the Poet with the faculties of the Analyist. He wrote charming little ballads, and was a curious disentangler of evidence—criminal evidence, for instance—and fond of problems and cipher. The union is indubitable; but I scarcely think it should have been so much dwelt upon. Every man of fine intellect of the highest class includes a capacity more or less for all branches of inquiry. Carlyle was distinguished in arithmetic long before he became the Teacher which we hail him as, now. On the other hand, inventors in the regions of mechanics partake of something poetic in their inspiration. Brindley was as eccentric as Goldsmith. Watt would muse over a tea-kettle as Rossseau did over *la pervenche*, or over the lake into which he dropped sentimental tears. One very curious theory was hit upon by a solid critic a little while ago to explain Poe's two-handedness. He knew that Poe wrote fine poetry—he knew Poe made subtle calculations; and what was his inference? *Credite posteri!* He insisted that the calculating faculty was *the* fact, and that the poetry was calculation! I scarcely ever remember a more curious instance of the " cart being put before the horse"—by the ass! Nothing can be more clear, to be sure, than that Poe employed a great deal of ingenuity and calculation in the finishing of his Tales and polishing of his poems. But all this leaves the poetic inspiration pure at the bottom as the essential fact. Otherwise, if we are to make the calculating the predominant faculty, we may look out for a volume of Sonnets by Cocker! Poe has admitted us, in one of his essays, to the *genesis* of "The Raven," and has even told us which stanza he wrote first, and on what mechanical principles he managed the arrangement of the story. But surely all this presupposes the pure creative genius necessary to the conception?

Keeping the distinction in view, we shall easily see that all his Tales—analytic and other—resolve themselves into poems, instead of the poems resolving themselves into machinery. The "Gold Bug," for example, makes a most ingenious use of cipher, but the cipher is only *matériel*. Without creative genius mere cipher is an affair for the Foreign Office—which still remains a very inferior place to Parnassus. The same remark applies to his other poetical exercises—for such they are—in Mesmerism, Physics, Circumstantial Evidence, &c. Far from being a narrow student of the details of these, he always has clearly an eye in using them to the poetic goal or result.

However, it is with his Poems that our main business is just now. I should say that he was a true poet, first of all. I mean simply, that his view of a piece of scenery, or an event, or a condition of human suffering or joy, will tell itself to you from his lips in a music inseparable from it, and, by dint of perception into the heart of the feelings which such scenery, or event, or condition would naturally awaken in every human soul. There is no occasion for going into recondite inquiries about the "nature of the poet." We see how GOETHE had tired of all that when he tells Eckermann, "lively feeling of situations and power to express them make the poet." I say, take the verses "To Helen," "The Bridal Ballad," "The Sleeper;" take these two lines,—

> The sad waters, sad and chilly,
> With the snows of the lolling lily,—

if we do not find poetry in these places, where are we to look for it? It is easy to talk about the "deep heart," &c., and there are half-a-dozen unreadable gentlemen always ready to assure one that poetry is gone to the dogs—all except their own; but submit Poe's volume to persons most habitually conversant with all poetry, and they will admit that the charm of it is in his book. Those who may deny that he is a *great*—have no right to deny that he is a *true* poet As *un gentilhomme est toujours gentilhomme*, so a real poet, of course, ranks with the family. The head of a family is perhaps a duke; but every cadet, however distant, shares the blood.

My remark on a point in his youthful poems extends to all his poems. Traces of spiritual emotion are not to be found there. Sorrow there is, but not divine sorrow. There is not any approach to the Holy —to the holiness which mingles with all Tennyson's poetry—as the Presence with the wine. And yet, when you view his poems simply as poems, this characteristic does not make itself felt as a want. It would seem as if he had only to deal with the Beautiful as a human aspirant. His soul thirsted for the "supernal loveliness." That thirst was to him religion—all the religion you discover in him. But if we cannot call him religious, we may say that he supplies the materials of worship. You want flowers and fruit for your altar; and wherever Poe's muse has passed, flowers and fruit are fairer and brighter.

With all this passion for the Beautiful, no poet was ever less voluptuous. He never profaned his genius, whatever else he profaned. "Irene," "Ulalume," "Lenore," "Annabel Lee," "Annie," are all gentle, and innocent, and fairy-like. A sound of music—rising as from an unseen Ariel—brings in a most pure and lovely figure—sad, usually; so delicate and dreamy are these conceptions, that indeed they hint only of some transcendent beauty—some region where passion has no place, where

> Music, and moonlight, and feeling,
> Are one,

as Shelley says.

Poe loved splendour,—he delighted in the gorgeous—in ancient birth—in tropical flowers—in southern birds—in castellated dwellings. The hero of his "Raven" sits on a "violet velvet lining;" the dead have "crested palls." He delighted, as Johnson says of Collins, "to gaze on the magnificence of golden palaces, to repose by the waterfalls of Elysian gardens." His scenery is everywhere magnificent. His genius is always waited upon with the splendour of an oriental monarch.

I have spoken of the tinge of melancholy which gives an effect like moonlight to all that he has done. I have said elsewhere that his "genius, like the eyes of a southern girl, is at once dark and luminous."* "The Raven," "Ulalume," "For Annie," all turn on death. And this melancholy, too, is of a heathen character. You might say that his book is *funestus*. The stamp of sorrow is upon it,—as cypress hung over the doors of a house among the ancients when death had entered there. Remembering this, one must admit that his range is narrow. He has, for instance, no humour—he had little sympathy with the various forms of man's life. No one can claim for him a rich dramatic humanity, such as makes much of the charm and some of the greatness of our great poet Browning. But he is perfectly poetic in his own province. If his circle is a narrow, it is a

* *Singleton Fontenoy*, vol. ii.

magic one. His poetry is sheer poetry, and borrows nothing from without, as didatic poetry does. For didactic poetry he had a very strong and a very natural dislike.

His melody is his own. You will find a music in each poem which is inseparable from the sentiment of it. He gives a certain musical air, as a soul, to each poem, but he works up the details of the execution like an artist. Witness "The Raven" or "The Bells." Everything he has done is finished in detail, and has received its final touches. He had an exquisite eye for proportion, and every little poem is carved like a cameo.

Such are the hints which I have to prefix to this American poet. And with three-times-three from a select band of his admirers he is now launched on the English public!

JAMES HANNAY.

London, November, 1852.

PREFATORY NOTICE.

DURING the summer of 1867 I had the opportunity (which I had often wished for) of expressing in print my estimate and admiration of the works of the American poet Walt Whitman.* Like a stone dropped into a pond, an article of that sort may spread out its concentric circles of consequences. One of these is the invitation which I have received to edit a selection from Whitman's writings; virtually the first sample of his work ever published in England, and offering the first tolerably fair chance he has had of making his way with English readers on his own showing. Hitherto, such readers—except the small percentage of them to whom it has happened to come across the poems in some one of their American editions—have picked acquaintance with them only through the medium of newspaper extracts and criticisms, mostly short-sighted, sneering, and depreciatory, and rather intercepting than forwarding the candid construction which people might be willing to put upon the poems, alike in their beauties and their aberrations. Some English critics, no doubt, have been more discerning—as W. J. Fox, of old, in the *Dispatch*, the writer of the notice in the *Leader*, and of late two in the

* See *The Chronicle* for 6th July 1867, article *Walt Whitman's Poems*.

Pall Mall Gazette and the *London Review;** but these have been the exceptions among us, the great majority of the reviewers presenting that happy and familiar critical combination—scurrility and superciliousness.

As it was my lot to set down so recently several of the considerations which seem to me most essential and most obvious in regard to Whitman's writings, I can scarcely now recur to the subject without either repeating something of what I then said, or else leaving unstated some points of principal importance. I shall therefore adopt the simplest course—that of summarising the critical remarks in my former article; after which, I shall leave without further development (ample as is the amount of development most of them would claim) the particular topics there glanced at, and shall proceed to some other phases of the subject.

Whitman republished in 1867 his complete poetical works in one moderate-sized volume, consisting of the whole *Leaves of Grass*, with a sort of supplement thereto named *Songs before Parting*,† and of the *Drum Taps*, with its *Sequel*. It has been intimated that he does not expect to write any more poems, unless it might be in expression of the religious side of man's nature. However, one poem on the last American harvest sown and reaped by those who had been soldiers in the great war, has already appeared since the volume in question, and has been republished in England.

Whitman's poems present no trace of rhyme, save in a couple or so of chance instances. Parts of them, indeed, may be regarded as a warp of prose amid the weft of poetry,

---

* Since this Prefatory Notice was written [in 1868], another eulogistic review of Whitman has appeared—that by Mr. Robert Buchanan, in the *Broadway*.

† In a copy of the book revised by Whitman himself, which we have seen, this title is modified into *Songs of Parting*.

such as Shakespeare furnishes the precedent for in drama. Still there is a very powerful and majestic rhythmical sense throughout.

Lavish and persistent has been the abuse poured forth upon Whitman by his own countrymen; the tricklings of the British press give but a moderate idea of it. The poet is known to repay scorn with scorn. Emerson can, however, from the first be claimed as on Whitman's side; nor, it is understood after some inquiry, has that great thinker since then retreated from this position in fundamentals, although his admiration may have entailed some worry upon him, and reports of his recantation have been rife. Of other writers on Whitman's side, expressing themselves with no measured enthusiasm, one may cite Mr. M. D. Conway; Mr. W. D. O'Connor, who wrote a pamphlet named *The Good Grey Poet;* and Mr. John Burroughs, author of *Walt Whitman as Poet and Person*, published quite recently in New York. His thorough-paced admirers declare Whitman to be beyond rivalry *the* poet of the epoch; an estimate which, startling as it will sound at the first, may nevertheless be upheld, on the grounds that Whitman is beyond all his competitors a man of the period, one of audacious personal ascendant, incapable of all compromise, and an initiator in the scheme and form of his works.

Certain faults are charged against him, and, as far as they are true, shall frankly stand confessed—some of them as very serious faults. Firstly, he speaks on occasion of gross things in gross, crude, and plain terms. Secondly, he uses some words absurd or ill-constructed, others which produce a jarring effect in poetry, or indeed in any lofty literature. Thirdly, he sins from time to time by being obscure, fragmentary, and agglomerative—giving long strings of successive and detached items, not, however, devoid of a certain primitive effectiveness. Fourthly, his self-assertion is boundless; yet not always to be understood as strictly or merely personal to himself, but sometimes as vicarious, the poet speaking on behalf of all men, and every man and woman. These and any other faults appear most harshly on a cursory reading; Whitman is a poet who bears and needs to be read as a whole, and then the volume and torrent of his power carry the disfigurements along with it, and away.

The subject-matter of Whitman's poems, taken individually, is absolutely miscellaneous: he touches upon any and every subject. But he has prefixed to his last edition an "Inscription" in the following terms, showing that the key-words of the whole book are two—"One's-self" and "En Masse:"—

> Small is the theme of the following chaut, yet the greatest—namely, ONE'S-SELF; that wondrous thing, a simple separate person. That, for the use of the New World, I sing.
> Man's physiology complete, from top to toe, I sing. Not physiognomy alone, nor brain alone, is worthy for the Muse: I say the form complete is worthier far. The female equally with the male I sing.
> Nor cease at the theme of One's-self. I speak the word of the modern, the word EN MASSE.
> My days I sing, and the lands—with interstice I knew of hapless war.
> O friend, whoe'er you are, at last arriving hither to commence, I feel through every leaf the pressure of your hand, which I return. And thus upon our journey linked together let us go.

The book, then, taken as a whole, is the poem both of Personality and of Democracy; and, it may be added, of American nationalism. It is *par excellence* the modern poem. It is distinguished also by this peculiarity—that in it the most literal view of things is continually merging into the most rhapsodic or passionately abstract. Picturesqueness it has, but mostly of a somewhat patriarchal kind, not deriving from the "word-painting" of the *littérateur;* a certain echo of the old Hebrew poetry may even be caught in it, extra-modern though it is. Another most prominent and pervading quality of the book is the exuberant physique of the author. The conceptions are throughout those of a man in robust health, and might alter much under different conditions.

Further, there is a strong tone of paradox in Whitman's writings. He is both a realist and an optimist in extreme measure: he contemplates evil as in some sense not existing, or, if existing, then as being of as much importance as anything else. Not that he is a materialist; on the contrary, he is a most strenuous assertor of the soul, and, with the soul, of the body as its infallible associate and vehicle in the present frame of things. Neither does he drift into fatalism or indifferentism; the energy of his temperament, and ever-fresh sympathy with national and other developments, being an effectual bar to this. The paradoxical element of the poems is such that one may sometimes find them in conflict with what has preceded, and would not be much surprised if they said at any moment the reverse of whatever they do say. This is mainly due to the multiplicity of the aspects of things, and to the immense width of relation in which Whitman stands to all sorts and all aspects of them.

But the greatest of this poet's distinctions is his absolute and entire originality. He may be termed formless by those who, not without much reason to show for themselves, are wedded to the established forms and ratified refinements of poetic art; but it seems reasonable to enlarge the canon till it includes so great and startling a genius, rather than to draw it close and exclude him. His work is practically certain to stand as archetypal for many future poetic efforts —so great is his power as an originator, so fervid his initiative. It forms incomparably the *largest* performance of our period in poetry. Victor Hugo's *Légende des Siècles* alone might be named with it for largeness, and even that with much less of a new starting-point in conception and treatment. Whitman breaks with all precedent. To what he himself perceives and knows he has a personal relation of the intensest kind: to anything in the way of prescription, no relation at all. But he is saved from isolation by the depth of his Americanism; with the movement of his predominant nation he is moved. His comprehension, energy, and tenderness are all extreme, and all inspired by actualities. And, as for poetic genius, those who, without being ready to concede that faculty to Whitman, confess his iconoclastic boldness and his Titanic power of temperament, working in the sphere of poetry, do in effect confess his genius as well.

Such, still further condensed, was the critical summary which I gave of Whitman's position among poets. It remains to say something a little more precise of the particular qualities of his works. And first, not to slur over defects, I shall extract some sentences from a letter which a friend, most highly entitled to form and express an opinion on any poetic question—one, too, who abundantly upholds the greatness of Whitman as a poet—has addressed to me with regard to the criticism above condensed. His observations, though severe on this individual point, appear to me not other than correct. "I don't think that you quite put strength enough into your blame on one side, while you make at least enough of minor faults or eccentricities. To me it seems always that Whitman's great flaw is a fault of debility, not an excess of strength—I mean his bluster. His own personal and national self-reliance and arrogance, I need not tell you, I applaud, and sympathise and rejoice in; but the blatant ebullience of feeling and speech, at times, is feeble for so great a poet of so great a people. He is in part certainly the poet of democracy; but not wholly, *because* he tries so openly to be, and asserts so violently that he is—always as if he was fighting the case out on a platform. This is the only thing I really or greatly dislike or revolt from. On the whole" (adds my correspondent), "my admiration and enjoyment of his greatness grow keener and warmer every time I think of him"—a feeling, I may be permitted to observe, which is fully shared by myself, and, I suppose, by all who consent in any adequate measure to recognise Whitman, and to yield themselves to his influence.

To continue. Besides originality and daring, which have been already insisted upon, width and intensity are leading characteristics of his writings—width both of subject-matter and of comprehension, intensity of self-absorption into what the poet contemplates and expresses. He scans and presents an enormous panorama, unrolled before him as from a mountain-top; and yet, whatever most large or most minute or casual thing his eye glances upon, that he enters into with a depth of affection which identifies him with it for a time, be the object what it may. There is a singular interchange also of actuality and of ideal substratum and suggestion. While he sees men, with even abnormal exactness and sympathy, as men, he sees them also "as trees walking," and admits us to perceive that the whole show is in a measure spectral and unsubstantial, and the mask of a larger and profounder reality beneath it, of which it is giving perpetual intimations and auguries. He is the poet indeed of literality, but of passionate and significant literality, full of indirections as well as directness, and of readings between the lines. If he is the 'cutest of Yankees, he is also as truly an enthusiast as any the most typical poet. All his faculties and performance glow into a white heat of brotherliness; and there is a *poignancy* both of tenderness and of beauty about his finer works which discriminates them quite as much as their modernness, audacity, or any other exceptional point. If the reader wishes to see the great and more intimate powers of Whitman in their fullest expression, he may consult the *Nocturn for the Death of Lincoln;* than which it would be difficult to find anywhere a purer, more elevated, more poetic, more ideally abstract, or at the same time more pathetically personal, threnody—uniting the thrilling chords of grief, of beauty, of triumph, and of final unfathomed satisfaction. With all his singularities, Whitman is a master of words and of sounds: he has them at his command—made for, and instinct with, his purpose—messengers of unsurpassable sympathy and intelligence between himself and his readers. The entire book may be called the pæan of the natural man—not of the merely physical, still less of the disjunctively intellectual or spiritual man, but of him who, being a man first and foremost, is therein also a spirit and an intellect.

There is a singular and impressive intuition or revelation of Swedenborg's: that the whole of heaven is in the form of one man, and the separate societies of heaven in the forms of the several parts of man. In a large sense, the general drift of Whitman's writings, even down to the passages which read as most bluntly physical, bear a striking correspondence or analogy to this dogma. He takes man, and every organism and faculty of man, as the unit—the datum—from which all that we know, discern, and speculate, of abstract and supersensual, as well as of concrete and sensual, has to be computed. He knows of nothing nobler than that unit man; but, knowing that, he can use it for any multiple, and for any dynamical extension or recast.

Let us next obtain some idea of what this most remarkable poet—the founder of *American* poetry rightly to be so called, and the most sonorous poetic voice of the tangibilities of actual and prospective democracy—is in his proper life and person.

Walt Whitman was born at the farm-village of West Hills, Long Island, in the State of New York, and about thirty miles distant from the capital, on the 31st of May 1819. His father's family, English by origin, had already been settled in this locality for five generations. His mother, named Louisa van Velsor, was of Dutch extraction, and came from Cold Spring, Queen's County, about three miles from West Hills. "A fine-looking old lady" she has been termed in her advanced age. A large family ensued from the marriage. The father was a farmer, and afterwards a carpenter and builder; both parents adhered in religion to "the great Quaker iconoclast, Elias Hicks." Walt was schooled at Brooklyn, a suburb of New York, and began life at the age of thirteen, working as a printer, later on as a country teacher, and then as a miscellaneous press-writer in New York. From 1837 to 1848 he had, as Mr. Burroughs too promiscuously expresses it, "sounded all experiences of life, with all their passions, pleasures, and abandonments." In 1849 he began travelling, and became at New Orleans a newspaper editor, and at Brooklyn, two years afterwards, a printer. He next followed his father's business of carpenter and builder. In 1862, after the breaking-out of the great Civil War, in which his enthusiastic unionism and also his anti-slavery feelings attached him inseparably though not rancorously to the good cause of the North, he undertook the nursing of the sick and wounded in the field, writing also a correspondence in the *New York Times*. I am informed that it was through Emerson's intervention that he obtained the sanction of President Lincoln for this purpose of charity, with authority to draw the ordinary army rations; Whitman stipulating at the same time that he would not receive any remuneration for his services. The first immediate occasion of his going down to camp was on behalf of his brother, Lieutenant-Colonel George W. Whitman, of the 51st New York Veterans, who had been struck in the face by a piece of shell at Fredericksburg. From the spring of 1863 this nursing, both in the field and more especially in hospital at Washington, became his "one daily and nightly occupation;" and the strongest testimony is borne to his measureless self-devotion and kindliness in the work, and to the unbounded fascination, a kind of magnetic attraction and ascendency, which he exercised over the patients, often with the happiest sanitary results. Northerner or Southerner, the belligerents received the same tending from him. It is said that by the end of the war he had personally ministered to upwards of 100,000 sick and wounded. In a Washington hospital he caught, in the summer of 1864, the first illness he had ever known, caused by poison absorbed into the system in attending some of the worst cases of gangrene. It disabled him for six months. He returned to the hospitals towards the beginning of 1865, and obtained also a clerkship in the Department of the Interior. It should be added that, though he never actually joined the army as a combatant, he made a point of putting down his name on the enrolment-lists for the draft, to take his chance as it might happen for serving the country in arms. The reward of his devotedness came at the end of June 1865, in the form of dismissal from his clerkship by the minister, Mr. Harlan, who learned that Whitman was the author of the *Leaves of Grass;* a book whose outspokenness, or (as the official chief considered it) immorality, raised a holy horror in the ministerial breast. The poet, however, soon obtained another modest but creditable post in the office of the Attorney-General. He still visits the hospitals on Sundays, and often on other days as well.

The portrait of Mr. Whitman reproduced in the present volume is taken from an engraving after a daguerreotype given in the original *Leaves of Grass*. He is much above the average size, and noticeably well-proportioned—a model of physique and of health, and, by natural consequence, as fully and finely related to all physical facts by his bodily constitution as to all mental and spiritual facts by his mind and his consciousness. He is now, however, old-looking for his years, and might even (according to the statement of one of his enthusiasts, Mr. O'Connor) have passed for being beyond the age for the draft when the war was going on. The same gentleman, in confutation of any inferences which might be drawn from the *Leaves of Grass* by a Harlan or other Holy Willie, affirms that "one more irreproachable in his relations to the other sex lives not upon this earth"—an assertion which one must take as one finds it, having neither confirmatory nor traversing evidence at hand. Whitman has light blue eyes, a florid complexion, a fleecy beard now grey, and a quite peculiar sort of magnetism about him in relation to those with whom he comes in contact. His ordinary appearance is masculine and cheerful: he never shows depression of spirits, and is sufficiently undemonstrative, and even somewhat silent in company. He has always been carried by predilection towards the society of the common people; but is not the less for that open to refined and artistic impressions—fond of operatic and other good music, and discerning in works of art. As to either praise or blame of what he writes, he is totally indifferent, not to say scornful—having in fact a very decisive opinion of his own concerning its calibre and destinies. Thoreau, a very congenial spirit, said of Whitman, "He is Democracy;" and again, "After all, he suggests something a little more than human." Lincoln broke out into the exclamation, "Well, *he* looks like a man!" Whitman responded to the instinctive appreciation of the President, considering him (it is said by Mr. Burroughs) " by far the noblest and purest of the political characters of the time;" and, if anything can cast, in the eyes of posterity, an added halo of brightness round the unsullied personal qualities and the great doings of Lincoln, it will assuredly be the written monument reared to him by Whitman.

The best sketch that I know of Whitman as an accessible human individual is that given by Mr. Conway.* I borrow from it the following few details. "Having occasion to visit New York soon after the appearance of Walt Whitman's book, I was urged by some friends to search him out. . . . The day was excessively hot, the thermometer at nearly 100°, and the sun blazed down as only on sandy Long Island can the sun blaze. . . . I saw stretched upon his back, and gazing up straight at the terrible sun, the man I was seeking. With his grey clothing, his blue-grey shirt, his iron-grey hair, his swart sunburnt face and bare neck, he lay upon the brown-and-white grass—for the sun had burnt away its greenness—and was so like the earth upon which he rested that he seemed almost enough a part of it for one to pass by without recognition. I approached him, gave my name and reason for searching him out, and asked him if he did not find the sun rather hot. 'Not at all too hot,' was his reply; and he confided to me that this was one of his favourite places and attitudes

* In the *Fortnightly Review*, 15th October 1866.

for composing 'poems.' He then walked with me to his home, and took me along its narrow ways to his room. A small room of about fifteen feet square, with a single window looking out on the barren solitudes of the island; a small cot; a wash-stand with a little looking-glass hung over it from a tack in the wall; a pine table with pen, ink, and paper on it; an old line-engraving representing Bacchus, hung on the wall, and opposite a similar one of Silenus; these constituted the visible environments of Walt Whitman. There was not, apparently, a single book in the room. . . . The books he seemed to know and love best were the Bible, Homer, and Shakespeare: these he owned, and probably had in his pockets while we were talking. He had two studies where he read; one was the top of an omnibus, and the other a small mass of sand, then entirely uninhabited, far out in the ocean, called Coney Island. . . . The only distinguished contemporary he had ever met was the Rev. Henry Ward Beecher, of Brooklyn, who had visited him. . . . He confessed to having no talent for industry, and that his forte was 'loafing and writing poems:' he was poor, but had discovered that he could, on the whole, live magnificently on bread and water. . . . On no occasion did he laugh, nor indeed did I ever see him smile."

The first trace of Whitman as a writer is in the pages of the *Democratic Review* in or about 1841. Here he wrote some prose tales and sketches—poor stuff mostly, so far as I have seen of them, yet not to be wholly confounded with the commonplace. One of them is a tragic school-incident, which may be surmised to have fallen under his personal observation in his early experience as a teacher. His first poem of any sort was named *Blood Money*, in denunciation of the Fugitive Slave Law, which severed him from the

Democratic party. His first considerable work was the *Leaves of Grass*. He began it in 1853, and it underwent two or three complete rewritings prior to its publication at Brooklyn in 1855, in a quarto volume—peculiar-looking, but with something perceptibly artistic about it. The type of that edition was set up entirely by himself. He was moved to undertake this formidable poetic work (as indicated in a private letter of Whitman's, from which Mr. Conway has given a sentence or two) by his sense of the great materials which America could offer for a really American poetry, and by his contempt for the current work of his compatriots—"either the poetry of an elegantly weak sentimentalism, at bottom nothing but maudlin puerilities or more or less musical verbiage, arising out of a life of depression and enervation as their result; or else that class of poetry, plays, &c., of which the foundation is feudalism, with its ideas of lords and ladies, its imported standard of gentility, and the manners of European high-life-below-stairs in every line and verse." Thus incited to poetic self-expression, Whitman (adds Mr. Conway) "wrote on a sheet of paper, in large letters, these words, 'Make the Work,' and fixed it above his table, where he could always see it whilst writing. Thenceforth every cloud that flitted over him, every distant sail, every face and form encountered, wrote a line in his book."

The *Leaves of Grass* excited no sort of notice until a letter from Emerson[*] appeared, expressing a deep sense of its power and magnitude. He termed it "the most extraordinary piece of wit and wisdom that America has yet con-

---

[*] Mr. Burroughs (to whom I have recourse for most biographical facts concerning Whitman) is careful to note, in order that no misapprehension may arise on the subject, that, up to the time of his publishing the *Leaves of Grass*, the author had not read either the essays or the poems of Emerson.

tributed." The edition of about a thousand copies sold off in less than a year. Towards the end of 1856 a second edition in 16mo appeared, printed in New York, also of about a thousand copies. Its chief feature was an additional poem beginning "A Woman waits for me." It excited a considerable storm. Another edition, of about four to five thousand copies, duodecimo, came out at Boston in 1860-61, including a number of new pieces. The *Drum Taps*, consequent upon the war, with their *Sequel*, which comprises the poem on Lincoln, followed in 1865; and in 1867, as I have already noted, a complete edition of all the poems, including a supplement named *Songs before Parting*. The first of all the *Leaves of Grass*, in point of date, was the long and powerful composition entitled *Walt Whitman*—perhaps the most typical and memorable of all of his productions, but shut out from the present selection for reasons given further on. The final edition shows numerous and considerable variations from all its precursors; evidencing once again that Whitman is by no means the rough-and-ready writer, panoplied in rude art and egotistic self-sufficiency, that many people suppose him to be. Even since this issue, the book has been slightly revised by its author's own hand, with a special view to possible English circulation. The copy so revised has reached me (through the liberal and friendly hands of Mr. Conway) after my selection had already been decided on; and the few departures from the last printed text which might on comparison be found in the present volume are due to my having had the advantage of following this revised copy. In all other respects I have felt bound to reproduce the last edition, without so much as considering whether here and there I might personally prefer the readings of the earlier issues.

The selection here offered to the English reader contains

a little less than half the entire bulk of Whitman's poetry. My choice has proceeded upon two simple rules: first, to omit entirely every poem which could with any tolerable fairness be deemed offensive to the feelings of morals or propriety in this peculiarly nervous age; and, second, to include every remaining poem which appeared to me of conspicuous beauty or interest. I have also inserted the very remarkable prose preface which Whitman printed in the original edition of *Leaves of Grass*, an edition that has become a literary rarity. This preface has not been reproduced in any later publication, although its materials have to some extent been worked up into poems of a subsequent date.* From this prose composition, contrary to what has been my rule with any of the poems, it has appeared to me permissible to omit two or three short phrases which would have shocked ordinary readers, and the retention of which, had I held it obligatory, would have entailed the exclusion of the preface itself as a whole.

A few words must be added as to the indecencies scattered through Whitman's writings. Indecencies or improprieties —or, still better, deforming crudities—they may rightly be termed; to call them immoralities would be going too far. Whitman finds himself, and other men and women, to be a compound of soul and body; he finds that body plays an extremely prominent and determining part in whatever he and other mundane dwellers have cognisance of; he perceives this to be the necessary condition of things, and therefore, as he fully and openly accepts it, the right condition; and he knows of no reason why what is universally seen and known, necessary and right, should not also be allowed and proclaimed in speech. That such a view of the matter is entitled to a great deal of weight, and at any rate to candid

---

* Compare, for instance, the Preface, pp. 38, 39, with the poem *To a Foiled Revolter or Revoltress*, p. 133.

consideration and construction, appears to me not to admit of a doubt; neither is it dubious that the contrary view, the only view which a mealy-mouthed British nineteenth century admits as endurable, amounts to the condemnation of nearly every great or eminent literary work of past time, whatever the century it belongs to, the country it comes from, the department of writing it illustrates, or the degree or sort of merit it possesses. Tenth, second, or first century before Christ—first, eighth, fourteenth, fifteenth, sixteenth, seventeenth, or even eighteenth century A.D.—it is still the same: no book whose subject-matter admits as possible of an impropriety according to current notions can be depended upon to fail of containing such impropriety,—can, if those notions are accepted as the canon, be placed with a sense of security in the hands of girls and youths, or read aloud to women; and this holds good just as much of severely moral or plainly descriptive as of avowedly playful, knowing, or licentious books. For my part, I am far from thinking that earlier state of literature, and the public feeling from which it sprang, the wrong ones—and our present condition the only right one. Equally far, therefore, am I from indignantly condemning Whitman for every startling allusion or expression which he has admitted into his book, and which I, from motives of policy, have excluded from this selection; except, indeed, that I think many of his tabooed passages are extremely raw and ugly on the ground of poetic or literary art, whatever aspect they may bear in morals. I have been rigid in exclusion, because it appears to me highly desirable that a fair verdict on Whitman should now be pronounced in England on poetic grounds alone; and because it was clearly impossible that the book, with its audacities of topic and of expression included, should run the same chance of justice, and of circulation through refined minds and hands, which may possibly be accorded to it after the rejection of all such peccant poems. As already intimated, I have not in a single instance excised any *parts* of poems: to do so would have been, I conceive, no less wrongful towards the illustrious American than repugnant, and indeed unendurable, to myself, who aspire to no Bowdlerian honours. The consequence is, that the reader loses *in toto* several important poems, and some extremely fine ones—notably the one previously alluded to, of quite exceptional value and excellence, entitled *Walt Whitman*. I sacrifice them grudgingly; and yet willingly, because I believe this to be the only thing to do with due regard to the one reasonable object which a selection can subserve—that of paving the way towards the issue and unprejudiced reception of a complete edition of the poems in England. For the benefit of misconstructionists, let me add in distinct terms that, in respect of morals and propriety, I neither admire nor approve the incriminated passages in Whitman's poems, but, on the contrary, consider that most of them would be much better away; and, in respect of art, I doubt whether even one of them deserves to be retained in the exact phraseology it at present exhibits. This, however, does not amount to saying that Whitman is a vile man, or a corrupt or corrupting writer; he is none of these.

The only division of his poems into sections, made by Whitman himself, has been noted above: *Leaves of Grass*, *Songs before Parting*, supplementary to the preceding, and *Drum Taps*, with their *Sequel*. The peculiar title, *Leaves of Grass*, has become almost inseparable from the name of Whitman; it seems to express with some aptness the simplicity, universality, and spontaneity of the poems to which it is applied. *Songs before Parting* may indicate that these compositions close Whitman's poetic roll. *Drum Taps* are, of course, songs of the Civil War, and their *Sequel* is mainly on the same theme: the chief poem in this last section being the one on the death of Lincoln. These titles all apply to fully arranged series of compositions. The present volume is not in the same sense a fully arranged series, but a selection; and the relation of the poems *inter se* appears to me to depend on altered conditions, which, however narrowed they are, it may be as well frankly to recognise in practice. I have therefore redistributed the poems (a latitude of action which I trust the author may not object to), bringing together those whose subject-matter seems to warrant it, however far separated they may possibly be in the original volume. At the same time, I have retained some characteristic terms used by Whitman himself, and have named my sections respectively—

1. Chants Democratic (poems of democracy).
2. Drum Taps (war songs).
3. Walt Whitman (personal poems).
4. Leaves of Grass (unclassified poems).
5. Songs of Parting (missives).

The first three designations explain themselves. The fourth, *Leaves of Grass*, is not so specially applicable to the particular poems of that section here as I should have liked it to be; but I could not consent to drop this typical name. The *Songs of Parting*, my fifth section, are compositions in which the poet expresses his own sentiment regarding his works, in which he forecasts their future, or consigns them to the reader's consideration. It deserves mention that, in the copy of Whitman's last American edition revised by his own hand, as previously noticed, the series termed *Songs of Parting* has been recast, and made to consist of poems of the same character as those included in my section No. 5.

Comparatively few of Whitman's poems have been endowed by himself with titles properly so called. Most of them are merely headed with the opening words of the poems themselves—as "I was looking a long while;" "To get betimes in Boston Town;" "When lilacs last in the door-yard bloomed;" and so on. It seems to me that in a selection such a lengthy and circuitous method of identifying the poems is not desirable: I should wish them to be remembered by brief, repeatable, and significant titles. I have therefore supplied titles of my own to such pieces as bear none in the original edition: wherever a real title appears in that edition, I have retained it.

With these remarks I commend to the English reader the ensuing selection from a writer whom I sincerely believe to be, whatever his faults, of the order of *great* poets, and by no means of pretty good ones. I would urge the reader not to ask himself, and not to return any answer to the questions, whether or not this poet is like other poets—whether or not the particular application of rules of art which is found to hold good in the works of those others, and to constitute a part of their excellence, can be traced also in Whitman. Let the questions rather be—Is he powerful? Is he American? Is he new? Is he rousing? Does he feel and make me feel? I entertain no doubt as to the response which in due course of time will be returned to these questions and such as these, in America, in England, and elsewhere—or to the further question, "Is Whitman then indeed a true and a great poet?" Lincoln's verdict bespeaks the ultimate decision upon him, in his books as in his habit as he lives—"Well, *he* looks like a man."

Walt Whitman occupies at the present moment a unique position on the globe, and one which, even in past time, can have been occupied by only an infinitesimally small number of men. He is the one man who entertains and professes respecting himself the grave conviction that he is the actual and prospective founder of a new poetic literature, and a great one—a literature proportional to the material vastness and the unmeasured destinies of America: he believes that the Columbus of the continent or the Washington of the States was not more truly than himself in the future a founder and upbuilder of this America. Surely a sublime conviction, and expressed more than once in magnificent words—none more so than the lines beginning

"Come, I will make this continent indissoluble." *

Were the idea untrue, it would still be a glorious dream, which a man of genius might be content to live in and die for: but is it untrue? Is it not, on the contrary, true, if not absolutely, yet with a most genuine and substantial approximation? I believe it *is* thus true. I believe that Whitman is one of the huge, as yet mainly unrecognised, forces of our time; privileged to evoke, in a country hitherto still asking for its poet, a fresh, athletic, and American poetry, and predestined to be traced up to by generation after generation of believing and ardent—let us hope not servile—disciples.

"Poets are the unacknowledged legislators of the world." Shelley, who knew what he was talking about when poetry was the subject, has said it, and with a profundity of truth. Whitman seems in a peculiar degree marked out for "legis-

---

* See the poem headed *Love of Comrades*, p. 308.

lation" of the kind referred to. His voice will one day be potential or magisterial wherever the English language is spoken—that is to say, in the four corners of the earth; and in his own American hemisphere, the uttermost avatars of democracy will confess him not more their announcer than their inspirer.

1868.   W. M. ROSSETTI.

N.B.—The above prefatory notice was written in 1868, and is reproduced practically unaltered. Were it to be brought up to the present date, 1886, I should have to mention Whitman's books *Two Rivulets* and *Specimen-days and Collect*, and the fact that for several years past he has been partially disabled by a paralytic attack. He now lives at Camden, New Jersey.

1886.   W. M. R.

MEMOIR

Arthur Hugh Clough, born at Liverpool, Jan. 1, 1819, was educated at Rugby. His career there has been sketched by a distinguished schoolfellow, from whose interesting notice the following lines are extracted. Arthur Stanley thus writes:—

'Of all the scholars at Rugby School, in the time when Arnold's influence was at its height, there was none who so completely represented the place in all its phases as Clough. He had come there as a very young boy, and gradually worked his way from form to form till he reached the top of the school. He did not, like some of the more distinguished of his contemporaries, hold aloof from the common world of schoolboy life, but mingled freely in the games and sports of his schoolfellows. He received also into an unusually susceptible and eager mind the whole force of that electric shock which Arnold communicated to all his better pupils. Over the career of none of his pupils did Arnold watch with a livelier interest or a more sanguine hope. By none, during those last years of school life, or first years of college life, was that interest more actively reciprocated in the tribute of enthusiastic affection than by Clough.

'He came up to Oxford, and carried away the Balliol scholarship with a renown beyond that of any of his predecessors. I remember, even to this day, the reverberation of the profound sensation occasioned in the Common-room of that College, already famous, when his youthful English essay was read aloud to the assembled Fellows. From Balliol he was elected (1842) to a Fellowship at Oriel — a distinction still at that time retaining something of its original splendour, and rectifying the sometimes ill-adjusted balance (as had happened in Clough's case) of the honours of the University.'

Clough's residence at Oxford was cast at a time when one of the theological tempests, which during the last hundred years have so often arisen there, was raging at its fiercest. It was a controversy from which few could hold aloof — least of all, a mind lively, susceptible and speculative. And for awhile the movement of that day attracted him, by holding out the ideal of a more devoted and unselfish life, and a higher sense of duty, than the common. But he learned early to distrust a theory not resting on honest acceptance of our human nature, and was soon named as one of the foremost who battled for just freedom of opinion and speech, for liberation from what he esteemed archaeological formulas, for more conscientious fulfilment of obligation towards the students — for a wider course of studies, lastly, than those who had grown up under the older system were willing to contemplate. Hence all who longed for that more comprehensive university of which they have since seen the beginning, looked on Clough as amongst their leaders; and his influence was always towards whatever should incline others to a liberal view of the questions of the day, of the claims of the feeble, and the feelings of the poor; —verging gradually to what, in a phrase which now seems itself an echo from the past, were considered ' democratic tendencies.' Plainer living and higher thinking were the texts on which he gave us many a humorous and admirable lesson. In all his dealings, the most casual observer would have felt, here was a man who loved truth and justice, not coldly and afar off, as most, but with passion and intensely; and against what he judged wrong and meanness in high places, he fought with an unselfish courage and a spirit which did good to all honest hearts.

One instance is too characteristic of the man to be passed over. He always held in horror the selfish deductions which (he thought) were often made from some doctrines of Political Economy:— and when the Irish famine took place, he advocated the relief fund which was set up in Oxford in a very plain-spoken and vigorous pamphlet, urging the immediate suppression of certain academical luxurious habits, and, above all, requiring from us sympathy with the distressed as an imperious duty.

It would, however, be no true picture of Clough in his youth, that presented him mainly as a ' practical man;' indeed a certain unaptness or want of shrewd rapidity (as shown in his honours' examination), a sensitive fairness and chivalrous openness of dealing, marked him rather as the poet who walked the world's way as matter of duty, living a life, meanwhile, hidden with higher and holier things, with the friends and books he loved so fondly, with deep solitary thought, with Nature in her wildness and her majesty. Cast on days of change and developement, his strong moral impulses threw him into the sphere of warfare; yet he was no 'born reformer;' was diffident of his own conclusions; had no clean-cut decisive system, nay, thought experience proved the narrowness of such; and was beyond those fetters of 'logical consistency' which played so great a part in the controversies of the time. Many fragments of his verse show that whilst roused to a spirit of resolute self-reliance by what went on around him, he felt how much the war of conscience and conviction must be carried on within, until some clearer light should break upon the enquirer.

> O let me love my love unto myself alone,
> And know my knowledge to the world unknown;
> No witness to the vision call,
> Beholding unbeheld of all;
> And worship thee, with thee withdrawn apart,
> Whoe'er, whate'er thou art,
> Within the closest veil of mine own inmost heart.

Or, again, we find the voice of sound worldly wisdom expressing itself in the Siren strains which are not confined to the invitations of pleasure:

> Better it were, thou sayest, to consent;
> Feast while we may, and live ere life be spent;

> Close up clear eyes, and call the unstable sure,
> The unlovely lovely, and the filthy pure.

Here, too, 'there is much to be said on both sides;' but one can foretell the poet's answer.

To these years belongs, also, the series of poems published in 1849, (and now reprinted with omissions marked by the author), under the title *Ambarvalia*. This contains several pieces of which it has been justly said, 'that they will hold their place beside those of Tennyson and Browning':—to friends looking at the little volume, however, as an exhibition of Clough's own mind, we trace him characteristically in a certain caprice or overfantasy of taste, in a subtle and far-fetched mode of reasoning which returns to plain conclusions through almost paradoxical premises, in a singular toleration and largeness towards views opposed to his own; it may be added, in an honesty of mind which confesses itself not only perplexed with the 'riddle of the universe,' but indignant at the complacent explanations which those who proclaim it insoluble are too apt, he thought, to enforce upon the diffident.

But whilst this conflict went on within, towards friends what might be called the imaginative side of his nature was dominant. The sunshine and animating smiles which, many will remember, he brought with him into college society, came, not from ordinary and slighter causes, but from a heart to which affection was at once a delight and a necessity, and a mind 'haunted like a passion' by the loveliness of poetry or of scenery. During several summer vacations he had searched out the glens and heights, lakes and moors, of Wales, and Westmoreland, and Scotland, with that minute and reverent care, in absence of which travelling is idle, and with that love for the very soil and configuration of his country which almost always implies high-heartedness. And it was noticed that when speaking of spots of any special beauty or impressiveness—Grasmere, or Pont-y-Wern by Snowdon, or the lochs and valleys of the Western Highlands—his eyes brightened as at the thought of something personally dear, and his voice softened at names and remembrances which carried with them so much of poetry. And to this youthful enthusiasm for nature he united that other enthusiasm for energetic walks and venturesome wanderings, bathing, swimming, and out-of-doors existence in general, which may, perhaps, be claimed as an impulse peculiarly English.

All this, with much else, Clough summed up in his first published poem, brought out in the autumn of 1848, as if his farewell to his university. The *Bothie of Tober-Na-Vuolich* (as, for euphony's sake, he finally wished the Gaelic name to stand), is a true Long Vacation pastoral, in style and thought intensely Oxonian;—yet with this, which so much amused us at the time, are other and deeper features not less characteristic of the writer. Such are the profound and vital interest in the ancient masterworks of prose and poetry, which an Oxford man at least cannot recognize elsewhere in such reality; the profound sympathy with those who live by the labours we too slightingly call mechanical, and with minds which owe more to nature than to society or study; the delight in friendship and in solitude; the love of wild wandering, and the intense—not appreciation of, say rather 'acceptance in,' the natural landscape, in which Arthur Clough, more than any man known to the writer, seemed to have inherited a double portion of the spirit of William Wordsworth. A sense of fresh, healthy manliness; a scorn of base and selfish motives; a frank admiration for common life; a love of earth, not 'only for its earthly sake,' but for the divine and the eternal interfused in it—such, and other such, are the impressions left. These noble qualities are rare in any literature; they have a charm so great that, like Beauty before the Areopagus, they almost disarm the judgement. Viewed critically, Clough's work is wanting in art; the language and the thought are often unequal and incomplete; the poetical fusion into a harmonious whole, imperfect. Here, and in his other writings, one feels a doubt whether in verse he chose the right vehicle, the truly natural mode of utterance. It is poetry, however, which truly belongs to a very uncommon class. Even where the last touches have been given, the matter almost everywhere much outruns the workmanship: it should be judged by the thoughts awakened, rather than by the mode of expressing them.

Such writing, it might be imagined, from its merits equally with its faults, addresses itself to no numerous audience; yet the *Bothie* was quickly known and valued; and as a true man, from whom much might be hoped, the author was henceforth spoken of, not only in the sphere of friendship and of Oxford, but in many places where the life around them, from different circumstances, rendered men sensitive to his tone of thought:—in Northern England especially, in America, and in those wide regions over seas to which Englishmen have carried endurance of toil, and energy of intellect.

This poem has been already alluded to as the author's farewell to Oxford. Having held a tutorship in his college now for several years, and joined in all efforts onward, a sense that he had done his work in Oxford, that he was a little too alien in speculative and in practical thought from the tone of the University, to be of further use, or to find a fit abode there; that he might honourably seek a more unshackled career without, led Clough to withdraw, in 1848, from Oriel. There was much in the spirit of that day with which he could not reconcile himself:

> To finger idly some old Gordian knot,
> Unskill'd to sunder, and too weak to cleave,
> And with much toil attain to half-believe,

as he once expressed it, could not be his portion. Chivalrously generous in allowing liberty of opinion in others, he might now seek at least a fuller freedom for himself. Other half-external causes, it has been stated, cooperated in this; but more influential with so conscientious and brave a man, was the conviction of antagonism to the form of thought which Oxford exacted, or appeared to exact from her children. That world was not his friend, he fancied, nor that world's law. Yet this divergence was not such as ever estranged him in heart from that noble corporation which, more than any other of modern times, is apt to retain a life-long hold on the affections and the honour of its members; nor was it, again, such as, after his withdrawal, could be laid at rest within the bonds of some different system. This was no logical tangle, no scepticism in the common sense, no sudden imagined discovery, caprice of vanity, fanciful reverie, far less pride of heart or of intellect. Rather, if frank submission to the inexplicable mysteries of creation, if a reverence which feared expression, a faith in the eternal truth and justice, be the attributes of a religious mind, Clough possessed it with a reality uncommon in the followers of any religion. But the consciousness of the strange things of life, verbally recognized by most of us, and then explained by some phrase, or put by as unpractical, was to him the 'heavy and weary weight' which men like Wordsworth or Pascal felt it. The 'voyant trop pour nier, et trop peu pour s'assurer' of the greatest of French thinkers, as truly expressed Clough's conviction; and, convinced thus, it was with mingled perplexity and wrath that he listened to the popular solutions which he heard so confidently, often so threateningly vaunted — to the profane pretence of knowledge (as he thought it) disguised under the name of Providential schemes, or displayed in dogmatic formulas. Far other was the pure and lowly confession of man's incapacity to search out God, with which at this time he spoke in a few of his most characteristic and deeply-felt poems, which will be found in this collection. What pathetic tenderness, what manly courage, is concentrated in the lines referred to — how deep, practical, and modest a faith — how devout a submission! Those who knew Clough know how truly he has here rendered, not only the conviction, but the practice of a life of high and unwearied industry — a life in which the thought of self, except as regarded the fulfilment of duty, had no share; nor will they feel the phrase too serious, if it be added, that he who 'lived in the spirit of this creed' was surely already not far from the kingdom of Heaven.

The pages he then wrote contain the record of Clough's essential life during this second, or transitional, portion of that brief career, and have hence been dwelt on with greater minuteness. He meanwhile was spending the spring and summer of 1849 in Italy: drawn thither in part by the charm of that country to so sympathetic a student of the ancient literature; in part by the attraction which any effort to gain rational liberty exercises over all noble natures. Such efforts, or what seemed such, notably at this period engaged much of Clough's best thoughts and warmest sympathies. Thus in 1848 he wrote thus, in his half-humourous, half-pathetic strain, from Paris: —

'I do little else in the way of lionizing than wander about the Tuileries' chestnuts, and about bridges and streets, " pour savourer la république." I contemplate with infinite thankfulness the blue blouse garnished with red of the Garde Mobile, and emit a perpetual incense of devout rejoicing for the purified state of the Tuileries.' But a few days later comes the reverse of the picture — 'Ichabod, Ichabod, the glory has departed. Liberty, Equality, Fraternity, driven back by shopkeeping bayonet, hides her red cap in dingiest St. Antoine. Well-to-do-ism shakes her Egyptian scourge, to the tune of "ye are idle, ye are idle;"—the tale of bricks will be doubled, and the Moses and Aaron of Socialism can at the best only pray for plagues: which perhaps will come, paving-stones for *vivats*, and *émeutes* in all their quarters.

'Meantime the glory and the freshness of the dream is departed. The very Garde Mobile has changed its blouse for a bourgeoisie-prætorian uniform with distinctive green hired-soldier epaulets.

'The voice of Clubs is silent. Inquisitors only and stone walls of Vincennes list the words of Barbes. *Antirappel* Courtais no longer hushes the drum, which, as he said, "fâche le peuple." Wherefore, bring forth, ye millionaires, the three-months-hidden carriages; rub clean, ye new nobles, the dusty emblazonries: ride forth again, ye cavalier-escorted amazons, to your Bois de Boulogne. The world begins once more to move on its axis, and draw on its kid gloves. The golden age of the Republic displays itself now, you see, as a very vulgar parcel-gilt era.'

It is needless to add that a similar discouragement awaited Clough in Rome. Unable or unwilling to believe what at least bore the name Republic could really lead the crusade on behalf of despotism, he lingered on till the investment of Rome by a French army rendered departure impossible.

Many details of that memorable siege he recorded in letters sufficiently refuting the calumnies which England at that time was not ashamed to borrow from the natural enemies of freedom. He witnessed the patience and courage of the besieged, the self-restraint under privation and provocation, the firm, proud submission to overwhelming force, and a conquest where all of honour was with the defeated,—the high national qualities, in a word, with which Italy has made Europe familiar. 'Whether the Roman Republic will stand, I don't know,' he wrote during the struggle, 'but it has, under Mazzini's inspiration, shown a wonderful energy and a glorious generosity.' Readers will find many of Clough's impressions and feelings of that period recorded in the *Amours de Voyage* and other shorter pieces. Then, from the temporary triumph of shame and superstition, he turned to the Power which 'never did betray the heart that loved her,' and through the Italian Lakes and Switzerland wandered homewards to resume more active duties.

From a poem now written at Venice, may be taken a traveller's wish that he might

> In one unbroken passage borne
> To closing night from opening morn,
> Uplift at whiles slow eyes to mark
> Some palace front, some passing bark;
> Thro' windows catch the varying shore,
> And hear the soft turns of the oar.
> How light we move, how softly! ah,
> Were life but as the Gondola!

Though not altogether accomplished, something of this easy tenour of the happy life was in store for the writer during the twelve years of useful and energetic labour, which the 'blind Fury' Fate of the poet had measured out for him. At first indeed he found in the Wardenship of University Hall, London, an employment not altogether congenial to his disposition: yet even here, in the comparative solitude of the new abode, the discovery that withdrawal from Oxford had no ways shaken the affection of those he trusted, cheered the hours which, to a disposition so tenderly sensitive as Clough's, were apt to catch a gloom from the sight of unfamiliar walls and faces. This was, perhaps, the most lonely part of his life: and in the streets of London many strange passages of what he called the *philosophia metropolitana* presented themselves, and have found their way into verses of a peculiar pathos and sarcasm.

But such depressing humours came and went, whilst in the increased respect of those he most valued, whether alien from his tone of thought or not, he received now part of the reward with which truth recompenses self-sacrifice. Soon, too, when resident for a few months in America, whither in 1852 he went to try his fortunes, he found amongst the most distinguished men of Boston and its neighbourhood a renewal of the deep interest which he had aroused in his earlier companions. 'He had nothing of insular narrowness,' one of them writes, 'none of the prejudices which too often interfere with the capacity of English travellers or residents among us, to sympathize with and justly understand habits of life and thought so different from those to which they have been accustomed.' The friendships then formed were the main result — a sufficient result, Clough held it — of the trial: England drew him towards her before he could find a footing in the West, with the one irresistible word — homewards. Yet the resolution to return was not taken without some reluctance to quit the new world.

'I like America all the better,' (he wrote in 1853) 'for the comparison with England on my return. Certainly I think you were more right than I was willing to admit, about the position of the poorer classes here. Such is my first reimpression. However it will wear off soon enough, I daresay.

'There are deeper waters of ancient knowledge and experience about one here, and one is saved from the temptation of flying off into space; but I think you have, beyond all question, the happiest country going.'

An appointment, however, in the education department of the Privy Council-office decided him to return to England.

> ———The universal instinct of repose,
> The longing for confirm'd tranquillity,
> Inward and outward; humble, yet sublime;
> The life where hope and memory are as one:

—what life was ever wholly true to this great ideal? Yet in its most essential features, at peace with himself and with circumstances, happy in his home and the blessing of his children, Clough may be held to have fulfilled it.

A career such as this had been naturally watched by

his friends with a certain anxiety, heightened by the sight of a character at once so sensitive and so self-sacrificing, and by the warmth of affection which it excited. Henceforward, however, until failing health raised them, there was no cause for anxious thoughts. It was evident, indeed, that rest or leisure were not in his prospect; that not less than in his earlier days, Clough would be still, in its most emphatic and highest sense, a working man. His official employment was varied, but hardly diminished, by the Secretaryship to the Commission of Report on Military Education, which, in 1856, carried him again to France, and finally to Vienna. Meantime he gradually completed the long revision of Dryden's 'Translation of Plutarch,' begun in America; comparing that inaccurate though spirited text throughout with the original, and retouching it with a skill and taste in which his careful study of Chaucer and our early literature gave him a special mastery. These tasks were more than enough, as it proved, for a constitution never robust; and when, with his usual energetic sympathy for all that touched the welfare of the poor or the wretched, he further undertook much anxious work to assist his wife's cousin, Florence Nightingale, in her own arduous labours, Clough's health gave way, and travelling was prescribed.

His first journey, to Greece and Constantinople, was of great interest to so good a scholar; and he summed up the chief features on his return in a few lines placed in one of the *Tales*, of which the most complete are printed within this volume.

> Aware it might be first and last,
> I did it eagerly and fast;
> Counted the towns that lie like slain
> Upon the wide Boeotian plain;
> With wonder in the spacious gloom
> Stood of the Mycenaean tomb:
> From the Acro-Corinth watched the day
> Light the Eastern and the Western bay.
> Constantinople then had seen,
> Where 'mid her cypresses the queen
> Of the east sees flow thro' portal wide
> The steady streaming Scythian tide.
> To see the things which sick with doubt
> And comment one had learnt about,
> Was like clear morning after night,
> Or raising of the blind to sight.

Finding his health not thoroughly restored, after a short visit to England he returned southwards for the winter. By one of the Italian lakes he was struck by malaria fever, and with difficulty completed the journey to Florence, where it carried him off on November 13, 1861. He lies in the little cypress-crowded cemetery beyond the walls of the Fair City, on the side towards Fiesole.

This truly was a life of much performance, yet of more promise. Clough did the work of a man within his two and forty years; yet we must feel now the bitterness and irony of that fate which seemed to secure him outward prosperity, but never left him a brief interval in which, as one who best knew him said, 'to be himself,' and to realize for his own advantage, if not for ours, powers rarely given in such curiously subtle combination. Perhaps his speculative activity was beyond his powers of co-ordination, the discursive element of thought too dominant, the fear of partial conclusions over-scrupulous. But from what he might have been it is best to turn to what he was. It appears to the writer an idle demand, though now a demand often made, that a man should publish to the world the results of his thought or study : — to live a lofty life, within the limits of this existence, — to carry out for himself a perfect scheme, so far as human weakness may allow, is a far higher thing, as unhappily a far rarer : and in this aspect, those who knew him will confess it is no phrase of partial affection to say that Clough ranked with the best of his contemporaries. The reader will find many charming stanzas, some excellent, amongst those belonging to the later period of his life. Yet in the larger sense, it might be truly said, that he rather lived than wrote his poem. It must not be imagined that, with the more prosperous circumstances above noticed, he became false to his convictions, or, as some do, put away from himself as unpractical the thought of those deeper problems which had perplexed his earlier years, not less by the sense of their darkness than of their close and unavoidable pressure on our daily life ; that he now recoiled from them in fear, or forgot them in felicity. No one could be more conscience-pure from that self-deceiving concession to ease and cowardice by which honest doubt and insoluble difficulty are so often stifled. But with a modest reserve, the frequent companion of frank simplicity,— with a sense, it may be, of the increased perplexities which darken wider horizons, — he kept mainly to himself the results of his riper speculative experience; satisfied to express them henceforth only by a larger charity towards opponents, and an even more fervent earnestness on his own part to make truth and justice and generosity his sole guides for action. As said above, Clough lived his poem. Few, it has been observed, have looked on nature more entirely in the spirit which his favourite Wordsworth expressed in the immortal lines on Tintern: fewer, perhaps, in this age have more completely worked out his ideal, 'plain living and high thinking.' Let it not be said that Clough's gifts were inadequately realized, when he has left us this example.

It is a second, nay, to Fancy a more final farewell, thus to review the memories of lost affection. We would willingly, in his friend's pathetic phrase,

> Treasuring the look we cannot find,
> The words that are not heard again—

willingly linger yet a little more over the now visionary remembrance of outward form and manner; — the youthful blitheness and boyishness of heart with which he welcomed the sight of those he cared for, contrasted with the signs of age before its time in his scant and silvery hair: the gait, almost halting at times, which seemed hardly consistent with so much physical resolve and energy; the perplexed yet encouraging smile that met the speaker, if chance talk touched on matters of speculative or moral interest; the frown and furrows of the massive forehead at any tale of baseness or injustice; the sunny glance or healthy homely laughter at any word of natural kindness, or brilliancy, or innocent humour.

There were days, indeed,— months, perhaps — of darkness from more quarters than most men are accessible to: yet this was on the whole a happy life, though in a sense remote from the world's happiness. Here was little prosperity in common parlance; years of struggle and toil, fightings within and without, the *otia dia* of the poet within view only to be snatched away; no fame or recognition of abilities much beyond what he saw crown others with celebrity. But his mind was free from the 'last infirmity:' he lived in the inner light of a pure conscience, the healthfulness of duty fulfilled, the glorious liberty of absolute utter unworldliness. And even in the midnight of meditative troubles, the ever-youthful hope of the 'royal heart of innocence' was never wanting. Nor were other elements of human happiness absent within his home and without it,— society and solitude by turns, nature and poetry glorious throughout life as on the first day, friendships equal, open, and enduring,— reverence, even from many who knew him but slightly, for one so signalized and authenticated as a true Man by the broad seal of Nobleness. This must be reckoned the first, as it is the rarest, feature in human character. But in him it was equally balanced by another, which in such degree is hardly less rare, Tenderness. Clough might be said not so much to trust his friends, as to trust himself to them. Friendship in his eyes, as in the ancient days he felt with so deeply, was a high and sacred thing, a duty and a virtue in itself, and he guarded it with scrupulous sensitiveness. — It was natural that one so gifted should be looked up to with unusual warmth and honour. Many will remember how much Clough's opinion on acts or thoughts, on literature or on nature — remote from ordinary judgements or humorously paradoxical as it might be — was tacitly referred to; how often the difficulties and doubts of the tangled passages of life were laid before him for counsel. A resolution was not always ready, but they never failed to find that which is better than most men's decisive clearness — a judgement noble, tender, courageous, conscientious : — if not always practical advice, no little measure, at least, of that wisdom which is from above.

F. T. PALGRAVE

ARTHUR HUGH CLOUGH.

To win such love as Arthur Hugh Clough won in life, to leave so dear a memory as he has left, is a happiness that falls to few men. In America, as in England, his death is mourned by friends whose affection is better than fame, and who in losing him have met with an irreparable loss. Outside the circle of his friends his reputation had no large extent; but though his writings are but little known by the great public of readers, they are prized by all those of thoughtful and poetic temper to whose hands they have come, as among the most precious and original productions of the time. To those who knew him personally his poems had a special worth and charm, as the sincere expression of a character of the purest stamp, of rare truthfulness and simplicity, not less tender than strong, and of a genius thoroughly individual in its form, and full of the promise of a large career. He was by Nature endowed with subtile and profound powers of thought, with feeling at once delicate and intense, with lively and generous sympathies, and with conscientiousness so acute as to pervade and control his whole intellectual disposition. Loving, seeking, and holding fast to the truth, he despised all falseness and affectation. With his serious and earnest thinking was joined the play of a genial humor and the brightness of poetic fancy. Liberal in sentiment, absolutely free from dogmatism and pride of intellect, of a questioning temper, but of reverent spirit, faithful in the performance not only of the larger duties, but also of the lesser charities and the familiar courtesies of life, he has left a memory of singular consistency, purity, and dignity. He lived to conscience, not for show, and few men carry through life so white a soul.

A notice of Mr. Clough understood to be written by one who knew him well gives the outline of his life.

"Arthur Hugh Clough was educated at Rugby, to which school he went very young, soon after Dr. Arnold had been elected head-master. He distinguished himself at once by gaining the only scholarship which existed at that time, and which was open to the whole school under the age of fourteen. Before he was sixteen he was at the head of the fifth form, and, as that was the earliest age at which boys were then admitted into the sixth, had to wait for a year before coming under the personal tuition of the head-master. He came in the next (school) generation to Stanley and Vaughan, and gained a reputation, if possible, even greater than theirs. At the yearly speeches, in the last year of his residence, when the prizes are given away in the presence of the school and the friends who gather on such occasions, Arnold took the almost unexampled course of addressing him, (when he and two fags went up to carry off his load of splendidly bound books,) and congratulating him on having gained every honor which Rugby could bestow, and having also already distinguished himself and done the highest credit to his school at the University. He had just gained a scholarship at Balliol, then, as now, the blue ribbon of undergraduates.

"At school, although before all things a student, he had thoroughly entered into the life of the place, and before he left had gained supreme influence with the boys. He was the leading contributor to the 'Rugby Magazine'; and though a weakness in his ankles prevented him from taking a prominent part in the games of the place, was known as the best goal-keeper on record, a reputation which no boy could have gained without promptness and courage. He was also one of the best swimmers in the school, his weakness of ankle being no drawback here, and in his last half passed the crucial test of that day, by swimming from Swift's (the bathing-place of the sixth) to the mill on the Leicester road, and back again, between callings over.

"He went to reside at Oxford when the whole University was in a ferment. The struggle of Alma Mater to humble or cast out the most remarkable of her sons was at its height. Ward had not yet been arraigned for his opinions, and was a fellow and tutor of Balliol, and Newman was in residence at Oriel, and incumbent of St. Mary's.

"Clough's was a mind which, under any circumstances, would have thrown itself into the deepest speculative thought of its time. He seems soon to have passed through the mere ecclesiastical debatings to the deep questions which lay below them. There was one lesson — probably one only — which he had never been able to learn from his great master, namely, to acknowledge that there are problems which intellectually are not to be solved by man, and before these to sit down quietly. Whether it were from the harass of thought on such matters which interfered with his regular work, or from one of those strange miscarriages in the most perfect of examining machines, which every now and then deprive the best men of the highest honors, to the surprise of every one Clough missed his first class. But he completely retrieved this academical mishap shortly afterwards by gaining an Oriel fellowship. In his new college, the college of Pusey, Newman, Keble, Marriott, Wilberforce, presided over by Dr. Hawkins, and in which the influence of Whately, Davidson, and Arnold had scarcely yet died out, he found himself in the very centre and eye of the battle. His own convictions were by this time leading him far away from both sides in the Oxford contest; he, however, accepted a tutorship at the college, and all who had the privilege of attending them will long remember his lectures on logic and ethics. His fault (besides a shy and reserved manner) was that he was much too long-suffering to youthful philosophic coxcombry, and would rather encourage it by his gentle 'Ah! you think so?' or, 'Yes, but might not such and such be the case?'"

Clough was at Oxford in 1847, — the year of the terrible Irish famine, and with others of the most earnest men at the University he took part in an association which had for its object "Retrenchment for the sake of the Irish." Such a society was little likely to be popular with the comfortable dignitaries or the luxurious youth of the University. Many objections, frivolous or serious as the case might be, were raised against so subversive a notion as that of the self-sacrifice of the rich for the sake of the poor. Disregarding all personal considerations, Clough printed a pamphlet entitled, "A Consideration of Objections against the Retrenchment Association," in which he met the careless or selfish arguments of those who set themselves against the efforts of the society. It was a characteristic performance. His heart was deeply stirred by the harsh contrast between the miseries of the Irish poor and the wasteful extravagance of living prevalent at Oxford. He wrote with vehement indignation against the selfish pleas of the indifferent and the thoughtless possessors of wealth, wasters of the goods given them as a trust for others. His words were chiefly addressed to the young men at the University, — and they were not without effect. Such views of the rights and duties of property as he put forward, of the claims of labor, and of the responsibilities of the aristocracy, had not been often heard at Oxford. He was called a Socialist and a Radical, but it mattered little to him by what name he was known to those whose consciences were not touched by his appeal. "Will you say," he writes toward the end of this pamphlet, "this is all rhetoric and declamation? There is, I dare say, something too much in that kind. What with criticizing style and correcting exercises, we college tutors perhaps may be likely, in the heat of composition, to lose sight of realities, and pass into the limbo of the factitious, — especially when the thing must be done at odd times, in any case, and, if at all, quickly. But if I have been obliged to write hurriedly, believe me, I have obliged myself to think not hastily. And believe me, too, though I have desired to succeed in putting vividly and forcibly that which vividly and forcibly I felt and saw, still the graces and splendors of composition were thoughts far less present to my mind than Irish poor men's miseries, English poor men's hardships, and your unthinking indifference. Shocking enough the first and the second, almost more shocking the third."

It was about this time that the most widely known of his works, "The Bothie of Toper-na-Fuosich, a Long-Vacation Pastoral," was written. It was published in 1848, and though it at once secured a circle of warm admirers, and the edition was very soon exhausted, it "is assuredly deserving of a far higher popularity than it has ever attained." The poem was reprinted in America, at Cambridge, in 1849, and it may be safely asserted that its merit was more deeply felt and more generously acknowledged by American than by English readers. The fact that its essential form and local coloring were purely and genuinely English, and thus gratified the curiosity felt in this country concerning the social habits and ways of life in the mother-land, while on the other hand its spirit was in sympathy with the most liberal and progressive thought of the age, may sufficiently account for its popularity here. But the lovers of poetry found delight in it, apart from these characteristics, — in its fresh descriptions of Nature, its healthy manliness of tone, its scholarly construction, its lively humor, its large thought quickened and deepened by the penetrating imagination of the poet.

"Any one who has read it will acknowledge that a tutorship at Oriel was not the place for the author. The intense love of freedom, the deep and hearty sympathy with the foremost thought of the time, the humorous dealing with old formulas and conventionalisms grown meaningless, which breathe in every line of the 'Bothie,' show this clearly enough. He would tell in after-life, with much enjoyment, how the dons of the University, who, hearing that he had something in the press, and knowing that his theological views were not wholly sound, were looking for a publication on the Articles, were astounded by the appearance of that fresh and frolicsome poem. Oxford (at least the Oriel common room) and he were becoming more estranged daily. How keenly he felt the estrangement, not from Oxford, but from old friends, about this time, can be read only in his own words." It is in such poems as the "Qua Cursum Ventus," or the sonnet beginning, "Well, well, — Heaven bless you all from day to day!" that it is to be read. These, with a few other fugitive pieces, were printed, in company with verses by a friend, as one part of a small volume entitled, "Ambarvalia," which never attained any general circulation, although containing some poems which will take their place among the best of English poetry of this generation.

"*Qua Cursum Ventus.*

"As ships, becalmed at eve, that lay
  With canvas drooping, side by side,
Two towers of sail at dawn of day,
  Are scarce long leagues apart descried:

"When fell the night, upsprung the breeze,
  And all the darkling hours they plied,
Nor dreamt but each the self-same seas
  By each was cleaving side by side:

"E'en so —— But why the tale reveal
  Of those whom, year by year unchanged,
Brief absence joined anew to feel,
  Astounded, soul from soul estranged?

"At dead of night their sails were filled,
  And onward each rejoicing steered:
Ah, neither blame, for neither willed,
  Or wist, what first with dawn appeared!

"To veer, how vain! On, onward strain,
  Brave barks! In light, in darkness too,
Through winds and tides one compass guides:
  To that, and your own selves, be true!

"But, O blithe breeze! and O great seas!
  Though ne'er, that earliest parting past,
On your wide plain they join again,
  Together lead them home at last!

"One port, methought, alike they sought,
  One purpose hold where'er they fare:
O bounding breeze! O rushing seas!
  At last, at last, unite them there!"

"In 1848-49 the revolutionary crisis came on Europe, and Clough's sympathies drew him with great earnestness into the struggles which were going on. He was in Paris directly after the barricades, and in Rome during the siege, where he gained the friendship of Saffi and other leading Italian patriots." A part of his experiences and his thoughts while at Rome are interwoven with the story in his "Amours de Voyage," a poem which exhibits in extraordinary measure the subtilty and delicacy of his powers, and the fulness of his sympathy with the intellectual conditions of the time. It was first published in the "Atlantic Monthly" for 1858, and was at once established in the admiration of readers capable of appreciating its rare and refined excellence. The spirit of the poem is thoroughly characteristic of its author, and the speculative, analytic turn of his mind is represented in many passages of the letters of the imaginary hero. Had he been writing in his own name, he could not have uttered his inmost conviction more distinctly, or have given the clue to his intellectual life more openly than in the following verses: —

"I will look straight out, see things, not try to evade them:
Fact shall be Fact for me; and the Truth the Truth as ever,
Flexible, changeable, vague, and multiform and doubtful."

Or, again, —

"Ah, the key of our life, that passes all wards, opens all locks,
Is not *I will*, but *I must*. I must, — I must, — and I do it."

And still again, —

"But for the steady fore-sense of a freer and larger existence,
Think you that man could consent to be circumscribed here into action?
But for assurance within of a limitless ocean divine, o'er
Whose great tranquil depths unconscious the wind-tost surface
Breaks into ripples of trouble that come and change and endure not, —
But that in this, of a truth, we have our being, and know it,
Think you we men could submit to live and move as we do here?"

"To keep on doing right, — not to speculate only, but to act, not to think only, but to live," — was, it has been said, characteristic of the leading men at Oxford during this period. "It was not so much a part of their teaching as a doctrine woven into their being." And while they thus exercised a moral not less than an intellectual influence over their contemporaries and their pupils, they themselves, according to their various tempers and circumstances, were led on into new paths of inquiry or of life. Some of them fell into the common temptations of an English University career, and lost the freshness of energy and the honesty of conviction which first inspired them; others, holding their places in the established order of things, were able by happy faculties of character to retain also the vigor and simplicity of their early purposes; while others again, among whom was Clough, finding the restraints of the University incompatible with independence, gave up their positions at Oxford to seek other places in which they could more freely search for the truth and express their own convictions.

It was not long after his return from Italy that he became Professor of English Language and Literature at University College, London. He filled this place, which was not in all respects suited to him, until 1852. After resigning it, he took various projects into consideration, and at length determined to come to America with the intention of settling here, if circumstances should prove favorable. In November, 1852, he arrived in Boston. He at once established himself at Cambridge, proposing to give instruction to young men preparing for college, or to take on in more advanced studies those who had completed the collegiate course. He speedily won the friendship of those whose friendship was best worth having in Boston and its neighborhood. His thorough scholarship, the result of the best English training, and his intrinsic qualities caused his society to be sought and prized by the most cultivated and thoughtful men. He had nothing of insular narrowness, and none of the hereditary prejudices which too often interfere with the capacity of English travellers or residents among us to sympathize with and justly understand habits of life and of thought so different from those to which they have been accustomed. His liberal sentiments and his independence of thought harmonized with the new social conditions in which he found himself, and with the essential spirit of American life. The intellectual freedom and animation of this country were congenial to his disposition. From the beginning he took a large share in the interests of his new friends. He contributed several remarkable articles to the pages of the "North American Review" and of "Putnam's Magazine," and he undertook a work which was to occupy his scanty leisure for several years, the revision of the so-called Dryden's Translation of Plutarch's Lives. Although the work was undertaken simply as a revision, it turned out to involve little less labor than a complete new translation, and it was so accomplished that henceforth it must remain the standard version of this most popular of the ancient authors.

But all that made the presence of such a man a great gain to his new friends made his absence felt by his old ones as a great loss. In July, 1853, he received the announcement that a place had been obtained for him by their efforts in the Education Department of the Privy Council, and he was so strenuously urged to return to England, that, although unwilling to give up the prospect of a final settlement in America, he felt that it was best to go home for a time. Some months after his return he was married to the granddaughter of the late Mr. William Smith, M. P. for Norwich. He established himself in a house in London, and settled down to the hard routine-work of his office. In a private letter written not long after his return, he said, — "As for myself, whom you ask about, there is nothing to tell about me. I live on contentedly enough, but feel rather unwilling to be re-Englished, after once attaining that higher transatlantic development. However, *il faut s'y soumettre*, I presume, — though I fear I am embarked in the foundering ship. I hope to Heaven you 'll get rid of slavery, and then I should n't fear but you would really 'go ahead' in the long run. As for us and our inveterate feudalism, it is not hopeful."

In another letter about this time, he wrote, — "I like America all the better for the comparison with England on my return. Certainly I think you are more right than I was willing to admit, about the position of the poorer classes here. Such is my first reimpression. However, it will wear off soon enough, I dare say; so you must make the most of my admissions."

Again, a little later, he wrote, — "I do truly hope that you will get the North erelong thoroughly united against any further encroachments. I don't by any means feel that the slave-system is an intolerable crime, nor do I think that our system here is so much better; but it is clear to me that the only safe ground to go upon is that of your Northern States. I suppose the rich-and-poor difficulties must be creeping in at New York, but one would fain hope that European analogies will not be quite accepted even there."

His letters were reflections of himself, — full of thought, fancy, and pleasant humor, as well as of affectionateness and true feeling. Their character is hardly to be given in extracts, but a few passages may serve to illustrate some of these qualities.

"Ambrose Philips, the Roman Catholic, who set up the new St. Bernard Monastery at Charnwood Forest, has taken to spirit-rappings. He avers, *inter alia*, that a Buddhist spirit in misery held communication with him through the table, and entreated his confessor, Father Lorraine, to say three masses for him. Pray, convey this to T—— for his warning. For, moreover, it remains uncertain whether Father Lorraine did say the masses; so that perhaps T——'s deceased co-religionist is still in the wrong place."

Some time after his return, he wrote,— " Really, I may say I am only just beginning to recover my spirits after returning from the young and hopeful and humane republic, to this cruel, unbelieving, inveterate old monarchy. There are deeper waters of ancient knowledge and experience about one here, and one is saved from the temptation of flying off into space; but I think you have, beyond all question, the happiest country going. Still, the political talk of America, as one hears it here, is not always true to the best intentions of the country, is it?"

Writing on a July day from his office in Whitehall, he says, after speaking of the heat of the weather,— " Time has often been compared to a river: if the Thames at London represent the stream of traditional wisdom, the comparison will indeed be of an ill odor; the accumulated wisdom of the past will be proved upon analogy to be as it were the collected sewage of the centuries; and the great problem, how to get rid of it."

In March, 1854, he wrote,— " People talk a good deal about that book of Whewell's on the Plurality of Worlds. I recommend Fields to pirate it. Have you seen it? It is to show that Jupiter, Venus, Saturn, etc., are all pretty certainly uninhabitable,— being (Jupiter, Saturn, etc., to wit) strange washy limbos of places, where at the best only mollusks (or, in the case of Venus, salamanders) could exist. Hence we conclude we are the only rational creatures, which is highly satisfactory, and, what is more, quite Scriptural. Owen, on the other hand, I believe, and other scientific people, declare it a most presumptuous essay,— conclusions audacious, and reasoning fallacious, though the facts are allowed; and in that opinion I, on the ground that there are more things in heaven and earth than are dreamt of in the inductive philosophy, incline to concur."

Of his work he wrote,— " Well, I go on in the office, *operose nihil agendo*, very *operose*, and very *nihil* too. For lack of news, I send you a specimen of my labors." — " We are here going on much as usual, — occupied with nothing else but commerce and the money-market. I do not think any one is thinking audibly of anything else." — " I have read with more pleasure than anything else that I have read lately Kane's Arctic Explorations, *i. e.*, his second voyage, which is certainly a wonderful story. The whole narrative is, I think, very characteristic of the differences between the English and the American-English habits of command and obedience."

In the autumn of 1857, after speaking of some of the features of the Sepoy revolt, he said,— " I don't believe Christianity can spread far in Asia, unless it will allow men more than one wife,— which is n't likely yet out of Utah. But I believe the old Brahmin ' Touch not and taste not, and I am holier than thou, because I don't touch and taste,' may be got rid of. As for Mahometanism, it is a crystallized monotheism, out of which no vegetation can come. I doubt its being good even for the Central negro."

March, 1859. " Excuse this letter all about my own concerns. I am pretty busy, and have time for little else: such is our fate after forty. My figure 40 stands nearly three months behind me on the roadway, unwept, unhonored, and unsung, an *octavum lustrum* bound up and laid on the shelf. ' So-and-so is dead,' said a friend to Lord Melbourne of some author. ' Dear me, how glad I am! Now I can bind him up.' "

It was not until 1859 that the translation of Plutarch, begun six years before, was completed and published. It had involved much wearisome study, and gave proof of patient, exact, and elegant scholarship. Clough's life in the Council-Office was exceedingly laborious, and for several years his work was increased by services rendered to Miss Nightingale, a near relative of his wife. He employed " many hours, both before and after his professional duties were over, to aid her in those reforms of the military administration to which she has devoted the remaining energies of her overtasked life." For this work he was the better fitted from having acted, during a period of relief from his regular employment, as Secretary to a Military Commission appointed by Government shortly after the Crimean War to examine and report upon the military systems of some of the chief Continental nations. But at length his health gave way under the strain of continuous overwork. He had for a long time been delicate, and early in 1861 he was obliged to give up work, and was ordered to travel abroad. He went to Greece and Constantinople, and enjoyed greatly the charms of scenery and of association which he was so well fitted to appreciate. But the release from work had come too late. He returned to England in July, his health but little improved. In a letter written at that time he spoke of Lord Campbell's death, which had just occurred. "Lord Campbell's death is rather the characteristic death of the English political man. In the Cabinet, on the Bench, and at a dinner-party, busy, animated, and full of effort to-day, and in the early morning a vessel has burst. It is a wonder they last so long." But of himself he says, in words of striking contrast, — "My nervous energy is pretty nearly spent for to-day, so I must come to a stop. I have leave till November, and by that time I hope I shall be strong again for another good spell of work." After a happy three weeks in England, he went abroad again, and spent some time with his friends the Tennysons in Auvergne and among the Pyrenees. In September he was joined by his wife in Paris, and thence went with her through Switzerland to Italy. He had scarcely reached Florence before he became alarmingly ill with symptoms of a low malaria fever. His exhausted constitution never rallied against its attack. He sank gradually away, and died on the 13th of November. "I have leave till November, and by that time I hope I shall be strong again for another good spell of work." That hope is accomplished;—

"For sure in the wide heaven there is room
For love, and pity, and for helpful deeds."

He was buried in the little Protestant cemetery at Florence, a fit resting-place for a poet, the Protestant Santa Croce, where the tall cypresses rise over the graves, and the beautiful hills keep guard around.

"Every one who knew Clough even slightly," says one of his oldest friends, "received the strongest impression of the unusual breadth and massiveness of his mind. Singularly simple and genial, he was unfortunately cast upon a self-questioning age, which led him to worry himself with constantly testing the veracity of his own emotions. He has delineated in four lines the impression which his habitual reluctance to converse on the deeper themes of life made upon those of his friends who were attracted by his frank simplicity. · In one of his shorter poems he writes,—

'I said, My heart is all too soft;
He who would climb and soar aloft
Must needs keep ever at his side
The tonic of a wholesome pride.'

That expresses the man in a very remarkable manner. He had a kind of proud simplicity about him singularly attractive, and often singularly disappointing to those who longed to know him well. He had a fear, which many would think morbid, of leaning much on the approbation of the world. And there is one remarkable passage in his poems in which he intimates that men who live on the good opinion of others might even be benefited by a *crime* which would rob them of that evil stimulant:—

'Why, so is good no longer good, but crime
Our truest, best advantage, since it lifts us
Out of the stifling gas of men's opinion
Into the vital atmosphere of Truth,
Where He again is visible, though in anger.'

"So eager was his craving for reality and perfect sincerity, so morbid his dislike even for the unreal conventional forms of life, that a mind quite unique in simplicity and truthfulness represents *itself* in his poems as

'Seeking in vain, in all my store,
One feeling based on truth.'

"Indeed, he wanted to reach some guaranty for simplicity deeper than simplicity itself. We remember his principal criticism on America, after returning from his residence in Massachusetts, was, that the New-Englanders were much simpler than the English, and that this was the great charm of New-England society. His own habits were of the same kind, sometimes almost austere in their simplicity. Luxury he disliked, and sometimes his friends thought him even ascetic.

"This almost morbid craving for a firm base on the absolute realities of life was very wearing in a mind so self-conscious as Clough's, and tended to paralyze the expression of a certainly great genius. He heads some of his poems with a line from Wordsworth's great ode, which depicts perfectly the expression often written in the deep furrows which sometimes crossed and crowded his massive forehead: —

'Blank misgivings of a creature moving about
in worlds not realized.'

"Nor did Clough's great powers ever realize themselves to his contemporaries by any outward sign at all commensurate with the profound impression which they produced in actual life. But if his powers did not, there was much in his character that did produce its full effect upon all who knew him. He never looked, even in time of severe trial, to his own interest or advancement. He never flinched from the worldly loss which his deepest convictions brought on him. Even when clouds were thick over his own head, and the ground beneath his feet seemed crumbling away, he could still bear witness to an eternal light behind the cloud, and tell others that there is solid ground to be reached in the end by the weary feet of all who will wait to be strong. Let him speak his own farewell: —

'Say not the struggle nought availeth,
  The labor and the wounds are vain,
The enemy faints not nor faileth,
  And as things have been things remain.

'Though hopes were dupes, fears may be liars;
  It may be, in yon smoke concealed,
Your comrades chase e'en now the fliers,
  And but for you possess the field.

'For though the tired wave, idly breaking,
  Seems here no tedious inch to gain,
Far back, through creek and inlet making,
  Came, silent flooding in, the main.

'And not through eastern windows only,
  When daylight comes, comes in the light;
In front the sun climbs slow, — how slowly!
  But westward — look! the land is bright.'"

MEMOIR

OF

ARTHUR HUGH CLOUGH.

ARTHUR HUGH CLOUGH was born at Liverpool, January 1, 1819. He was the second son of James Butler Clough. His father belonged to an old Welsh family, who trace themselves back to Sir Richard Clough, known as agent at Antwerp to Sir Thomas Gresham. His mother's name was Anne Perfect. She was the daughter of John Perfect, a banker at Pontefract in Yorkshire.

When Arthur was four years old, his father migrated to Charleston in the United States, where he passed several years, and this was the home of Arthur's childhood till he went to school. A thoughtful and studious child, he soon showed a taste for reading. This he inherited from his mother, who early made him familiar with the stories of the old Greek heroes and statesmen, with the Odyssey and Iliad, with some of Walter Scott's novels, and waked his enthusiasm by the accounts of the sufferings of the early martyrs and the struggles of the Protestants.

In November 1828, Arthur was sent to school at Chester, and in the summer of 1829 he was removed to Rugby and came under the influence of Dr. Arnold. There he prospered. He gained a scholarship, open to the whole school under fourteen, and the only one which then existed. He was at the head of the fifth form at fifteen; and as sixteen was the earliest age at which boys were then admitted into the sixth, he had to wait a whole year for this. For a considerable time he was also the editor of 'The Rugby Magazine,' a periodical which absorbed much of the writing powers of the cleverer boys and to which he contributed constantly, chiefly poetry. Besides this he took an active part in some of the school games, and his name is handed down in William Arnold's 'Rules of Football,' as the best goal-keeper on record. He was also one of the first swimmers in the school, and was a very good runner. Among his school-fellows, in general, he gained a very high character; a sign of which is given by the story told by some of them at the time, that, when he left school for college almost every boy at Rugby contrived to shake hands with him at parting. Dr. Arnold also regarded him with increasing interest and satisfaction; and at the yearly speeches, in the last year of Clough's residence, he broke the rule of silence, to which he almost invariably adhered in the delivery of prizes, and congratulated him on having gained every honour which Rugby could bestow and done the highest credit to his school at the University. This was in allusion to his having gained the Balliol scholarship, then and now the highest honour which a schoolboy could obtain.

In November 1836 he gained the scholarship and the October following he went into residence at Oxford, when began the time which was essentially the turning point of his life. The University was then stirred to its depths by the great Tractarian movement. Mr. Ward, one of Clough's first friends at Oxford, was, as is well known, among the foremost of the party; and he was thus, at once, thrown into the very vortex of discussion. The accident of his passing from the Rugby of Arnold to the Oxford of Newman and Ward, drove him, while he ought to have been devoting himself to the ordinary work of an undergraduate reading for honours, and before he had attained his full intellectual development, to examine the deepest subjects that can occupy the human mind.

It is not difficult to understand into what trouble of spirit an impressionable nature must have been thrown by the storm that was raging round him and by contact with such powerful leaders. He himself said afterwards, that for two years he had been 'like a straw drawn up the draught of a chimney.' But his was not a character to accept any merely external system of authority, and the reaction which necessarily followed, drove him to start afresh in the search after truth. The spirit of doubt and struggle, yet of unshaken assurance in the final conquest of truth and good, comes out strongly in his poems written about this time.

The result of his disturbance of mind was naturally to distract his attention from his immediate studies, and to make his labour less productive. He disclosed but little to anyone of the mental struggle within him, but his family were aware that some great change was going on in him, and were anxious about his health, which evidently suffered. Yet he did read hard, even more so, perhaps, than most men of his time; and one of his friends records that the only bet he ever remembers making in his life was seven to one that Clough would get a first. His habits were at this time of Spartan simplicity: he had very cold rooms in Balliol on the ground floor; he is said to have passed a whole winter without a fire. He had a very high reputation as an undergraduate; and among his contemporaries and those immediately succeeding him, many were found to say that they owed more to him than to any other man.

From whatever cause, to the surprise both of undergraduates and of tutors, Clough missed his first class, which was a serious distress to his parents and friends, especially Dr. Arnold, who had looked forward to his achieving great distinction, and whose well-known dislike of the Tractarian movement made him doubly grieve at what he regarded as indirectly one of its consequences. Clough himself seems always to have felt a solid confidence in his own powers, and perhaps to have too little regarded the outward means of displaying them. Perhaps, too, he was somewhat conscious of that inaptitude to put himself forward to the best advantage, which many of his friends have noticed, and accepted it with his usual stoic philosophy. At any rate, his failure did not long produce the effects he most feared, of want of pupils; for through Dr. Arnold's kindness he was soon provided with profitable employment. In the autumn he tried unsuccessfully for a fellowship at Balliol. He continued, however, to reside at Oxford, and supported himself on the exhibition and scholarship which he still held. In the spring of 1842 he was elected fellow of Oriel, which was in every way a great and cheering success to him. He had as yet formed no definite views at variance with the principles of the Church. Though he had come to see the unimportance of many things commonly insisted on, he was not provided with any other scheme to set up; his habits and his affections all clung to the old ways; then and many years afterwards, he continued to feel that real liberality, width of view, and mental and moral cultivation were more commonly found among those nursed in the Anglican Church than in any exclusive sect, and probably the idea of any violent move, of quitting the home in which he had been reared, had never yet crossed his mind. His pleasure in his success in obtaining the fellowship was much enhanced by the satisfaction which it gave to Dr. Arnold, and in a practical way it was doubly valuable, because more troubles were now thickening round him and his family. Money difficulties pressed hard on his parents at this time; his help was much needed, and was unsparingly given. Other troubles soon came. The sudden death of his youngest and much-loved brother, when alone in Charleston, was followed within a year by that of his father.

The death of Dr. Arnold in June 1842 was a severe shock as well as a great grief to Clough, from its suddenness as well as from the intense reverence and affection he felt for him. 'He was for a long time more than a father to me,' were his own words.

In 1843 he was appointed tutor as well as fellow of Oriel, and especially endeared himself to his younger friends and pupils in this capacity. He took a warm and increasing interest in all social questions, and during this time also most of the poems in the little volume called 'Ambarvalia' were written.

Though his life passed on, thus with much of cheerful and active interest and work, it would seem, from his letters, that he was living at Oxford under a sense of intellectual repression. He evidently regarded teaching as his natural vocation, and had great enjoyment in it; but the sense of being bound by his position to silence on many important subjects probably oppressed him. Though everything in his outward circumstances combined to make it desirable for him to remain in his present position, yet by degrees his dissatisfaction with it became too strong to be endured. His was a nature 'which moveth all together, if it move at all;' and, once entered upon the course of free inquiry, nothing could stop the expansion of his thought in that direction. His absolute conscientiousness and intense unworldliness prevented the usual influences which slacken men's movements from telling upon his.

It is not very obvious what eventually decided him to quit Oxford at the precise moment when he did so. In the year 1847 he was powerfully stirred by the distress in Ireland at the time of the potatoe famine, as may be seen from the pamphlet on ' Retrenchment;' and the general ferment of his nature, as well as the ripening of opinions in his own mind, probably tended to make him more open to change. Emerson also visited England in this year. Clough became intimate with him, and his influence must have tended to urge him on in the direction in which he was already moving. Probably it was some half accidental confirmation of his own doubts as to the honesty and usefulness of his own course, which brought him at last almost suddenly face to face with the question whether he ought to resign his tutorship. After a correspondence with the head of his college—in speaking of whom he always expressed a strong sense of the uniform kindness which he had received from him under these trying circumstances—he eventually gave up his tutorship in 1848; and this done, though his fellowship had not yet expired, he began to feel his whole position hollow; and six months later (in October 1848), he resigned this likewise, and thus left himself unprovided with any present means of making a livelihood, and burdened besides with the payment of an annuity to which he had made himself liable for the sake of a friend. The sacrifice was greater to him than to many men, because he had no natural aptitude for making money. His power of literary production was always uncertain, and very little within his own control. His conscientious scruples interfered with his writing casually, as many would have done; for instance, we are told that he would not contribute to any paper or review with whose general principles he did not agree. He was, therefore, constrained to look out for some definite post in the line of education; and from the best chances in this department he had cut himself adrift by resigning his fellowship. He did, nevertheless, take this step, apparently with a certain lightness of heart and buoyancy, in singular contrast with what might be expected to be the feeling of a man taking a decision so important to his future life. It is clear that he 'broke away with delight' from what he felt to be the thraldom of his position in Oxford.

Immediately after laying down his tutorship, he made use of his leisure to go to Paris, in company with Emerson, where he spent a month in seeing the sights of the Revolution.

It was in September of this year (1848), when staying at home with his mother and sister in Liverpool, that he wrote his first long poem, the 'Bothie of Tober-na-Vuolich.' This was his utterance to the world on quitting Oxford, and not the theological pamphlet which was expected from him.

In the winter of 1848 he received an invitation to take the Headship of University Hall, London, an institution professing entirely unsectarian principles, founded for the purpose of receiving students attending the lectures at University College. His tenure of office was to date from October 1849, and he determined before this to take his first long holiday of travel, and to go to Rome. Thus his visit coincided accidentally with the siege of Rome by the French. At this time he wrote his second long poem, the 'Amours de Voyage.'

In October 1849 he returned to enter on his duties at University Hall. His new circumstances were, of course, very different from those of his Oxford life, and the change was in many respects painful to him. The step he had taken in resigning his fellowship, isolated him greatly; many of his old friends looked coldly on him, and the new acquaintances among whom he was thrown were often uncongenial to him. The transition from the intimate and highly refined society of Oxford to the bustling miscellaneous external life of London, to one not well furnished with friends, and without a home of his own, could hardly fail to be depressing. He had hoped for liberty of thought and action; he had found solitude, but not perfect freedom. Though not bound by any verbal obligations, he found himself expected to express agreement with the opinions of the new set among whom he had fallen, and this was no more possible to him here than it had been at Oxford. This was without doubt the dreariest, loneliest period of his life, and he became compressed and reserved to a degree quite unusual with him, both before and afterwards. He shut himself up, and went through his life in silence.

Yet here too he gradually formed some new and valuable friendships. Among these, his acquaintance with Mr. Carlyle was one of the most important; and to the end of his life he continued to entertain the warmest feeling for that great man. It was part of the sensitiveness of his character to shrink from going back on old impressions; and though he always retained his affection for his early friends, yet intercourse with fresh minds was often easier to him than with those to whom his former phases of life and thought were more familiar. In the autumn of 1850 he took advantage of his vacation to make a hasty journey to Venice, and during this interval he began his third long poem of 'Dipsychus,' which bears the mark of Venice in all its framework and its local colouring.

We have now mentioned, at the dates at which they were composed, all his longest works—the 'Bothie,' the 'Amours de Voyage,' and 'Dipsychus.' No other long work of his remains except the 'Mari Magno,' which is properly a collection of short poems, more or less united by one central idea, and bound together by their setting, as a series of tales related to each other by a party of companions on a sea voyage. The 'Ambarvalia,' poems written between 1840 and 1847, chiefly at Oxford, though without any setting at all, have something of the same inward coherence. They are all poems of the inner life, while the 'Mari Magno' poems deal with the social problems connected with the questions of love and marriage. His voyage to America, again, produced a cluster of little sea poems, closely linked together by one or two main thoughts.

It has often been a subject of surprise, that with such evident powers and even facility of production, Clough should have left so little behind him, even considering the shortness of his life, and that for such long periods he should have been entirely silent. We think the best explanation is to be found in his peculiar temper of mind, and we might say physical conformation of brain, which could not work unless under a combination of favourable circumstances. His brain though powerful was slow to concentrate itself, and could not carry on several occupations at once. Solitude and repose were necessary for production. This, combined with a certain inertia, a certain slowness of movement, constantly made it hard for him to get over the initial difficulties of self-expression, and would often, no doubt, cause him to delay too long and lose the passing inspiration or opportunity. But, once started, his very weight carried him on, as it did in the 'Bothie,' 'Amours,' 'Dipsychus,' and 'Mari Magno.'

After two years at University Hall, he was induced by several considerations to resign his post. He then went to America, and settled in October 1852 at Cambridge, Massachusetts. There he was welcomed with remarkable cordiality, and formed many friendships which lasted to the end of his life.

He wrote several articles at this time in the 'North American Review,' and in 'Putnam's Magazine,' and other magazines, and before long undertook a revision of the translation, known as Dryden's, of Plutarch's 'Lives,' for an American publisher. Thus he carried on a great deal of work, and was gradually making himself an assured position; and he would probably have felt no difficulty in settling down in America as his home, had not the offer of an examinership in the Education Office, which his friends obtained for him, come to draw him homewards again. The certainty of a permanent, though small income, the prospect of immediate marriage, and his natural affection for his own country, decided him to accept the place, and give up his chances in America, not without some regret, after he had gradually brought his mind to the idea of adopting a new country. His genuine democratic feeling rejoiced in the wider diffusion of prosperity and substantial comforts which he found in America; but he felt strongly the want of what he calls 'the deeper waters of ancient knowledge and experience' to be found in the old country.

In July 1853 he returned to England, and at once entered on the duties of his office. Henceforth his career was decided for him. He was freed from perplexing questions as to choice of occupation. His business life was simple, straightforward, and hard-working; but it was made up of little beyond official drudgery, and the fact of his entering the public service so late diminished his prospect of reaching higher posts. His immediate objects, however, were answered; and in June 1854 he married. For the next seven years he lived quietly at home; and during this time three children were born to him, who formed his chief and unfailing delight. No events of any moment marked this period; but it was one of real contentment. But, unfortunately, he was too willing and too anxious to take work of every sort, and to spend himself for others. Therefore he soon became involved in labours too exciting for a constitution already somewhat overtasked, nor was he ever able to yield himself wholly to the healthful indolence of private life. To a period of wasting thought and solitude succeeded one of over strenuous exertion; bracing indeed, but, for a man of his sympathetic temperament and laborious past life, too absorbing and engrossing.

Besides the work of the office, the translation of Plutarch, begun in America, absorbed a great part of his scanty leisure during five years after his return from America. In the spring of 1856 he was appointed secretary to a commission for examining the scientific military schools on the Continent. He visited, in consequence, the great schools for artillery and engineers in France, Prussia, and Austria. The travelling lasted about three months, and afforded him much occupation afterwards. But the work in which he took the deepest interest was that of his friend and relation, Miss Nightingale. He watched over every step in her various undertakings, affording her assistance not merely with advice, and little in his life gave him greater satisfaction than to be her active and trusted friend.

We see that his life, though uneventful, was full of work, and we can also understand why this period of his life produced no poetical result The conditions under which he could create were at this time wholly wanting. He had not time or strength or leisure of mind to spend on his natural gift of writing; and to his friends it must ever be a source of sorrow that his natural vocation, what he himself felt as such, was unfulfilled. He himself always looked forward to some time when greater opportunity might be granted him, when the various experiences of later life, the results of his later thought, might 'assort themselves upon the brain,' and be given out in some definite form. In the meantime he *waited*, not impatiently or unwillingly, for he was slow to draw conclusions, as he was also patient in hearing the views of others, and ready in his appreciation of them. Yet his mind did not fail to exercise a powerful influence upon others. All who knew him well will bear witness to the strong impression left by his character, and by the force and originality of his intellect. To describe his character would be impossible. Its charm was so personal that it seems to evaporate when translated into words. He was a singular combination of enthusiasm and calmness, of thoughtfulness and imagination, of speech and silence, of seriousness and humour.

But now this happy and peaceful though laborious life was approaching a too early close. There was never to be any complete opportunity given here for showing to the full what his best friends believed to be in him, and what his poems partly reveal. Probably ever since very early youth he had been subjected to a too severe moral and intellectual strain. His health, though good, had never been strong, and after 1859 it began to cause anxiety to his family, when a series of small illnesses and accidents combined to weaken his constitution.

In the autumn of 1860, finding himself seriously out of health, he obtained six months' leave from the Council Office. After several weeks' treatment at Malvern, which appeared to improve his health, in February 1861 he removed to Freshwater, in the Isle of Wight.

Further change of air, and still more change of scene, were ordered, and in the middle of April he went alone to Greece and Constantinople. Apparently he greatly enjoyed this journey, and no sooner was he again at leisure and in solitude than the old fountain of verse, so long dry within him, reopened afresh. During this journey he wrote the first and perhaps the second of the 'Mari Magno' stories. In June he returned for a few weeks to England; he seemed unable to bear any protracted absence, and to long for his home; yet he consented to quit it again in July and to go to Auvergne and the Pyrenees. There he was fortunate enough to join, though but for a short time, his friends Mr. and Mrs. Tennyson, whose companionship made his solitary wanderings pleasant, and to it he owed probably more than pleasure, some of the stimulus which produced the poems which were his last creations. While travelling in

Auvergne and the Pyrenees he composed all the remaining 'Mari Magno' tales, except the last, which was conceived and written entirely during his last illness. In the south of France he remained till the middle of September, when he went to Paris to join his wife. In Paris he spent a few days and then set out to travel through Switzerland to the Italian lakes, intending to stay some time at Florence, and reach Rome before the winter; but on the Italian lakes he caught a chill from which he did not recover, but grew gradually worse on the journey to Florence. Here they arrived on October 10, and here he took to his bed, unable longer to resist the fever. The fever, a sort of malaria, had its course, and appeared to give way. During the first three weeks he seemed perpetually occupied with a poem he was writing, the last in the volume of his poems; and when he began apparently to recover, and was able to sit up for several hours in the day, he insisted on trying to write it out, and when this proved too great an effort he begged to dictate it. But he broke down before it was finished, and returned to bed never to leave it again. A few days before his death he begged for a pencil and contrived to write down two verses, and quite to the end his thoughts kept hold of his poem. Fortunately it had all been completed and written out in pencil in the first stage of his illness, and was found after his death in his note-book.

The fever left him worn out, and then paralysis, with

which he had been threatened, struck him down. On the 13th of November he died, in his forty-third year.

He lies buried in the little Protestant cemetery, just outside the walls of Florence, looking towards Fiesole and the hills. 'Tall cypresses wave over the graves, and the beautiful hills keep guard around;' nowhere could there be a lovelier resting-place.

Titles in this Series

Criticism: General, Poetic, and Dramatic

1. Alfred Austin. THE POETRY OF THE PERIOD. 1870

2. Robert Buchanan. A LOOK ROUND LITERATURE. 1887

3. John William Cole. THE LIFE AND THEATRICAL TIMES OF CHARLES KEAN, F.S.A. 1859. (In two volumes)

4. E. S. Dallas. POETICS: AN ESSAY ON POETRY. 1852

5. E. S. Dallas. THE GAY SCIENCE. 1866

6. H. Buxton Forman. OUR LIVING POETS: AN ESSAY IN CRITICISM. 1871

7. Walter Hamilton. THE AESTHETIC MOVEMENT IN ENGLAND, third edition, 1882

8. R. H. Horne, editor. A NEW SPIRIT OF THE AGE, second edition. 1844. (In two volumes)

9. Madge Kendall. THE DRAMA. 1884. with DRAMATIC OPINIONS. 1890

10. Joseph A. Knight. A HISTORY OF THE STAGE DURING THE VICTORIAN ERA. 1901

11. Lord William Pitt Lennox. PLAYS, PLAYERS, AND PLAYHOUSES AT HOME AND ABROAD. 1881. (In two volumes)

12. Robert James Mann. TENNYSON'S "MAUD" VINDICATED: AN EXPLANATORY ESSAY. 1856

13. Mowbray Morris. ESSAYS IN THEATRICAL CRITICISM. 1882

14. Henry Neville. THE STAGE: ITS PAST AND PRESENT IN RELATION TO FINE ART. 1875

15. "Q" [Thomas Purnell]. DRAMATISTS OF THE PRESENT DAY. 1871

16. Walter Raleigh. STYLE. 1897

17. William Caldwell Roscoe. POEMS AND ESSAYS (volume two, ESSAYS, only). 1860

18. Clement Scott. THE DRAMA OF YESTERDAY & TODAY. 1899. (In two volumes)

19. James Field Stanfield. AN ESSAY ON THE STUDY AND COMPOSITION OF BIOGRAPHY. 1813

Parody, Satire, Literary Controversy, and Curiosa

20. Edward Bulwer-Lytton. THE NEW TIMON. 1846. with Algernon Charles Swinburne. SPECIMENS OF MODERN POETS. THE HEPTALOGIA, OR THE SEVEN AGAINST SENSE. 1880. with Algernon Charles Swinburne. "DISGUST: A DRAMATIC MONOLOGUE." 1898

21. [William E. Aytoun and Theodore Martin.] THE BOOK OF BALLADS: EDITED BY BON GAULTIER. 1845. with [William E. Aytoun.] FERMILIAN: OR THE STUDENT OF BADAJOZ: A SPASMODIC TRAGEDY BY T. PERCY JONES. 1854

22. James Carnegie. JONAS FISHER: A POEM IN BROWN AND WHITE. 1875. with [A. C. Swinburne.] THE DEVIL'S DUE: A LETTER TO THE EDITOR OF "THE EXAMINER." BY THOMAS MAITLAND. 1875

23. Philip James Bailey. THE AGE; A COLLOQUIAL SATIRE. 1858

24. [W. C. Bennett.] ANTI-MAUD. 1865. with [Eustace Clare Grenville Murray.] THE COMING K———. 1873. with [W. H. Mallock.] EVERY MAN HIS OWN POET. 1877

25. [John Burley Waring.] POEMS INSPIRED BY CERTAIN PICTURES AT THE ART TREASURES EXHIBITION, MANCHESTER. 1857. with [Anon.] THE LAUGHTER OF THE MUSES. 1869

26. Robert Buchanan. THE FLESHLY SCHOOL OF POETRY AND OTHER PHENOMENA OF THE DAY. 1872. with Algernon Charles Swinburne. UNDER THE MICROSCOPE. 1872

27. J. Rutter. THE NINETEENTH CENTURY, A POEM, IN TWENTY-NINE CANTOS. 1900

Collections of Critical Essays

28. William E. Fredeman, editor. VICTORIAN PREFACES AND INTRODUCTIONS: A FACSIMILE COLLECTION. 1986

29. Ira Bruce Nadel, editor. VICTORIAN FICTION: A COLLECTION OF ESSAYS FROM THE PERIOD. 1986

30. Ira Bruce Nadel, editor. VICTORIAN BIOGRAPHY: A COLLECTION OF ESSAYS FROM THE PERIOD. 1986

31. John F. Stasny, editor. VICTORIAN POETRY: A COLLECTION OF ESSAYS FROM THE PERIOD. 1986

32. William E. Fredeman, editor. THE VICTORIAN POETS: AN ALPHABETICAL COMPILATION OF THE BIO-CRITICAL INTRODUCTIONS TO THE VICTORIAN POETS FROM A. H. MILES'S "THE POETS AND POETRY OF THE NINETEENTH CENTURY." 1986